# SHIKIMORI'S
## not just a cutie

$(5)$

**KEIGO MAKI**

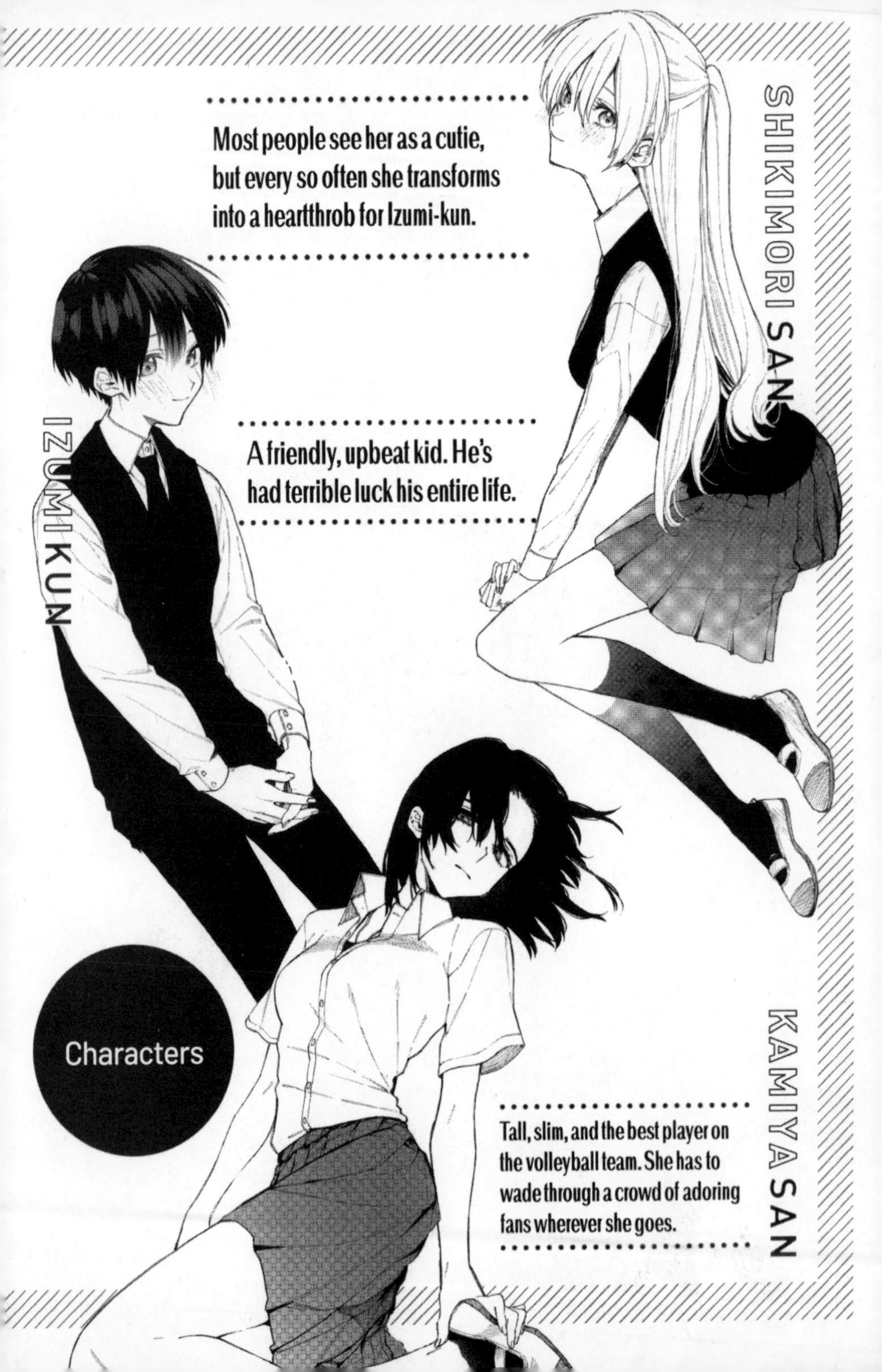
Characters
SHIKIMORI SAN
Most people see her as a cutie, but every so often she transforms into a heartthrob for Izumi-kun.
IZUMI KUN
A friendly, upbeat kid. He's had terrible luck his entire life.
KAMIYA SAN
Tall, slim, and the best player on the volleyball team. She has to wade through a crowd of adoring fans wherever she goes.

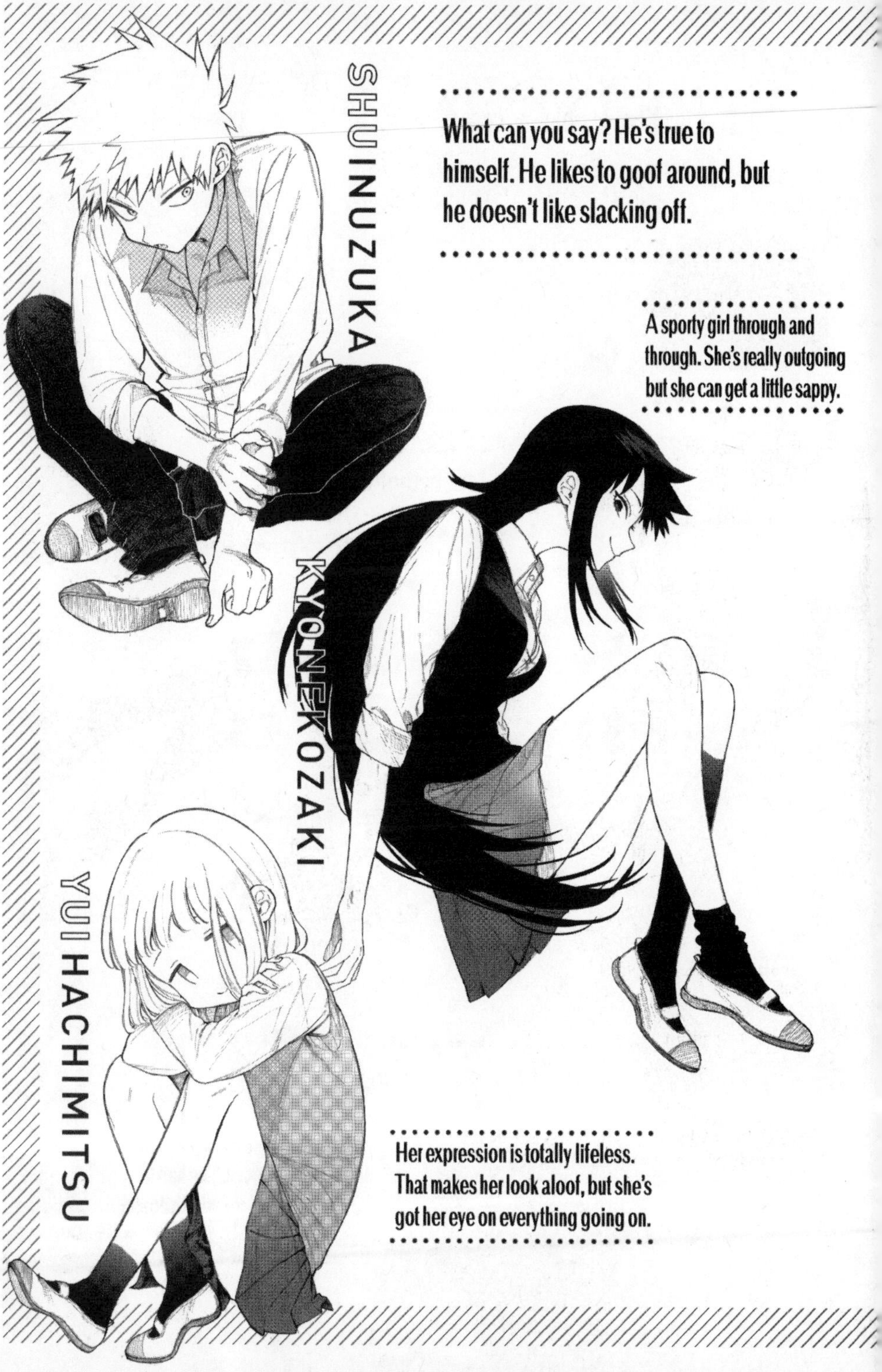
What can you say? He's true to himself. He likes to goof around, but he doesn't like slacking off.
SHU INUZUKA
A sporty girl through and through. She's really outgoing but she can get a little sappy.
KYO NEKOZAKI
Her expression is totally lifeless. That makes her look aloof, but she's got her eye on everything going on.
YUI HACHIMITSU

# SHIKIMORI'S
## not just a cutie

*volume.5*

# Contents

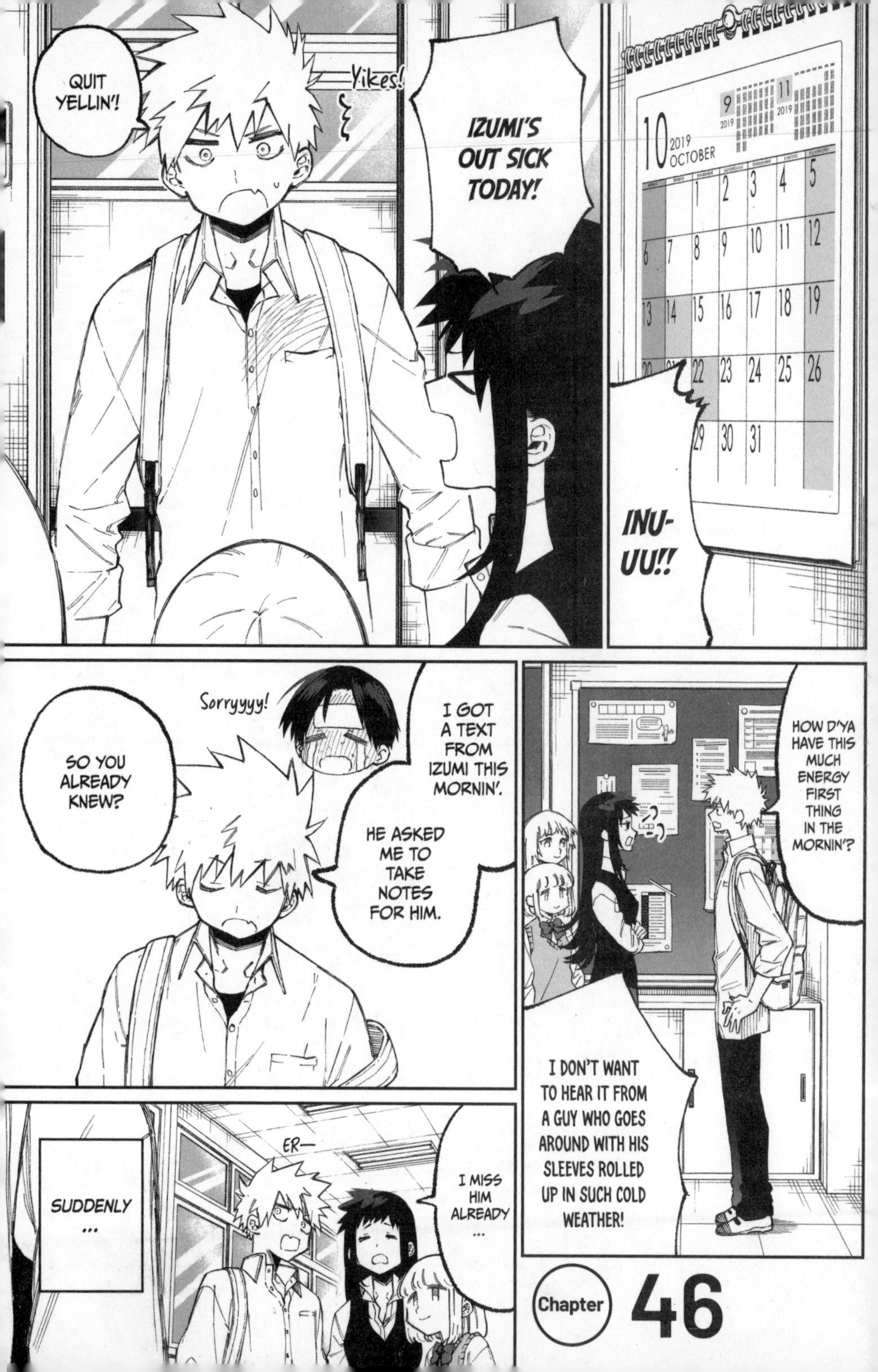
INU-UU!!
IZUMI'S OUT SICK TODAY!
Yikes!
QUIT YELLIN'!
HOW D'YA HAVE THIS MUCH ENERGY FIRST THING IN THE MORNIN'?
I DON'T WANT TO HEAR IT FROM A GUY WHO GOES AROUND WITH HIS SLEEVES ROLLED UP IN SUCH COLD WEATHER!
I GOT A TEXT FROM IZUMI THIS MORNIN'.
HE ASKED ME TO TAKE NOTES FOR HIM.
Sorryyyy!
SO YOU ALREADY KNEW?
I MISS HIM ALREADY...
ER—
SUDDENLY...
Chapter 46

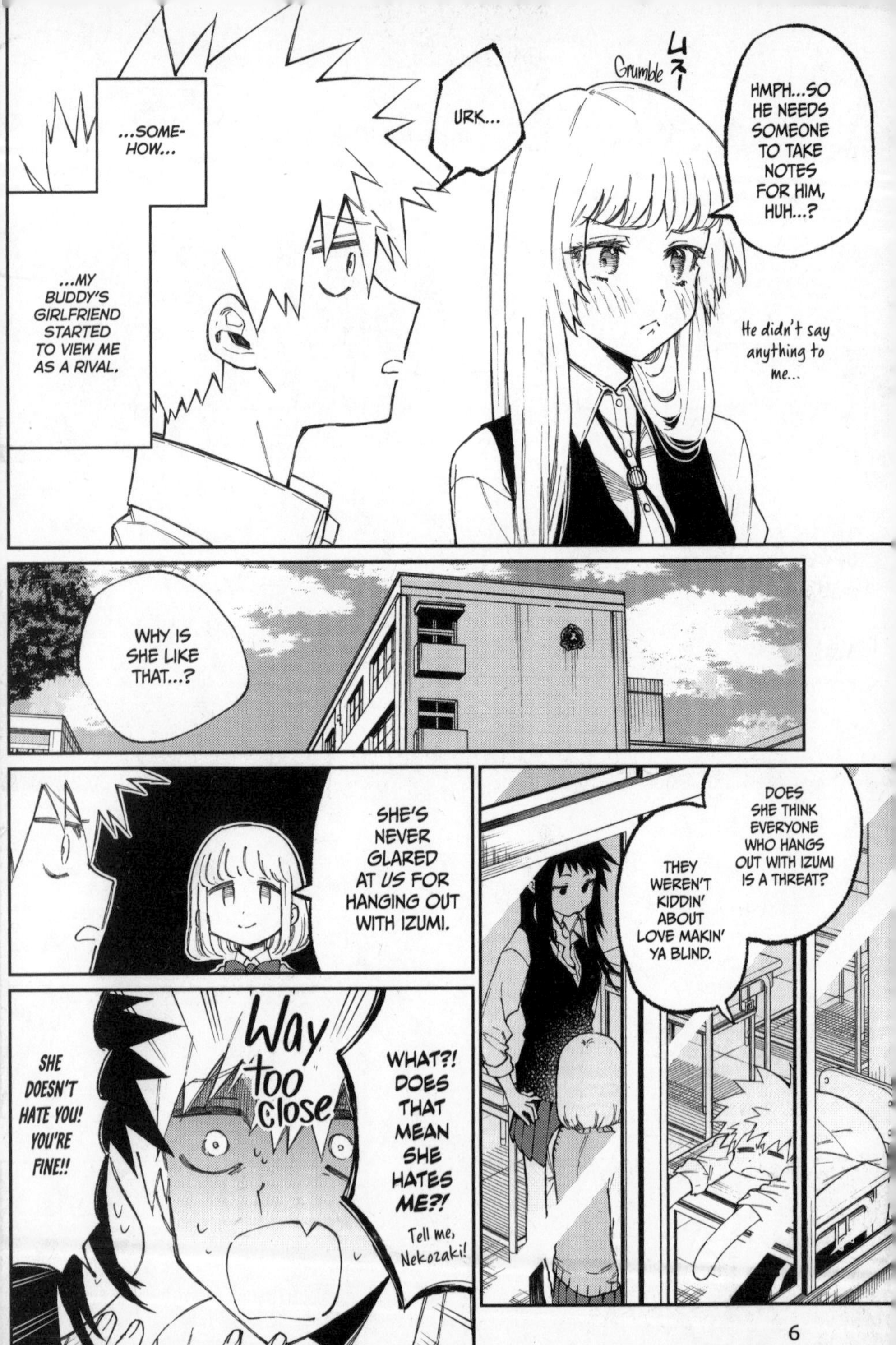
Grumble
HMPH...SO HE NEEDS SOMEONE TO TAKE NOTES FOR HIM, HUH...?
He didn't say anything to me...
URK...
...SOME-HOW...
...MY BUDDY'S GIRLFRIEND STARTED TO VIEW ME AS A RIVAL.
WHY IS SHE LIKE THAT...?
DOES SHE THINK EVERYONE WHO HANGS OUT WITH IZUMI IS A THREAT?
THEY WEREN'T KIDDIN' ABOUT LOVE MAKIN' YA BLIND.
SHE'S NEVER GLARED AT *US* FOR HANGING OUT WITH IZUMI.
WHAT?! DOES THAT MEAN SHE HATES *ME?!*
Tell me, Nekozaki!
Way too close
SHE DOESN'T HATE YOU! YOU'RE FINE!!

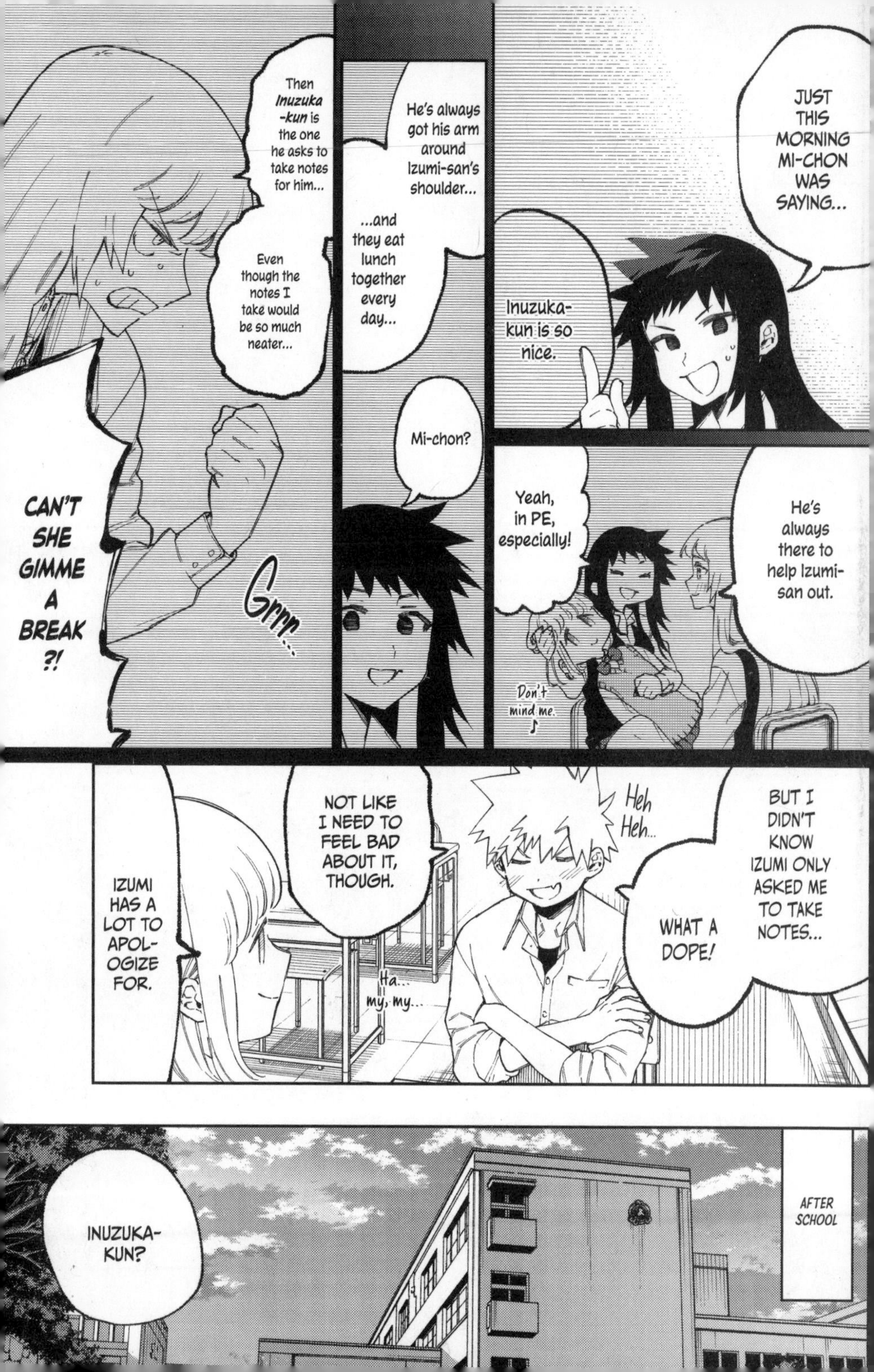
JUST THIS MORNING MI-CHON WAS SAYING...
Inuzuka-kun is so nice.
He's always there to help Izumi-san out.
Yeah, in PE, especially!
Don't mind me. ♪
He's always got his arm around Izumi-san's shoulder...
...and they eat lunch together every day...
Mi-chon?
Then *Inuzuka-kun* is the one he asks to take notes for him...
Even though the notes I take would be so much neater...
Grrr...
CAN'T SHE GIMME A BREAK?!
BUT I DIDN'T KNOW IZUMI ONLY ASKED ME TO TAKE NOTES...
WHAT A DOPE!
Heh Heh...
NOT LIKE I NEED TO FEEL BAD ABOUT IT, THOUGH.
IZUMI HAS A LOT TO APOLOGIZE FOR.
Ha... my, my...
AFTER SCHOOL
INUZUKA-KUN?

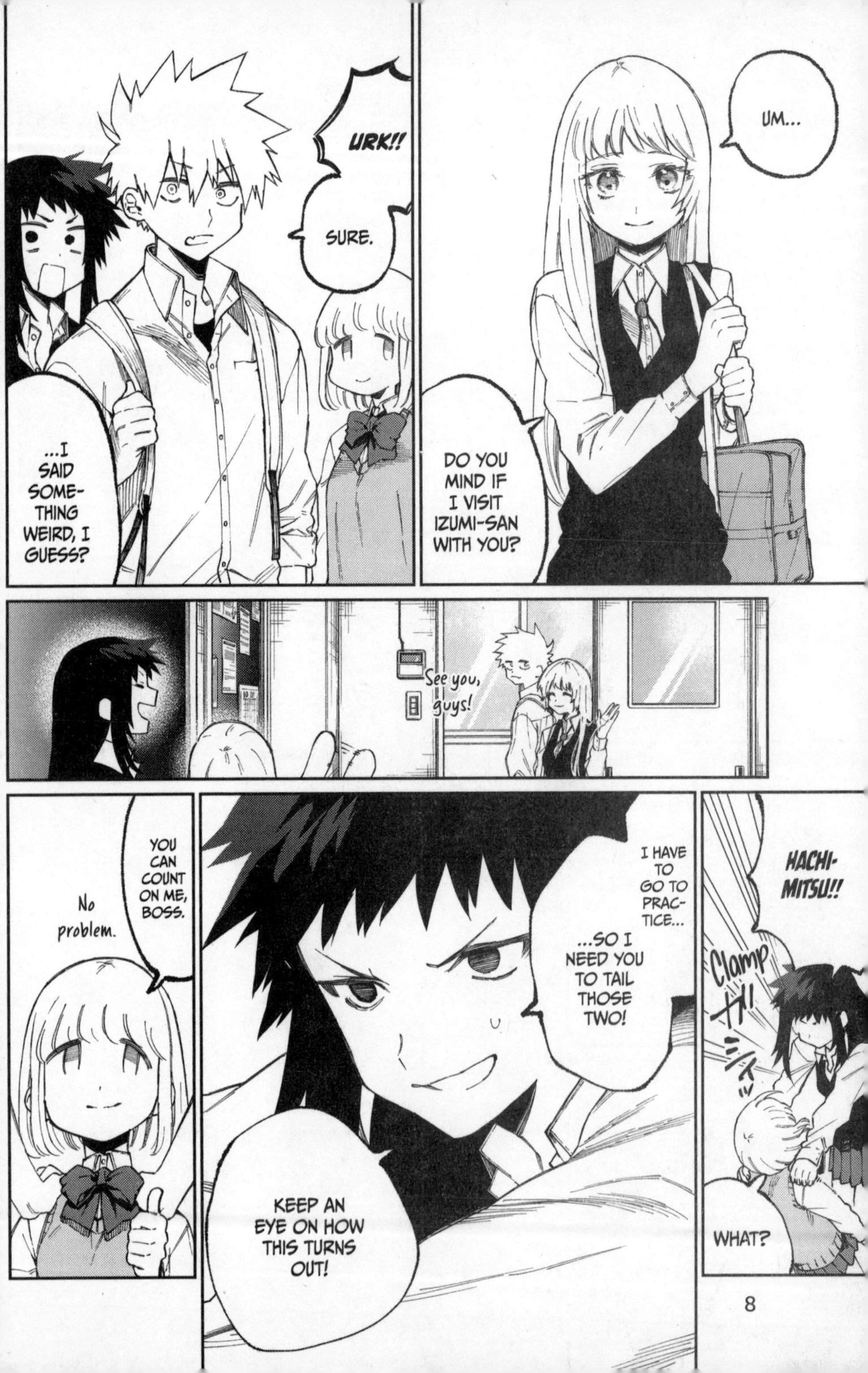
UM...
DO YOU MIND IF I VISIT IZUMI-SAN WITH YOU?
URK!!
SURE.
...I SAID SOME-THING WEIRD, I GUESS?
See you, guys!
HACHI-MITSU!!
Clamp
WHAT?
I HAVE TO GO TO PRAC-TICE...
...SO I NEED YOU TO TAIL THOSE TWO!
KEEP AN EYE ON HOW THIS TURNS OUT!
YOU CAN COUNT ON ME, BOSS.
No problem.

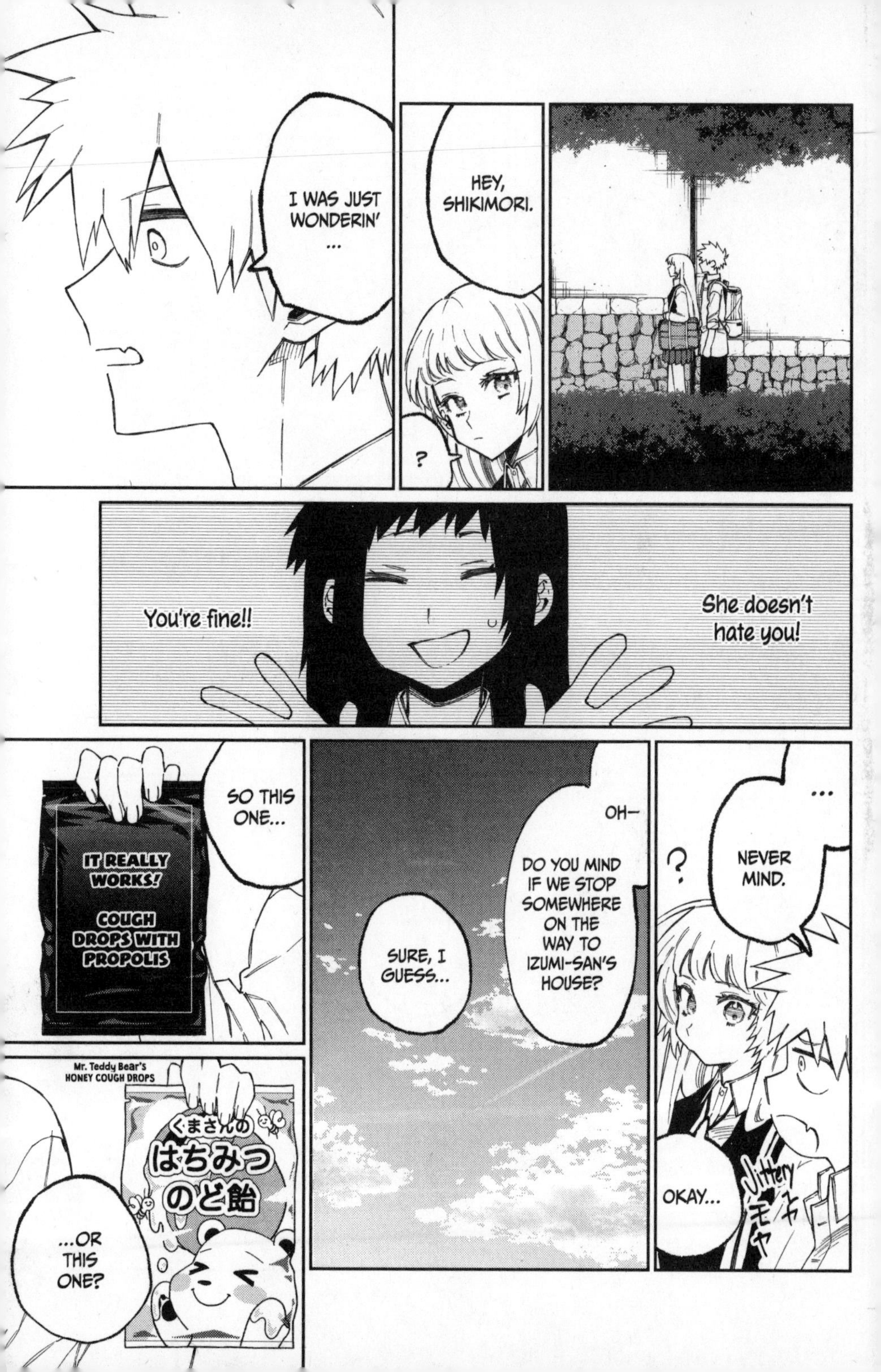
HEY, SHIKIMORI.
?
I WAS JUST WONDERIN' ...
She doesn't hate you!
You're fine!!
...
NEVER MIND.
?
OKAY...
Jittery
OH—
DO YOU MIND IF WE STOP SOMEWHERE ON THE WAY TO IZUMI-SAN'S HOUSE?
SURE, I GUESS...
SO THIS ONE...
IT REALLY WORKS!
COUGH DROPS WITH PROPOLIS
Mr. Teddy Bear's HONEY COUGH DROPS
くまさんの
はちみつ
のど飴
...OR THIS ONE?

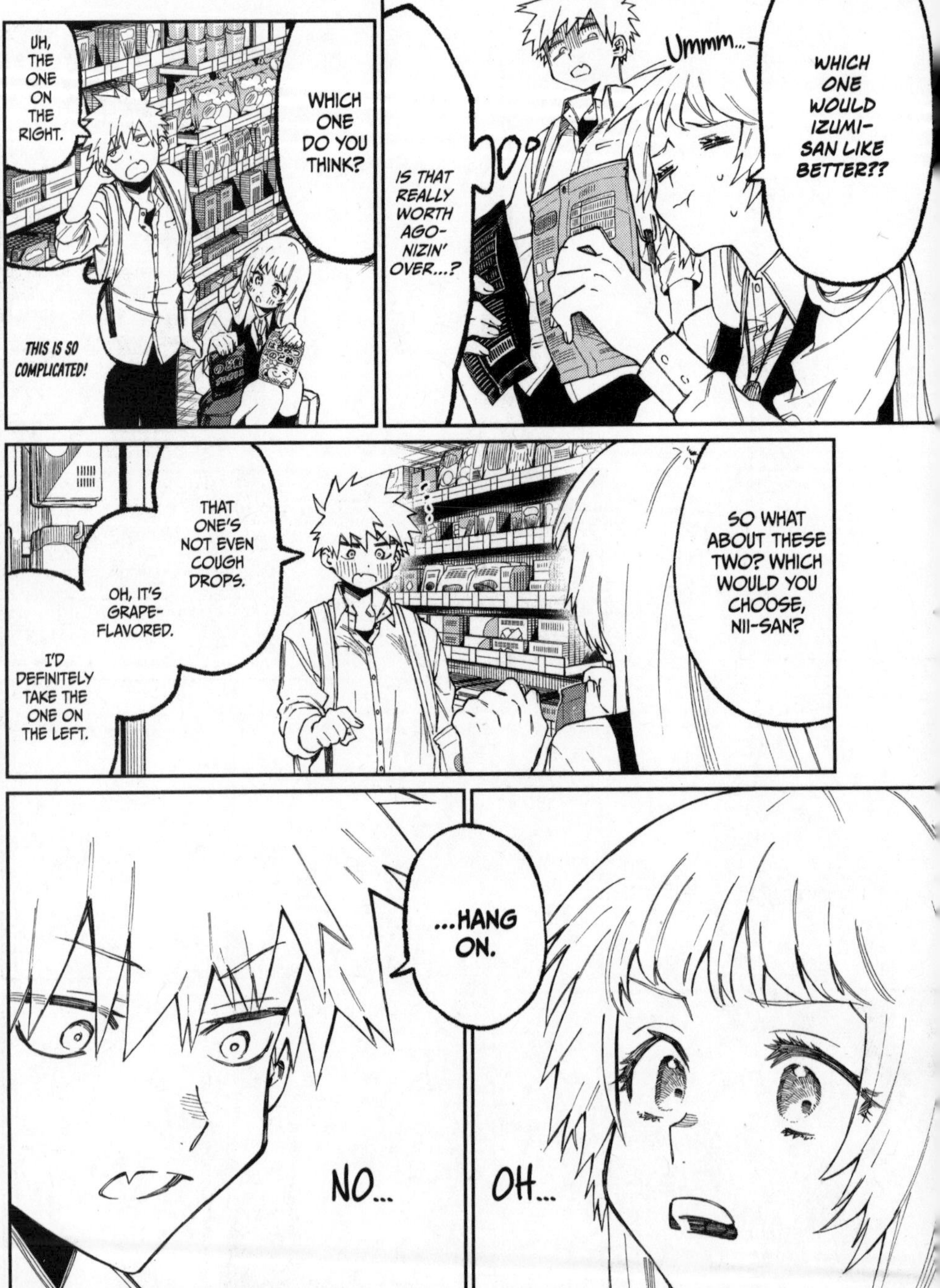
Ummm...
WHICH ONE WOULD IZUMI-SAN LIKE BETTER??
IS THAT REALLY WORTH AGO-NIZIN' OVER...?
WHICH ONE DO YOU THINK?
UH, THE ONE ON THE RIGHT.
THIS IS SO COMPLICATED!
SO WHAT ABOUT THESE TWO? WHICH WOULD YOU CHOOSE, NII-SAN?
THAT ONE'S NOT EVEN COUGH DROPS.
OH, IT'S GRAPE-FLAVORED.
I'D DEFINITELY TAKE THE ONE ON THE LEFT.
OH...
...HANG ON.
NO...

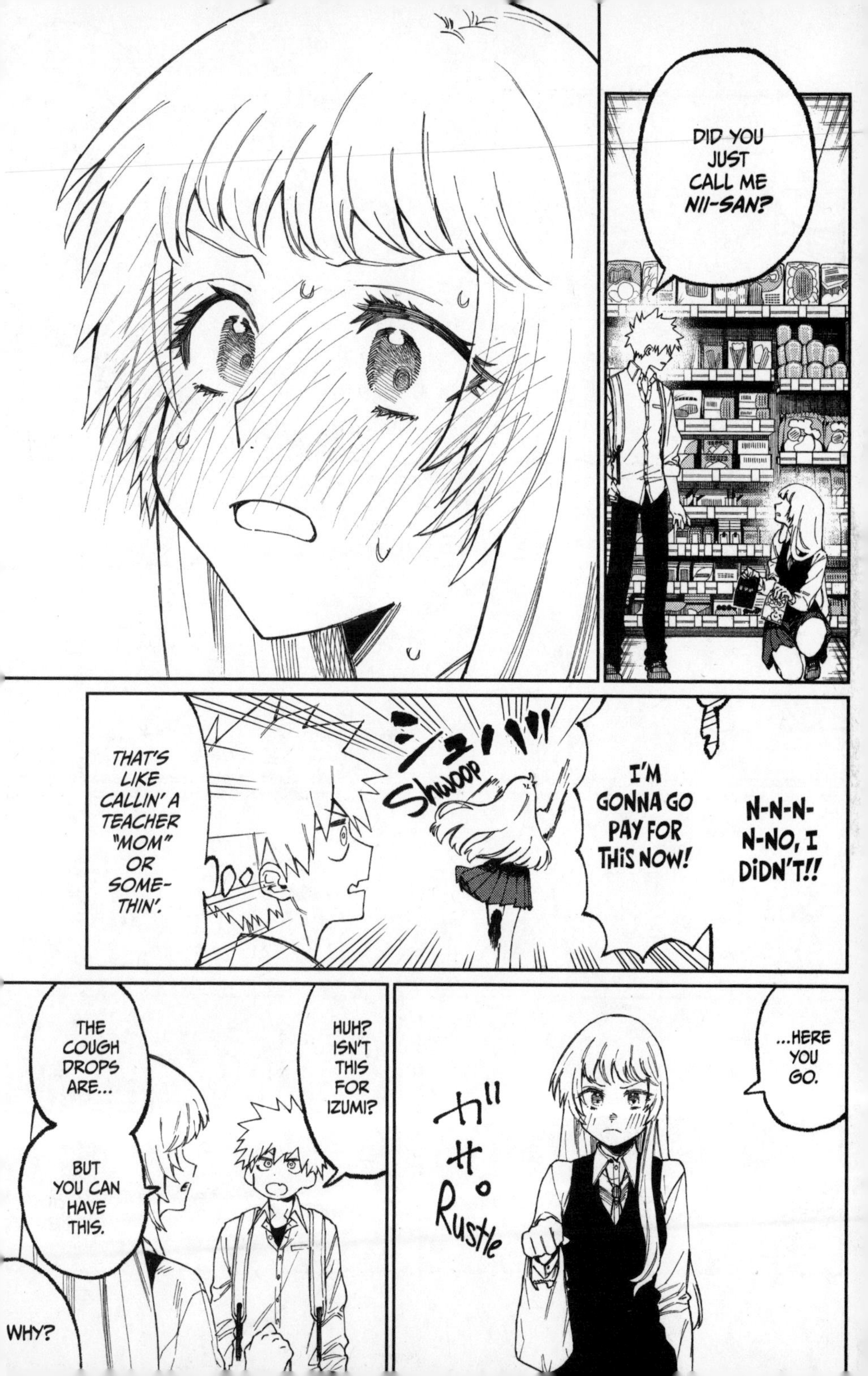
DID YOU JUST CALL ME NII-SAN?
N-N-N-N-NO, I DIDN'T!!
I'M GONNA GO PAY FOR THIS NOW!
シュバッ
Shwoop
THAT'S LIKE CALLIN' A TEACHER "MOM" OR SOME-THIN'.
...HERE YOU GO.
ガサ
Rustle
HUH? ISN'T THIS FOR IZUMI?
THE COUGH DROPS ARE...
BUT YOU CAN HAVE THIS.
WHY?

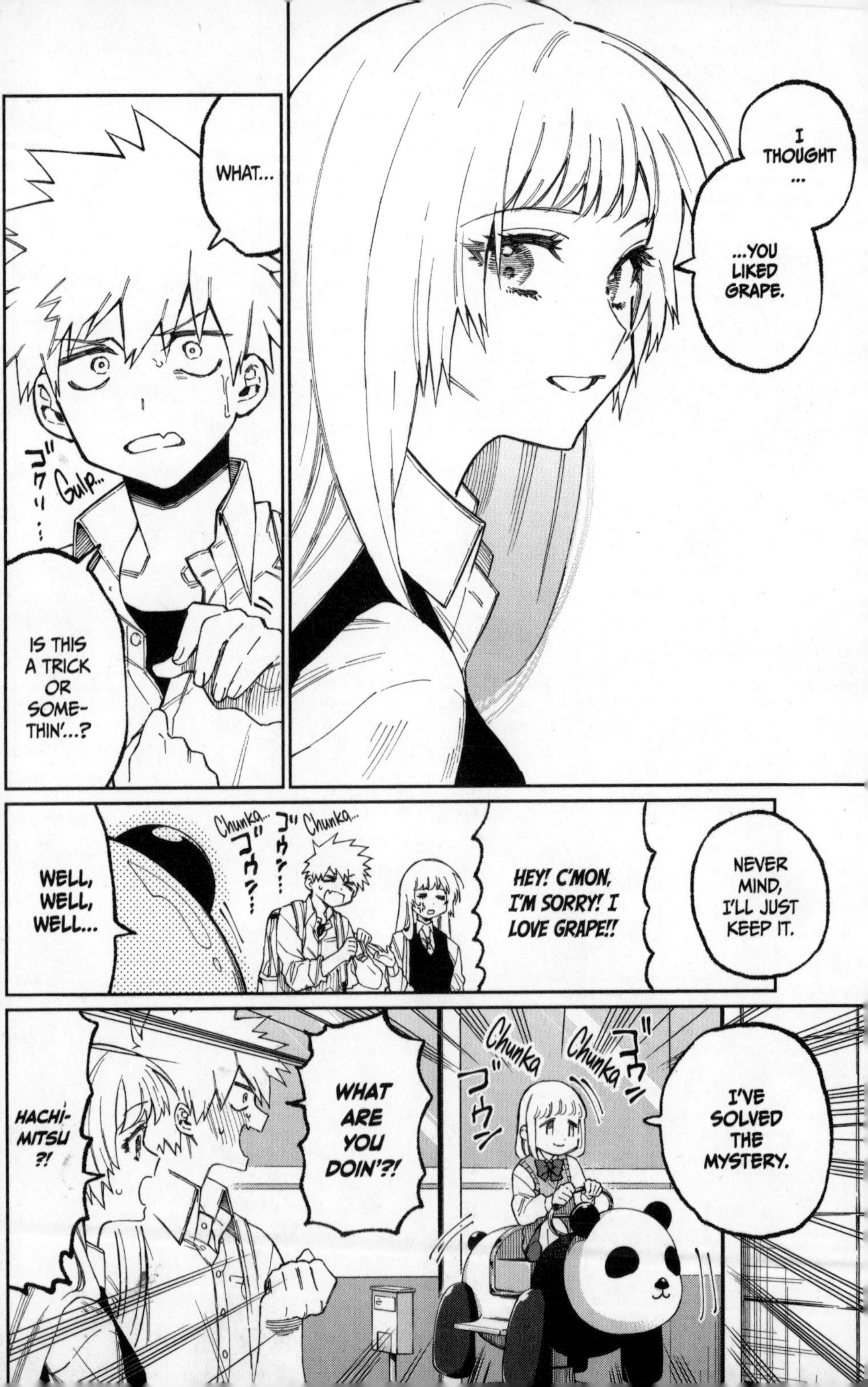
I THOUGHT ...
...YOU LIKED GRAPE.
WHAT...
Gulp...
IS THIS A TRICK OR SOME-THIN'...?
NEVER MIND, I'LL JUST KEEP IT.
HEY! C'MON, I'M SORRY! I LOVE GRAPE!!
Chunka...
Chunka...
WELL, WELL, WELL...
I'VE SOLVED THE MYSTERY.
Chunka
Chunka
WHAT ARE YOU DOIN'?!
HACHI-MITSU ?!

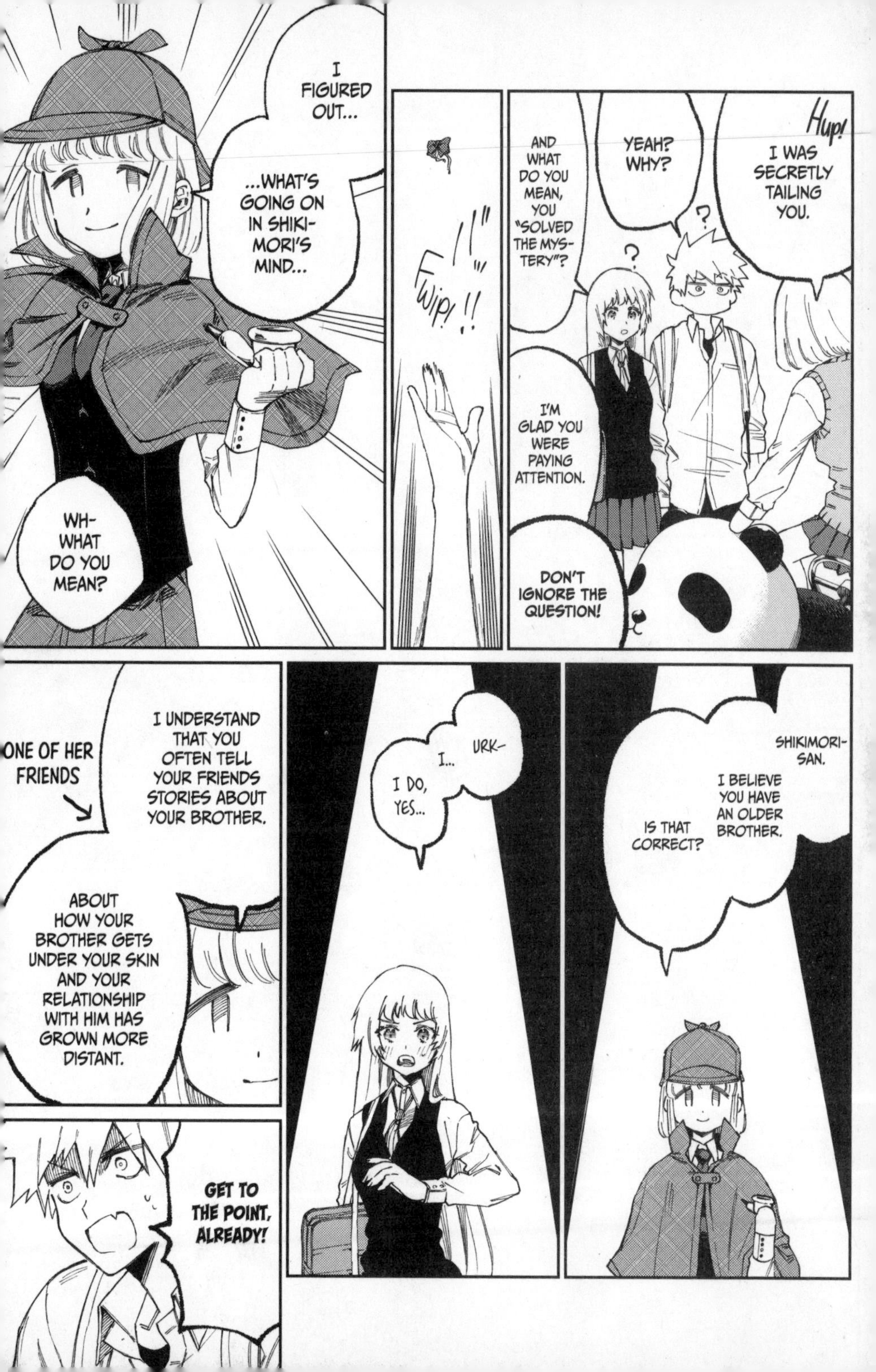

Hup!
I WAS SECRETLY TAILING YOU.
YEAH? WHY?
AND WHAT DO YOU MEAN, YOU "SOLVED THE MYS-TERY"?
I'M GLAD YOU WERE PAYING ATTENTION.
DON'T IGNORE THE QUESTION!
Fwip!!
I FIGURED OUT...
...WHAT'S GOING ON IN SHIKI-MORI'S MIND...
WH-WHAT DO YOU MEAN?
SHIKIMORI-SAN.
I BELIEVE YOU HAVE AN OLDER BROTHER.
IS THAT CORRECT?
URK-
I...
I DO, YES...
I UNDERSTAND THAT YOU OFTEN TELL YOUR FRIENDS STORIES ABOUT YOUR BROTHER.
ONE OF HER FRIENDS
ABOUT HOW YOUR BROTHER GETS UNDER YOUR SKIN AND YOUR RELATIONSHIP WITH HIM HAS GROWN MORE DISTANT.
GET TO THE POINT, ALREADY!

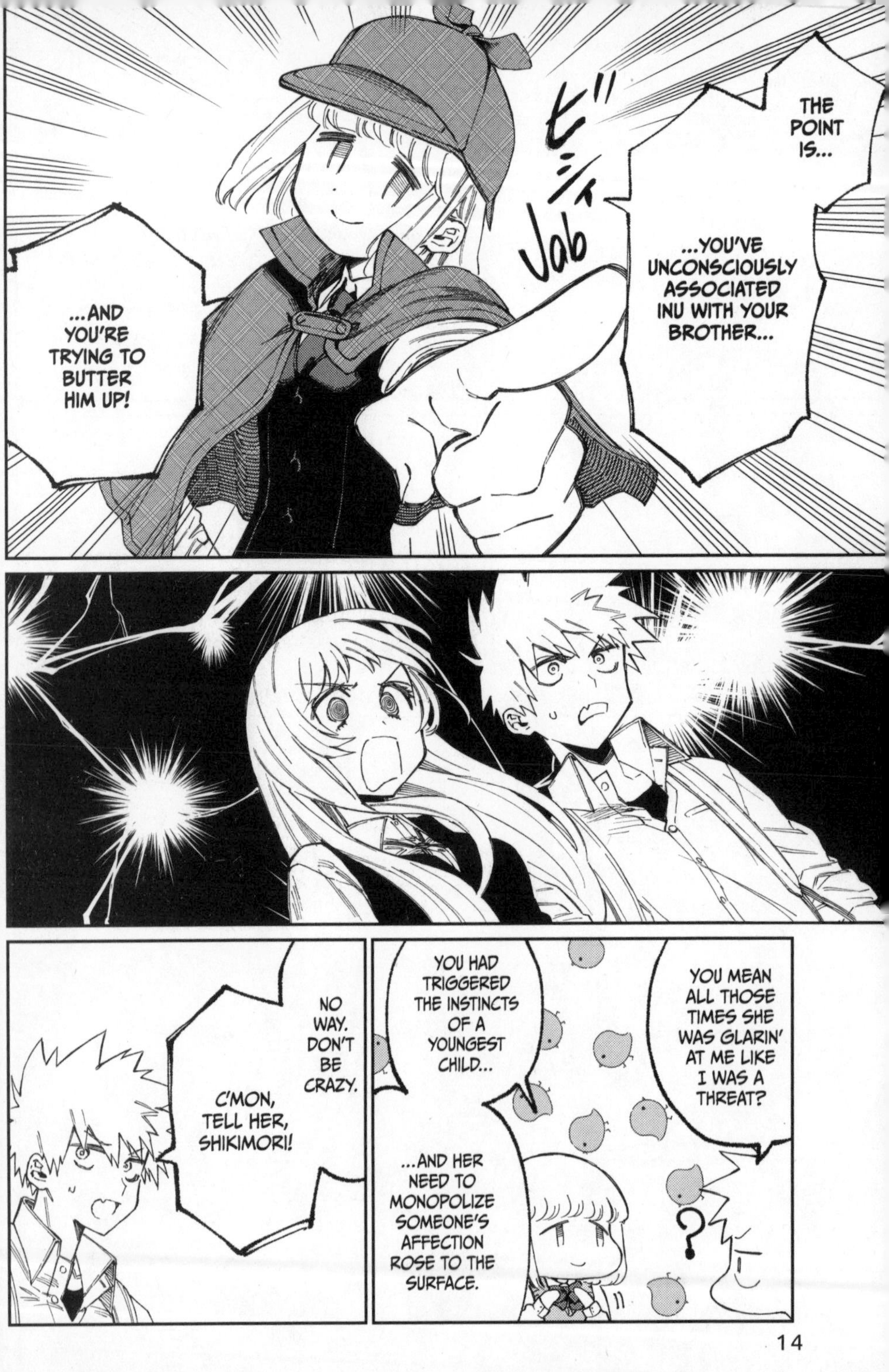
THE POINT IS...
Jab
...YOU'VE UNCONSCIOUSLY ASSOCIATED INU WITH YOUR BROTHER...
...AND YOU'RE TRYING TO BUTTER HIM UP!
YOU MEAN ALL THOSE TIMES SHE WAS GLARIN' AT ME LIKE I WAS A THREAT?
YOU HAD TRIGGERED THE INSTINCTS OF A YOUNGEST CHILD...
...AND HER NEED TO MONOPOLIZE SOMEONE'S AFFECTION ROSE TO THE SURFACE.
NO WAY. DON'T BE CRAZY.
C'MON, TELL HER, SHIKIMORI!

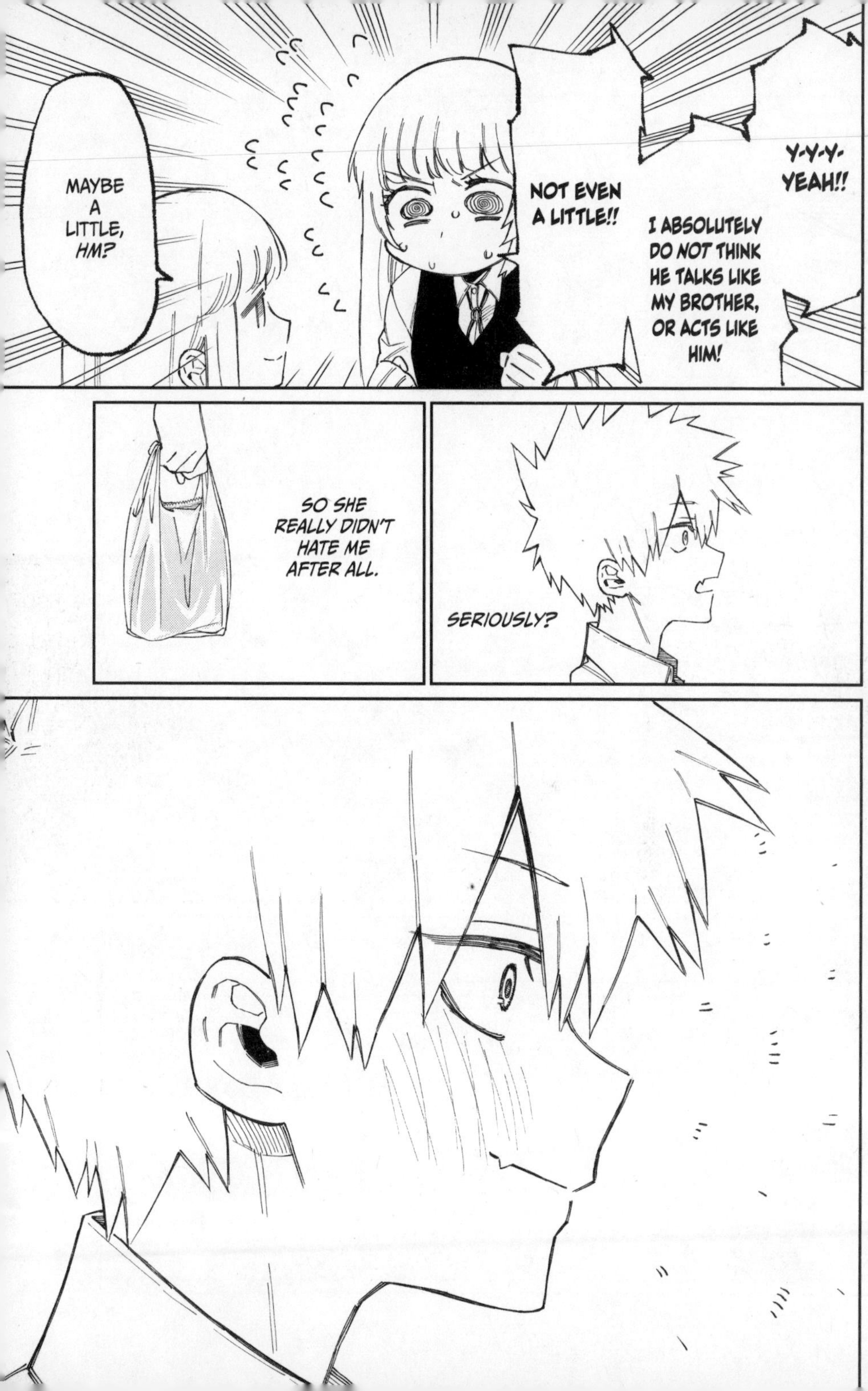
Y-Y-Y-YEAH!!
I ABSOLUTELY DO NOT THINK HE TALKS LIKE MY BROTHER, OR ACTS LIKE HIM!
NOT EVEN A LITTLE!!
MAYBE A LITTLE, HM?
SERIOUSLY?
SO SHE REALLY DIDN'T HATE ME AFTER ALL.

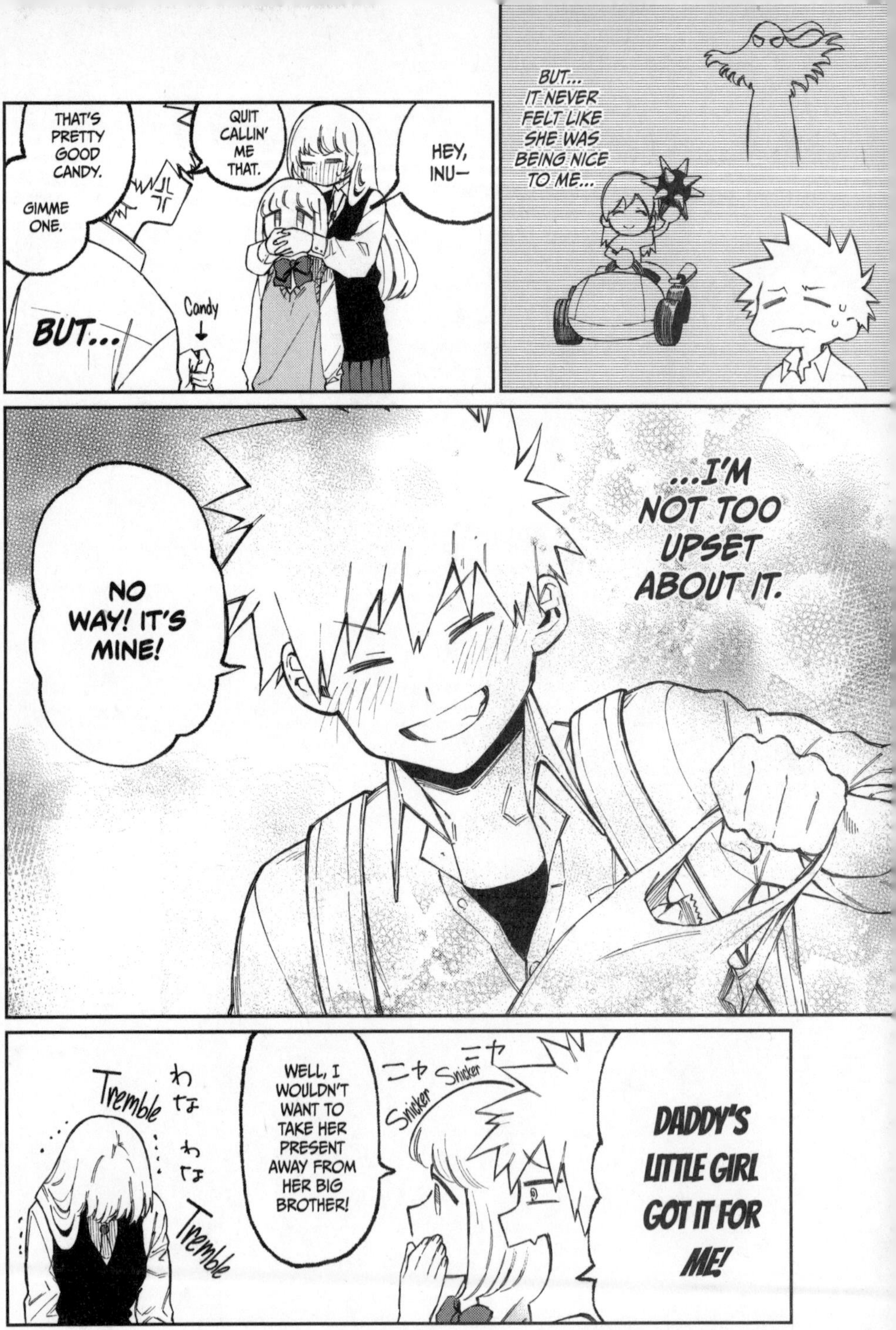

BUT... IT NEVER FELT LIKE SHE WAS BEING NICE TO ME...
HEY, INU—
QUIT CALLIN' ME THAT.
THAT'S PRETTY GOOD CANDY.
GIMME ONE.
Candy
BUT...
...I'M NOT TOO UPSET ABOUT IT.
NO WAY! IT'S MINE!
DADDY'S LITTLE GIRL GOT IT FOR ME!
ニヤ
Snicker
ニヤ
Snicker
WELL, I WOULDN'T WANT TO TAKE HER PRESENT AWAY FROM HER BIG BROTHER!
わな
Tremble
わな
Tremble

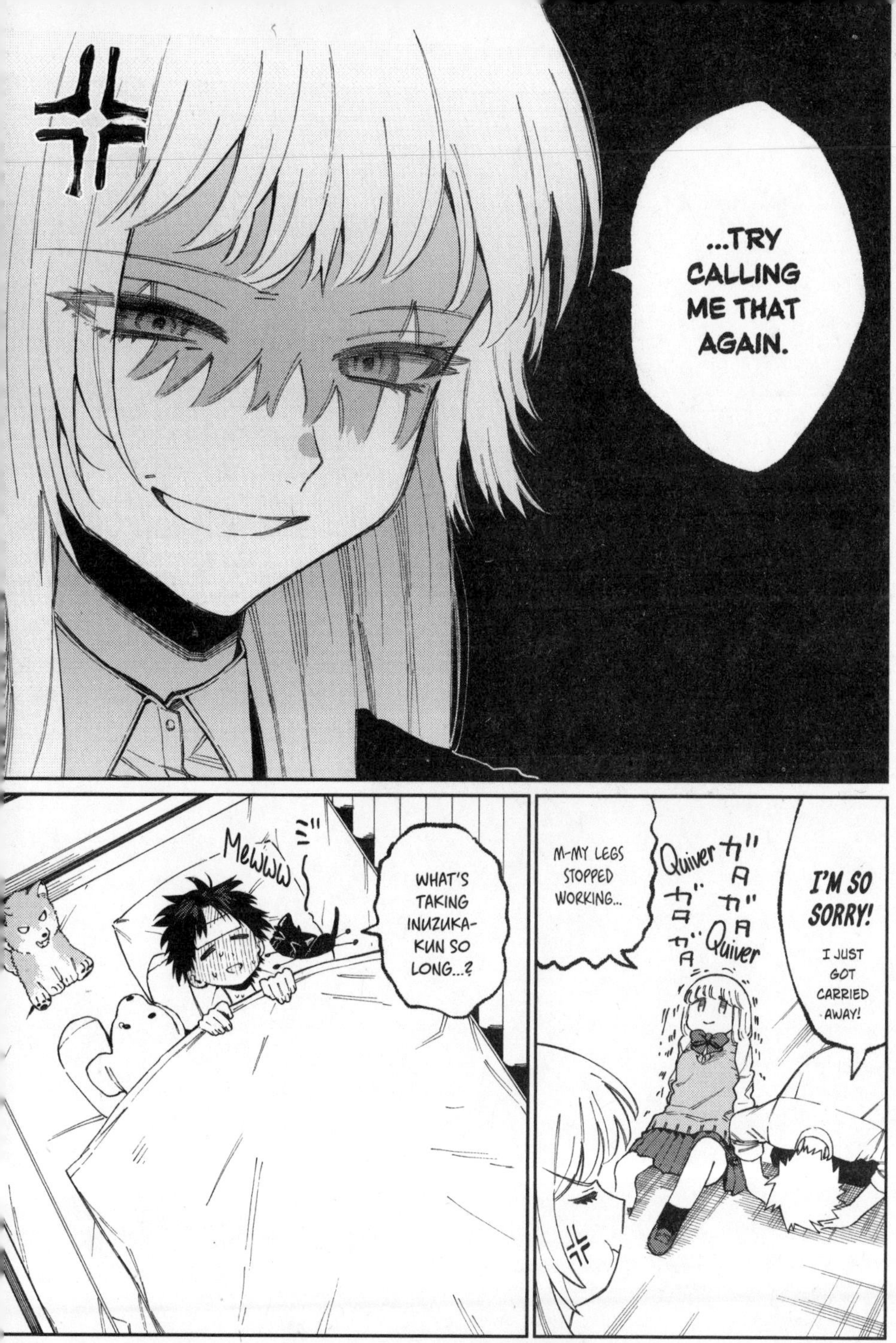
...TRY CALLING ME THAT AGAIN.
I'M SO SORRY!
I JUST GOT CARRIED AWAY!
Quiver ガタガタ
ガタガタ Quiver
M-MY LEGS STOPPED WORKING...
WHAT'S TAKING INUZUKA-KUN SO LONG...?
ジー
Mewww



Chapter 46 END

# SHIKIMORI'S Not just a cutie

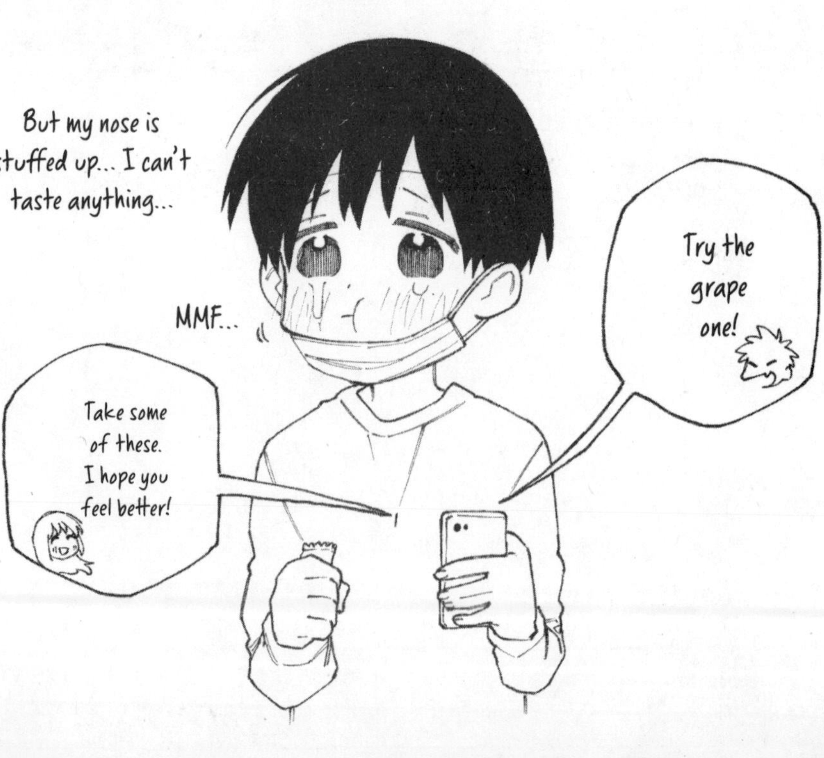
Try the grape one!
But my nose is stuffed up... I can't taste anything...
MMF...
Take some of these. I hope you feel better!

Chapter 47

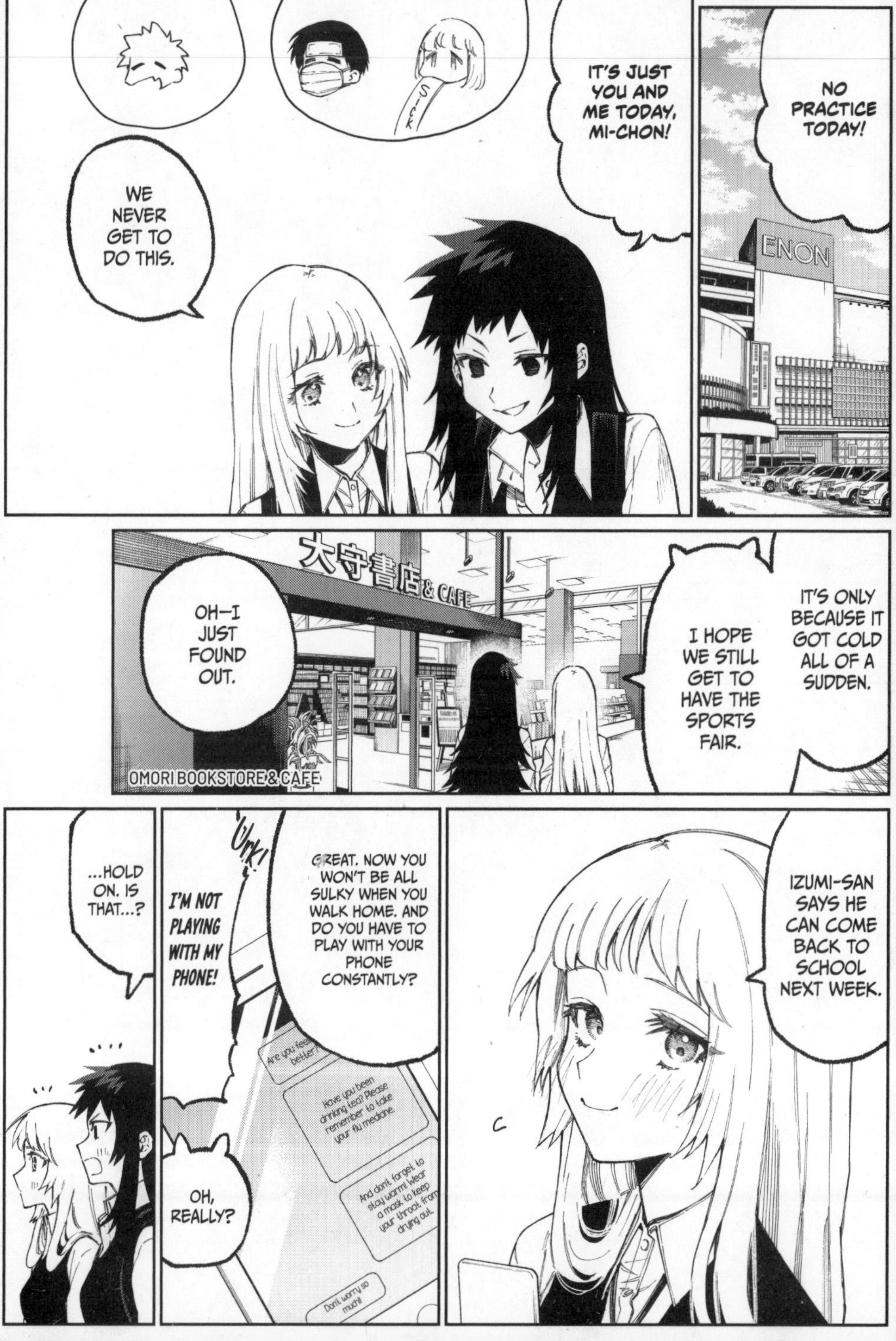

NO PRACTICE TODAY!
ENON
IT'S JUST YOU AND ME TODAY, MI-CHON!
GOT THE FLU IN OCTOBER
SICK
JOB
WE NEVER GET TO DO THIS.
IT'S ONLY BECAUSE IT GOT COLD ALL OF A SUDDEN.
I HOPE WE STILL GET TO HAVE THE SPORTS FAIR.
大守書店& CAFE
OH—I JUST FOUND OUT.
OMORI BOOKSTORE & CAFE
IZUMI-SAN SAYS HE CAN COME BACK TO SCHOOL NEXT WEEK.
GREAT. NOW YOU WON'T BE ALL SULKY WHEN YOU WALK HOME. AND DO YOU HAVE TO PLAY WITH YOUR PHONE CONSTANTLY?
Urk!
I'M NOT PLAYING WITH MY PHONE!
Have you been drinking tea? Please remember to take your flu medicine.
And don't forget to stay warm! Wear a mask to keep your throat from drying out.
Don't worry so much!!
OH, REALLY?
...HOLD ON. IS THAT...?
...

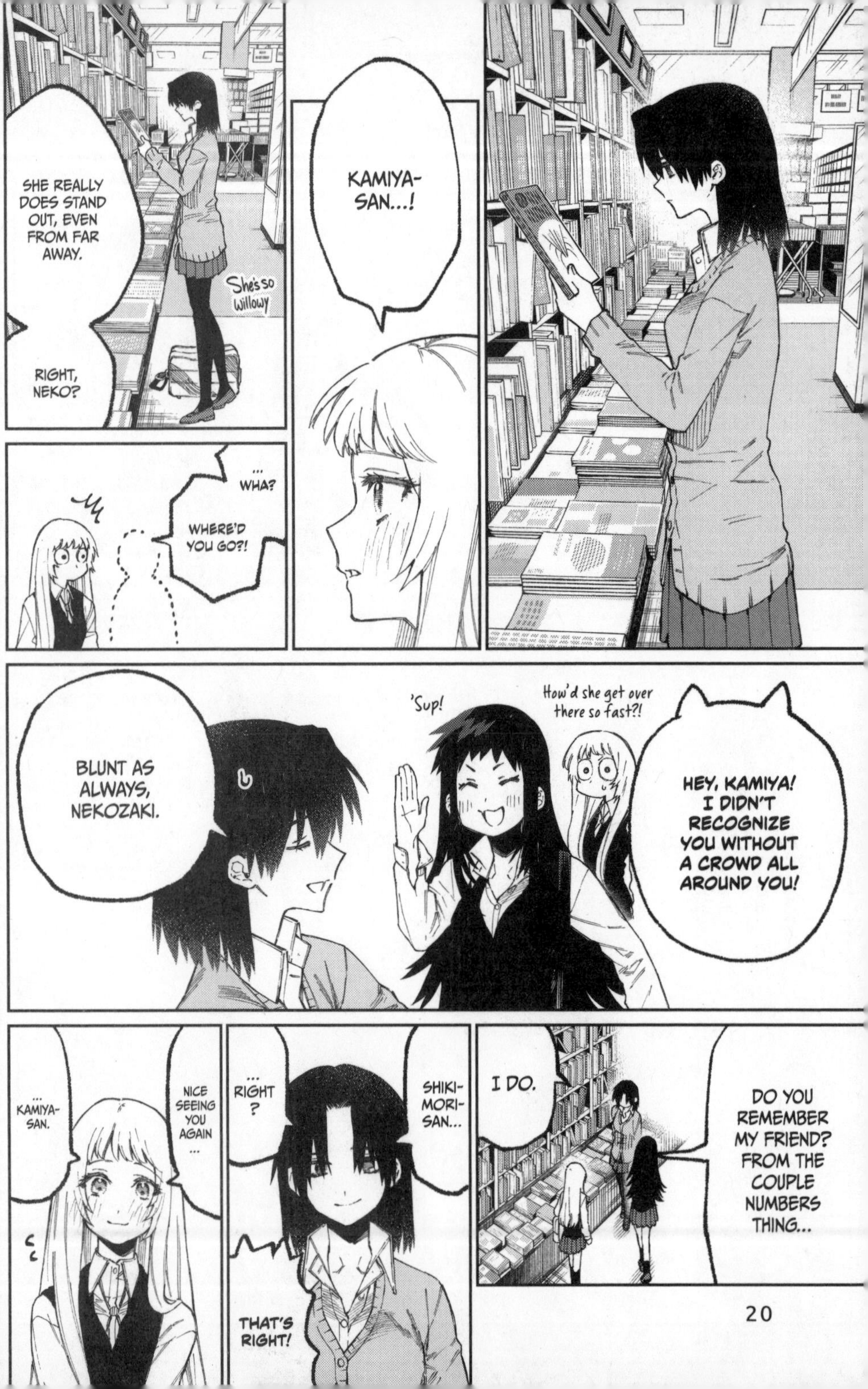
KAMIYA-SAN...!
SHE REALLY DOES STAND OUT, EVEN FROM FAR AWAY.
She's so willowy
RIGHT, NEKO?
... WHA?
WHERE'D YOU GO?!
HEY, KAMIYA! I DIDN'T RECOGNIZE YOU WITHOUT A CROWD ALL AROUND YOU!
How'd she get over there so fast?!
'Sup!
BLUNT AS ALWAYS, NEKOZAKI.
DO YOU REMEMBER MY FRIEND? FROM THE COUPLE NUMBERS THING...
I DO.
SHIKI-MORI-SAN...
... RIGHT?
THAT'S RIGHT!
NICE SEEING YOU AGAIN ...
... KAMIYA-SAN.

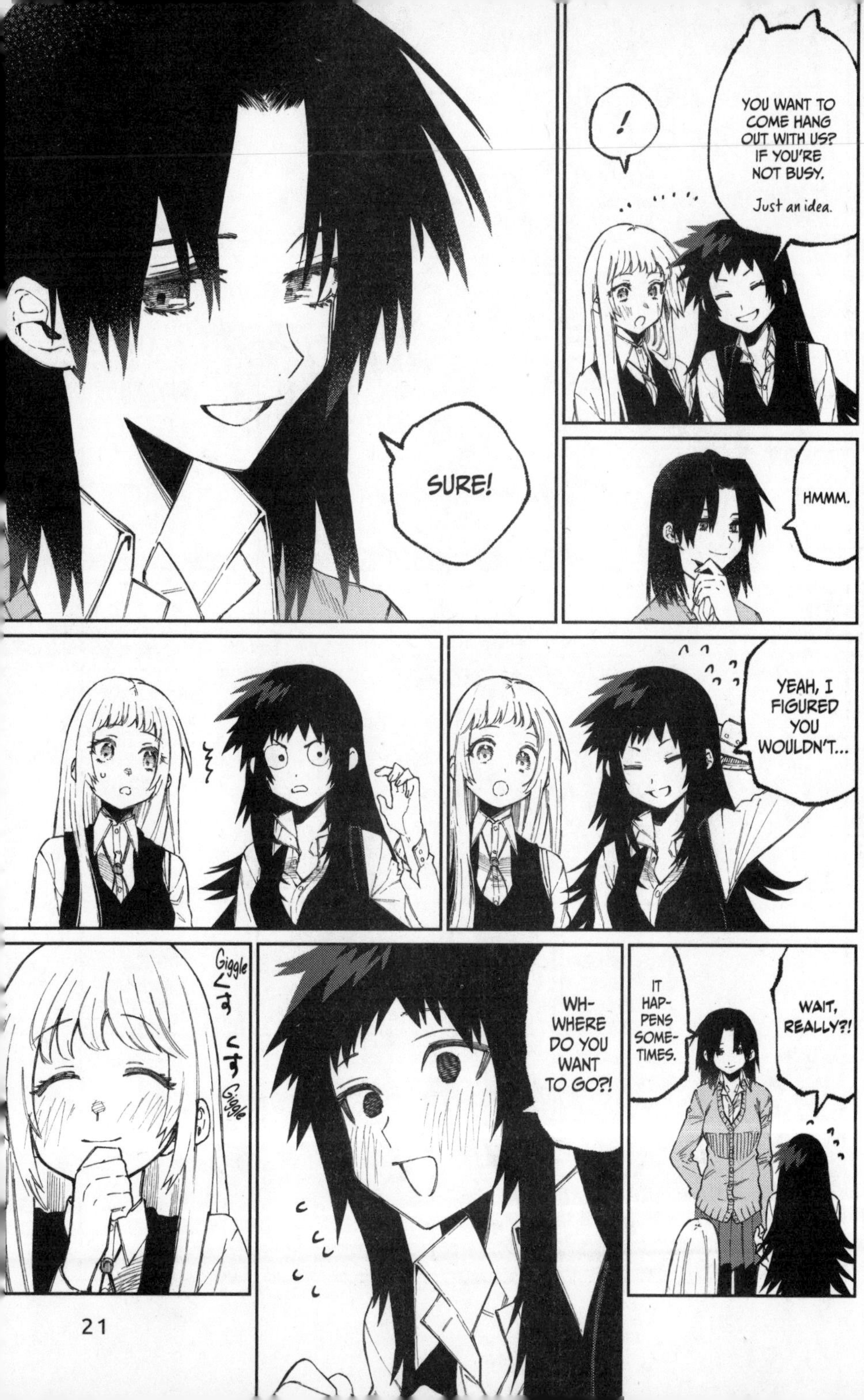
YOU WANT TO COME HANG OUT WITH US? IF YOU'RE NOT BUSY.
Just an idea.
!
HMMM.
SURE!
YEAH, I FIGURED YOU WOULDN'T...
WAIT, REALLY?!
IT HAP-PENS SOME-TIMES.
WH-WHERE DO YOU WANT TO GO?!
Giggle くす
くす Giggle

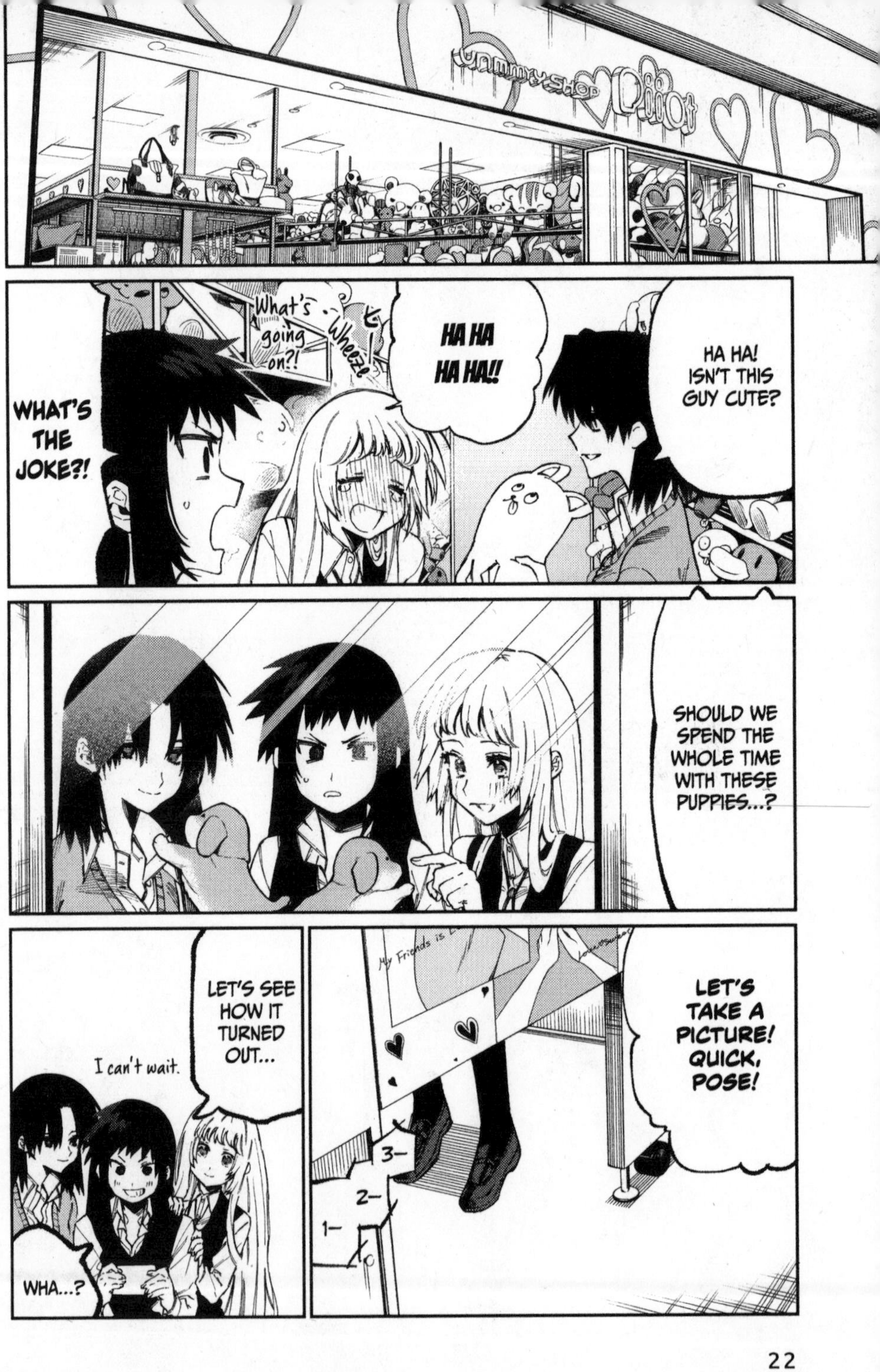
HA HA! ISN'T THIS GUY CUTE?
HA HA HA HA!!
Wheeze
What's going on?!
WHAT'S THE JOKE?!
SHOULD WE SPEND THE WHOLE TIME WITH THESE PUPPIES...?
LET'S TAKE A PICTURE! QUICK, POSE!
My Friends is
3—
2—
1—
LET'S SEE HOW IT TURNED OUT...
I can't wait.
WHA...?

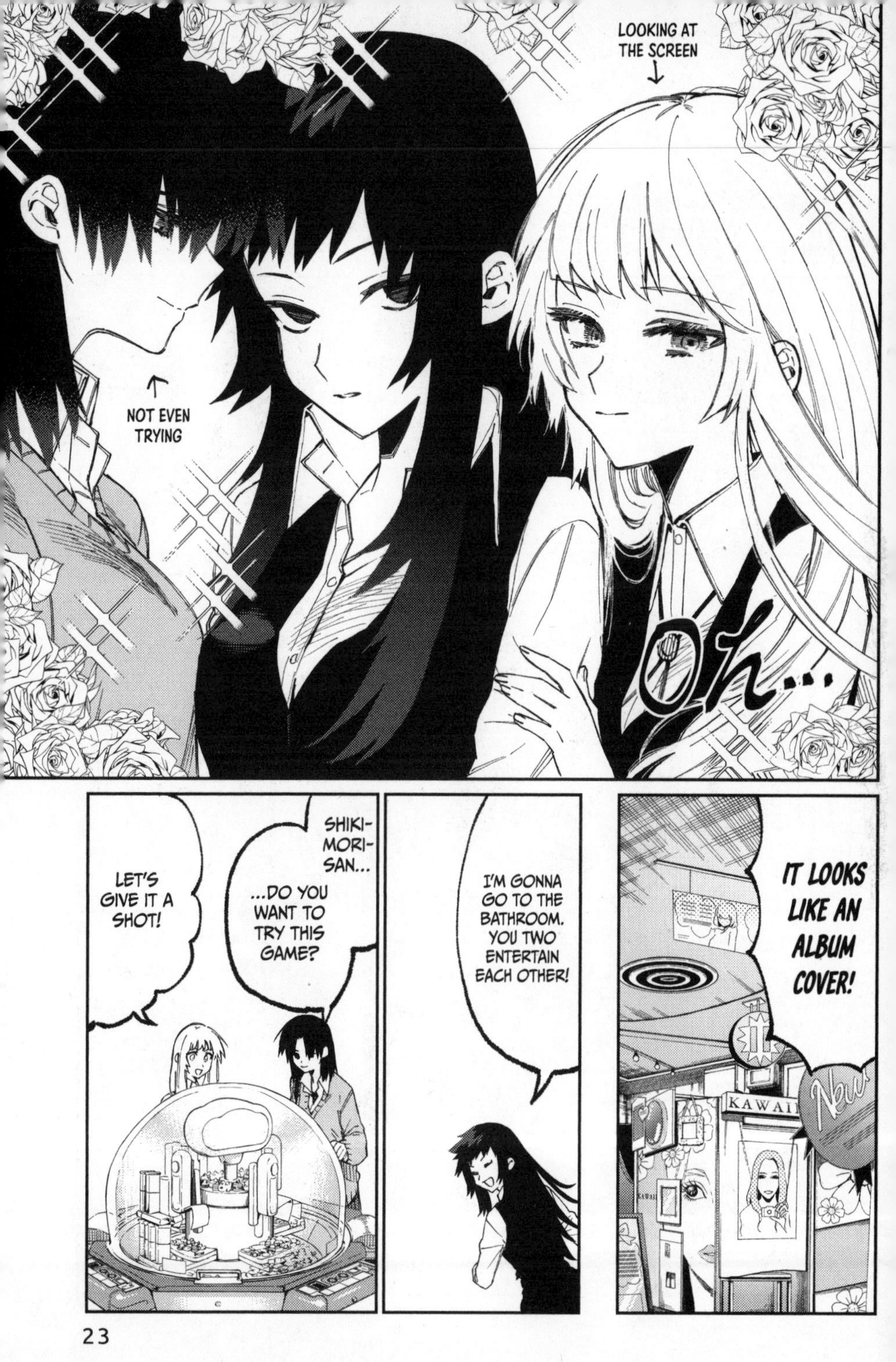
LOOKING AT THE SCREEN
Oh...
NOT EVEN TRYING
IT LOOKS LIKE AN ALBUM COVER!
KAWAII
I'M GONNA GO TO THE BATHROOM. YOU TWO ENTERTAIN EACH OTHER!
SHIKIMORI-SAN...
...DO YOU WANT TO TRY THIS GAME?
LET'S GIVE IT A SHOT!

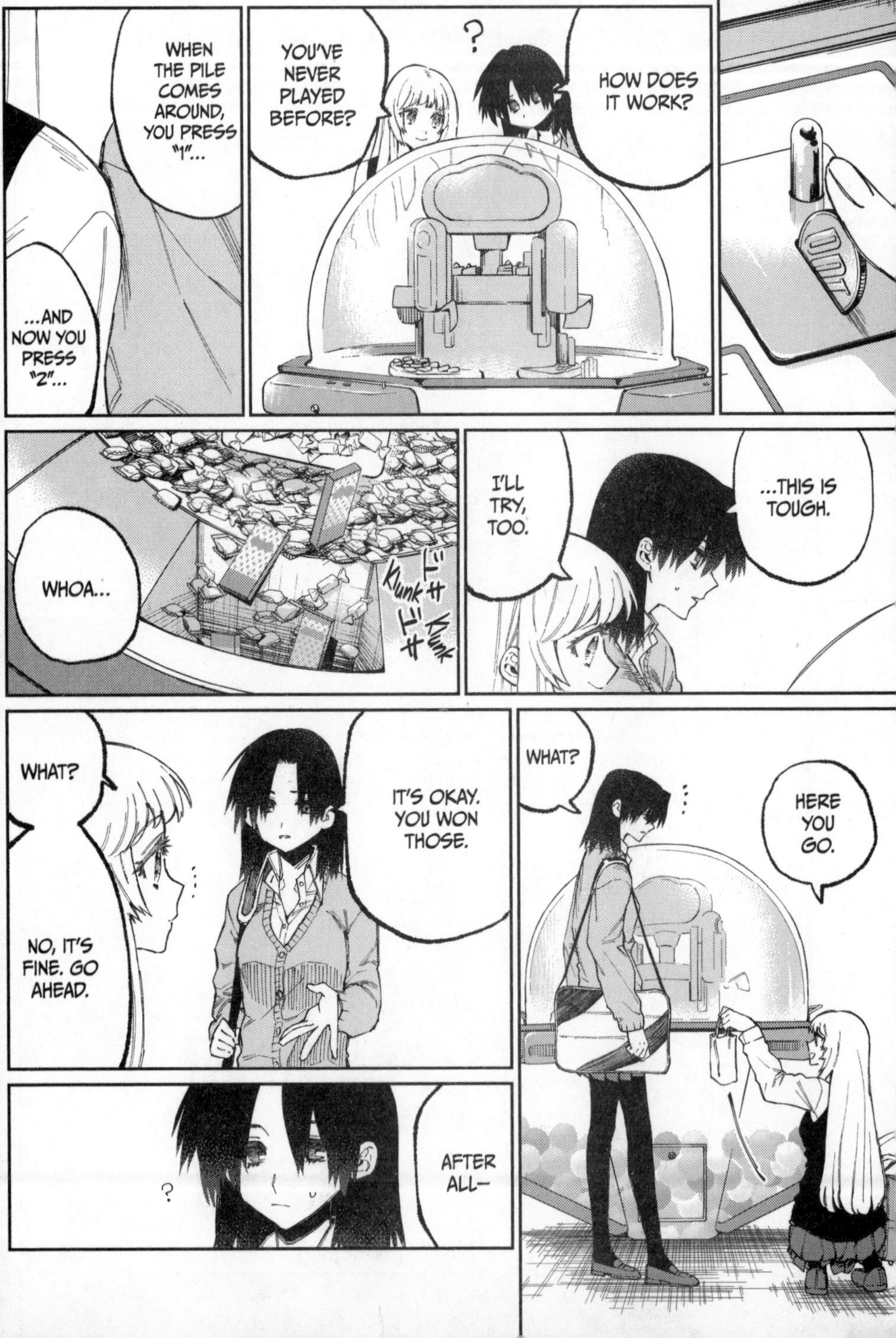
HOW DOES IT WORK?
?
YOU'VE NEVER PLAYED BEFORE?
WHEN THE PILE COMES AROUND, YOU PRESS "1"...
...AND NOW YOU PRESS "2"...
...THIS IS TOUGH.
I'LL TRY, TOO.
Klunk
Klunk
WHOA...
HERE YOU GO.
WHAT?
IT'S OKAY. YOU WON THOSE.
WHAT?
NO, IT'S FINE. GO AHEAD.
AFTER ALL—
?

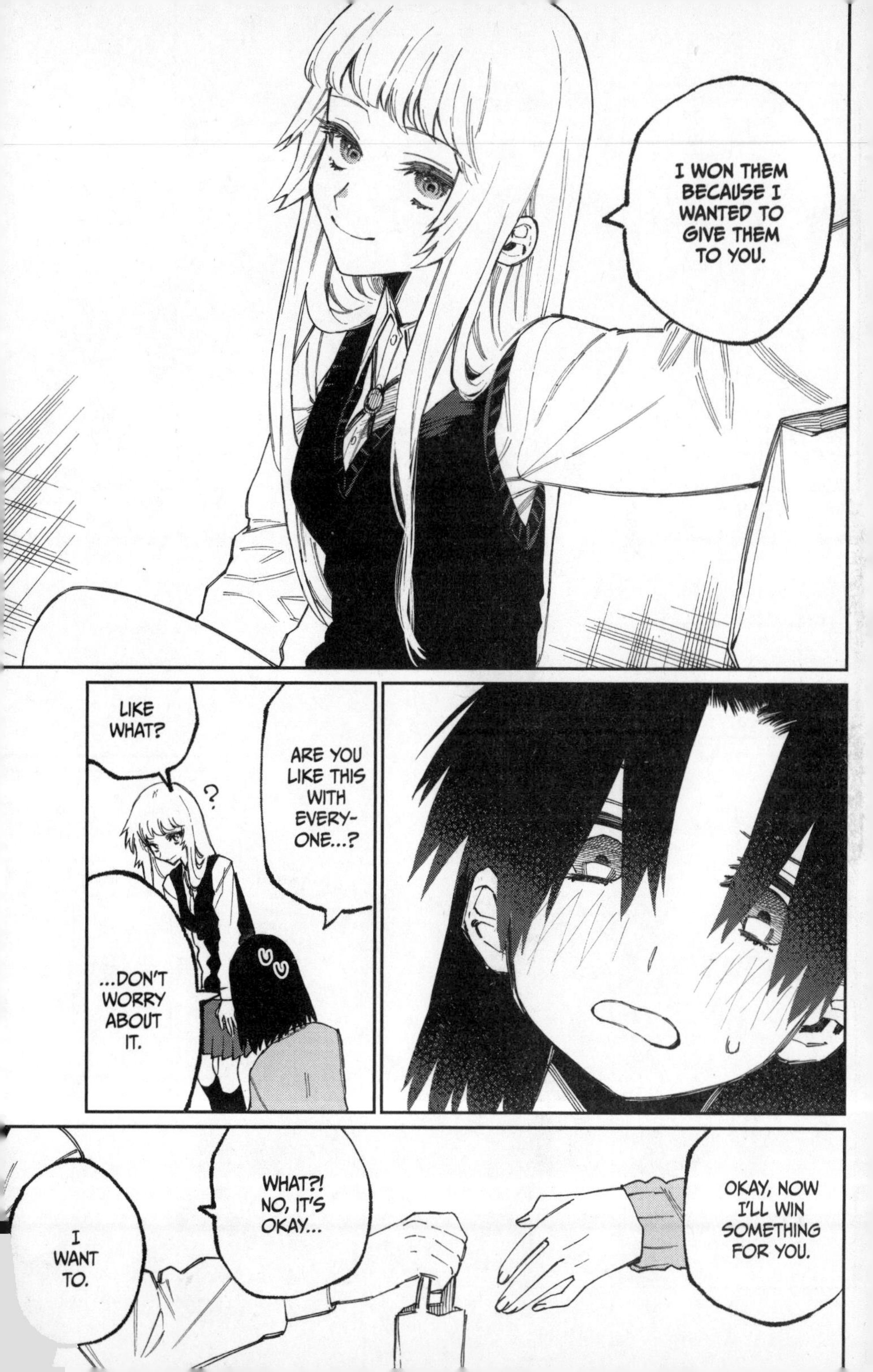
I WON THEM BECAUSE I WANTED TO GIVE THEM TO YOU.
ARE YOU LIKE THIS WITH EVERY-ONE...?
LIKE WHAT?
...DON'T WORRY ABOUT IT.
OKAY, NOW I'LL WIN SOMETHING FOR YOU.
WHAT?! NO, IT'S OKAY...
I WANT TO.

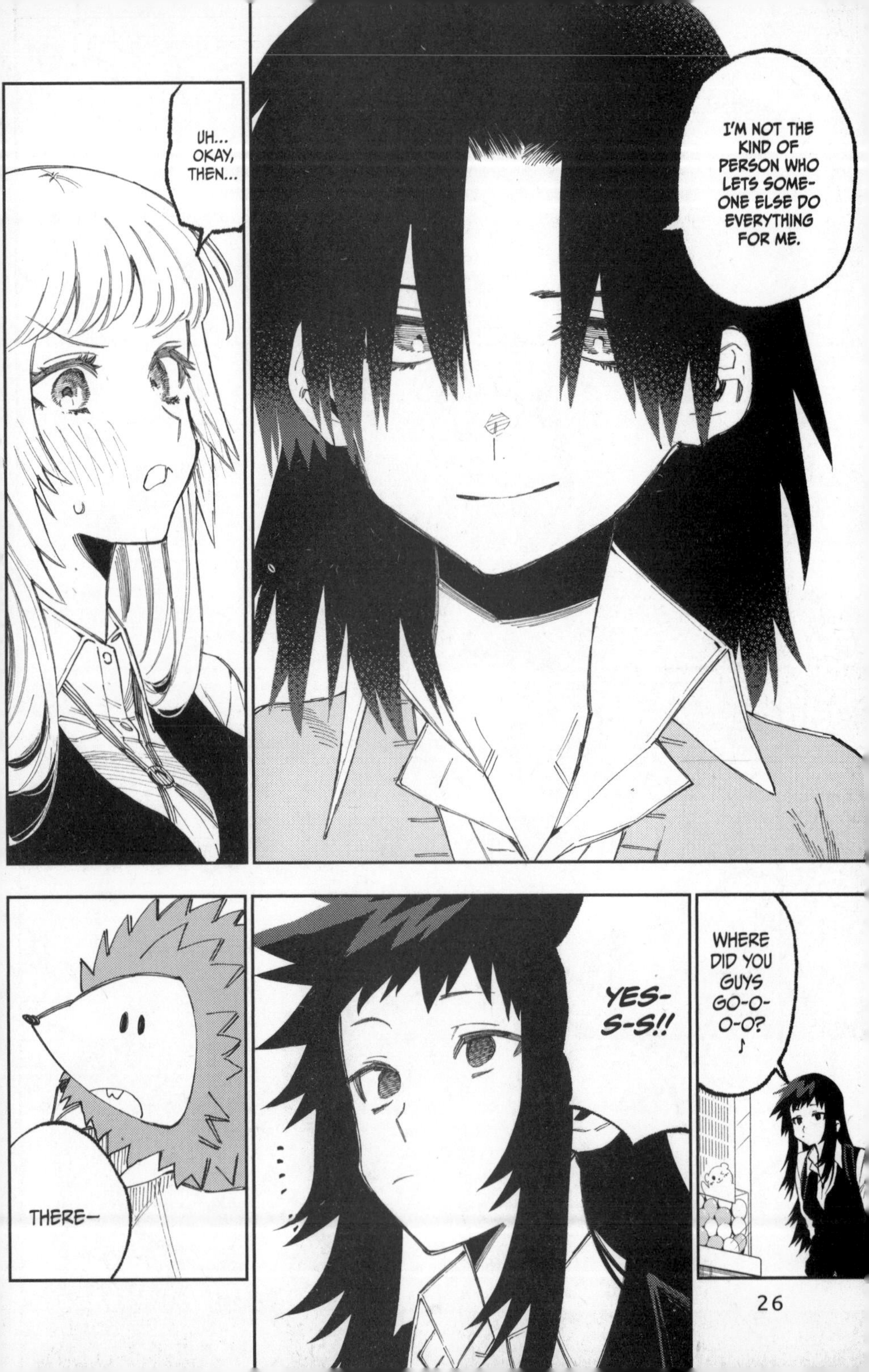
I'M NOT THE KIND OF PERSON WHO LETS SOME-ONE ELSE DO EVERYTHING FOR ME.
UH... OKAY, THEN...
WHERE DID YOU GUYS GO-O-O-O-O? ♪
YES-S-S!!
....
THERE—

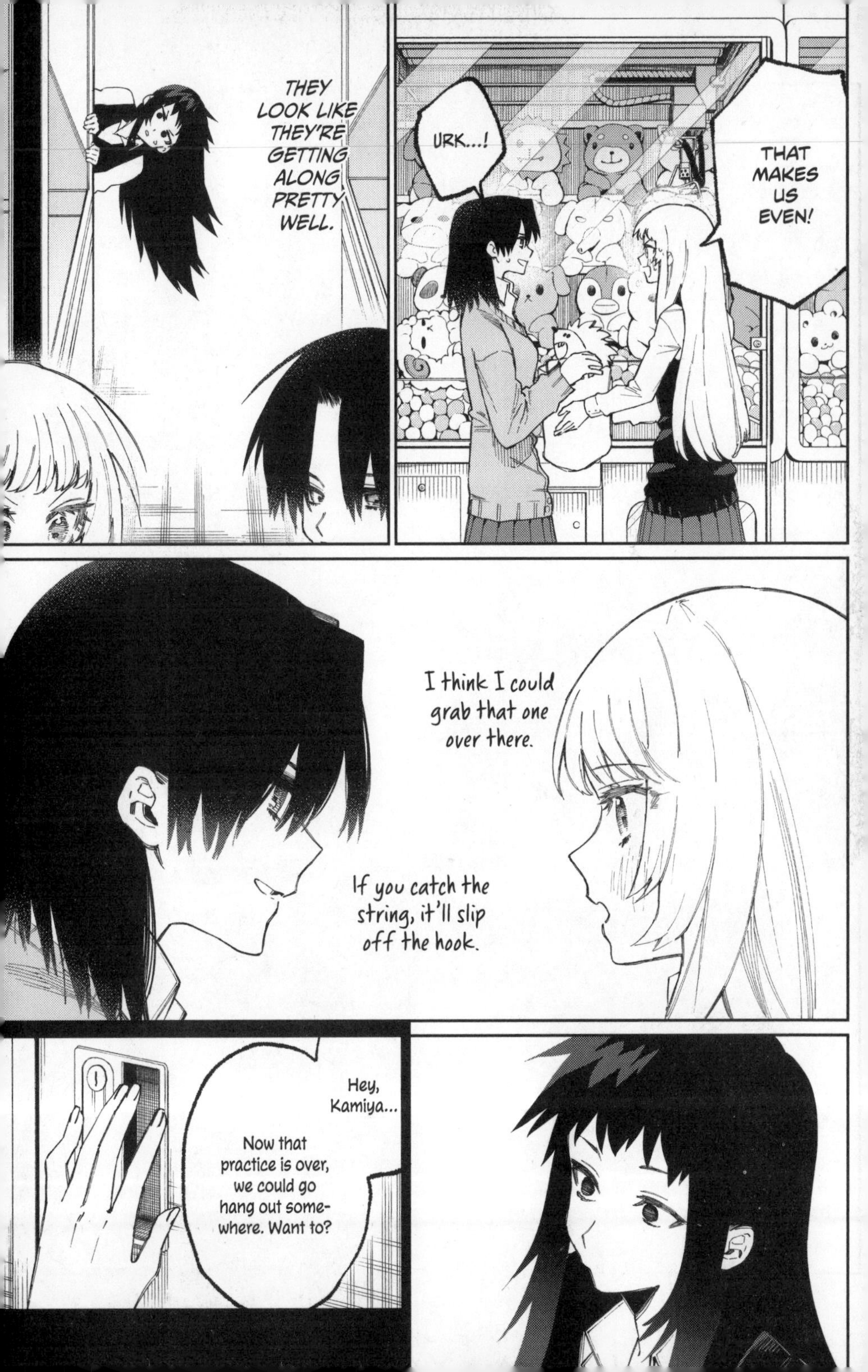
THAT MAKES US EVEN!
URK...!
THEY LOOK LIKE THEY'RE GETTING ALONG PRETTY WELL.
I think I could grab that one over there.
If you catch the string, it'll slip off the hook.
Hey, Kamiya...
Now that practice is over, we could go hang out some-where. Want to?

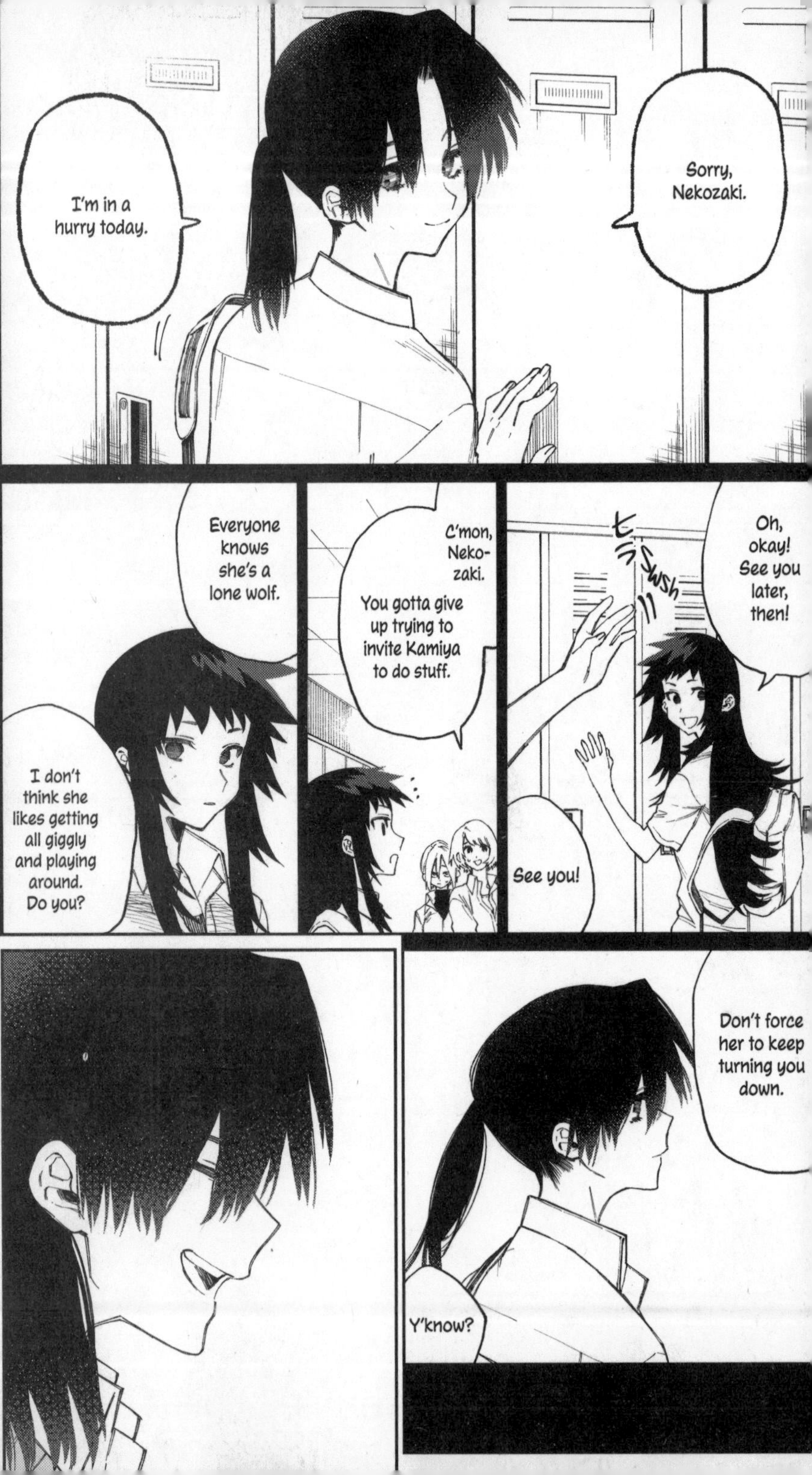
Sorry, Nekozaki.
I'm in a hurry today.
Oh, okay! See you later, then!
Swsh
See you!
C'mon, Neko-zaki.
You gotta give up trying to invite Kamiya to do stuff.
Everyone knows she's a lone wolf.
I don't think she likes getting all giggly and playing around. Do you?
Don't force her to keep turning you down.
Y'know?

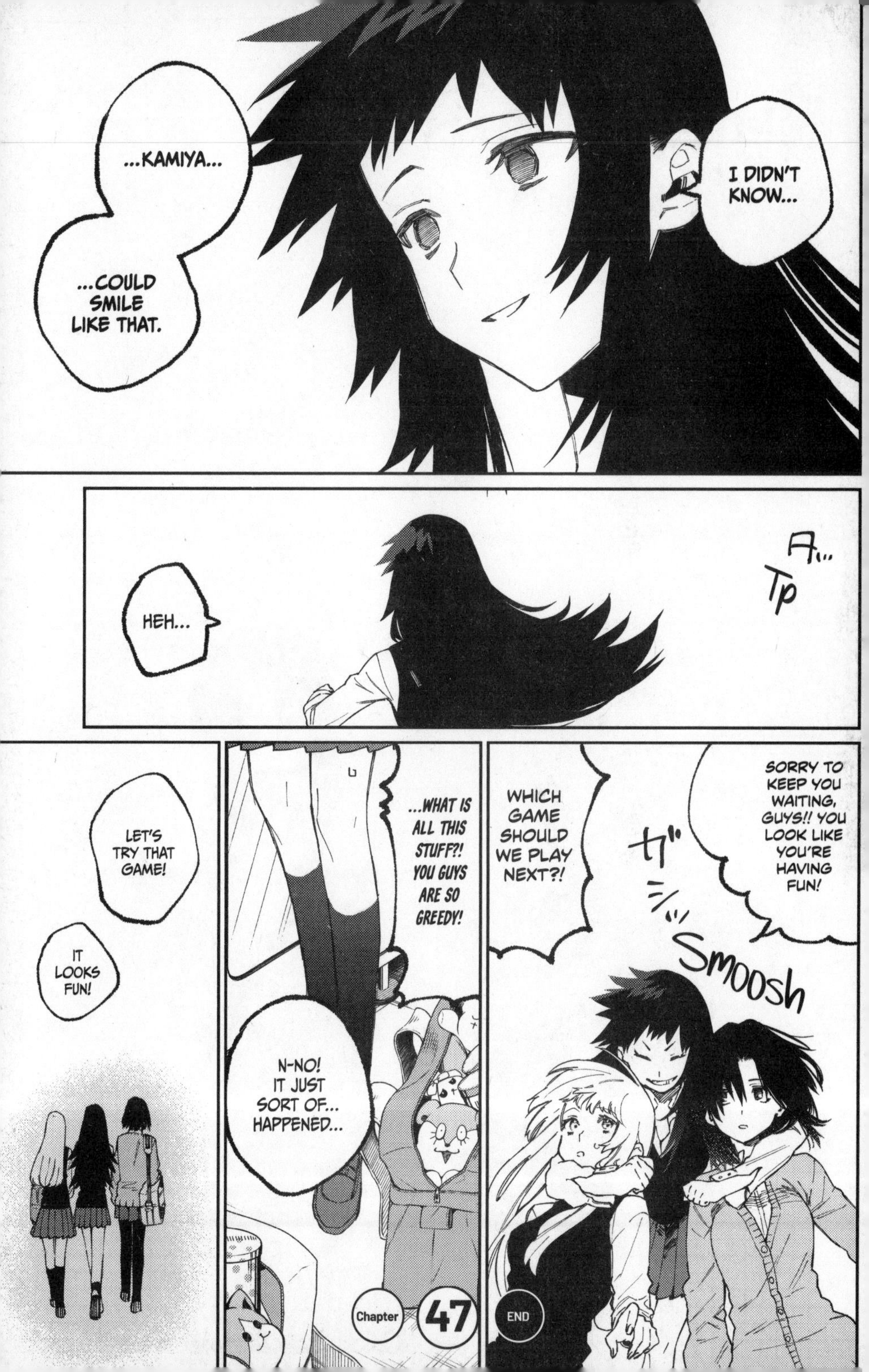
I DIDN'T KNOW...
...KAMIYA...
...COULD SMILE LIKE THAT.
A...
Tp
HEH...
SORRY TO KEEP YOU WAITING, GUYS!! YOU LOOK LIKE YOU'RE HAVING FUN!
ガ
Smoosh
WHICH GAME SHOULD WE PLAY NEXT?!
...WHAT IS ALL THIS STUFF?! YOU GUYS ARE SO GREEDY!
N-NO! IT JUST SORT OF... HAPPENED...
LET'S TRY THAT GAME!
IT LOOKS FUN!
Chapter 47 END

SHIKIMORI'S

Not just a cutie

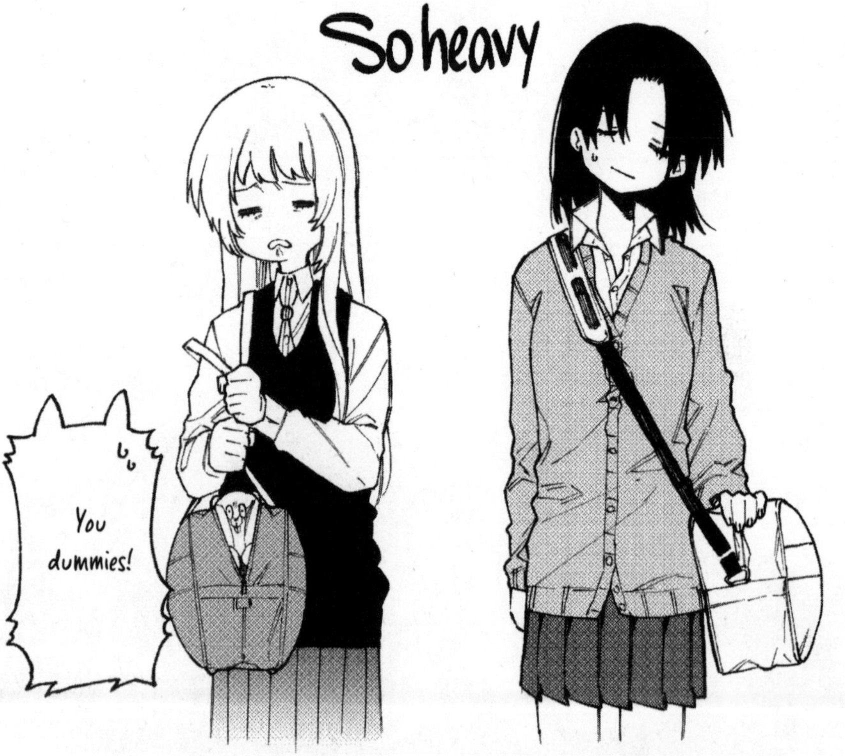
So heavy
You dummies!

# Chapter 48

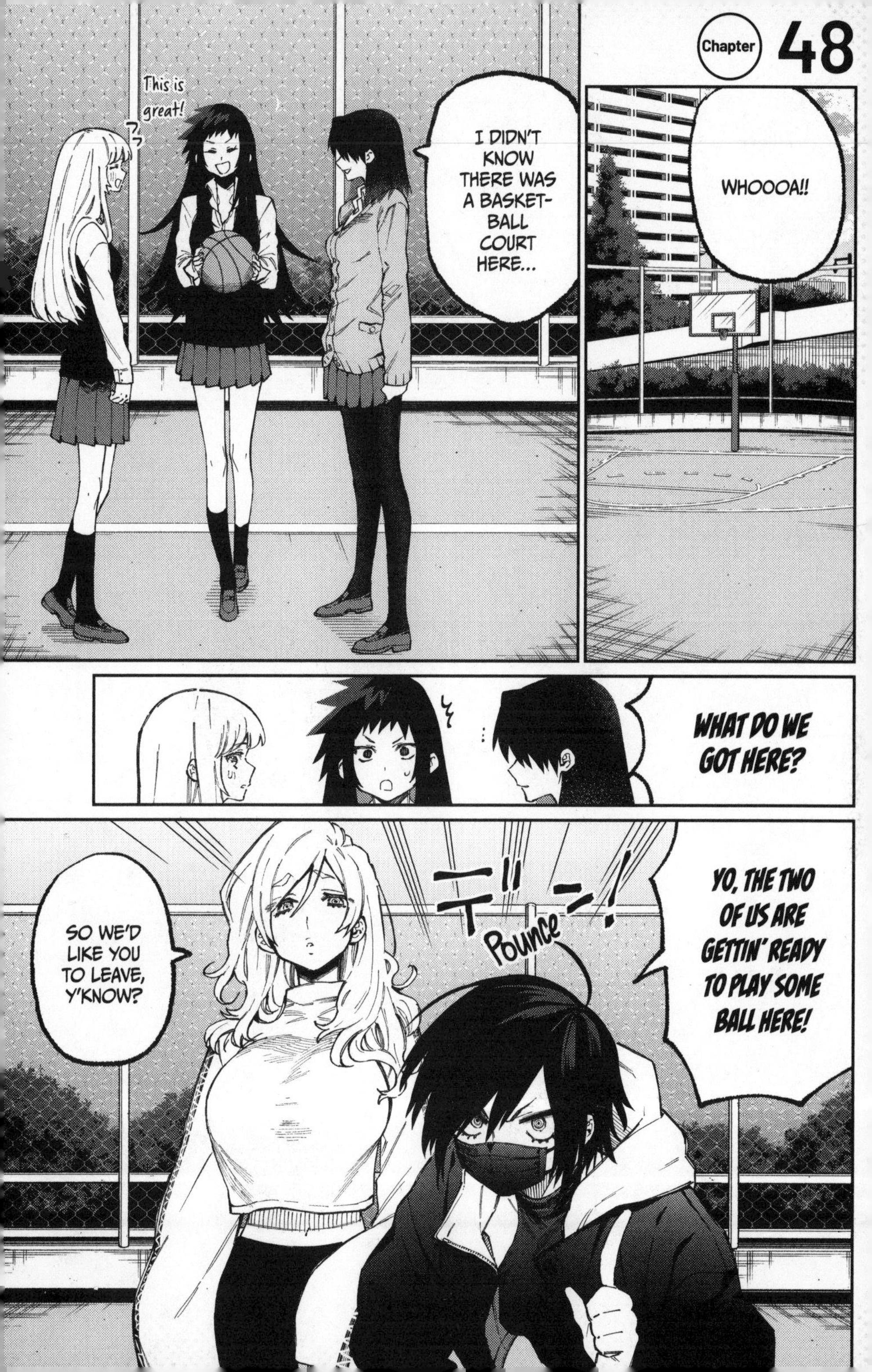
WHOOOA!!
I DIDN'T KNOW THERE WAS A BASKET-BALL COURT HERE...
This is great!
WHAT DO WE GOT HERE?
YO, THE TWO OF US ARE GETTIN' READY TO PLAY SOME BALL HERE!
Pounce
SO WE'D LIKE YOU TO LEAVE, Y'KNOW?

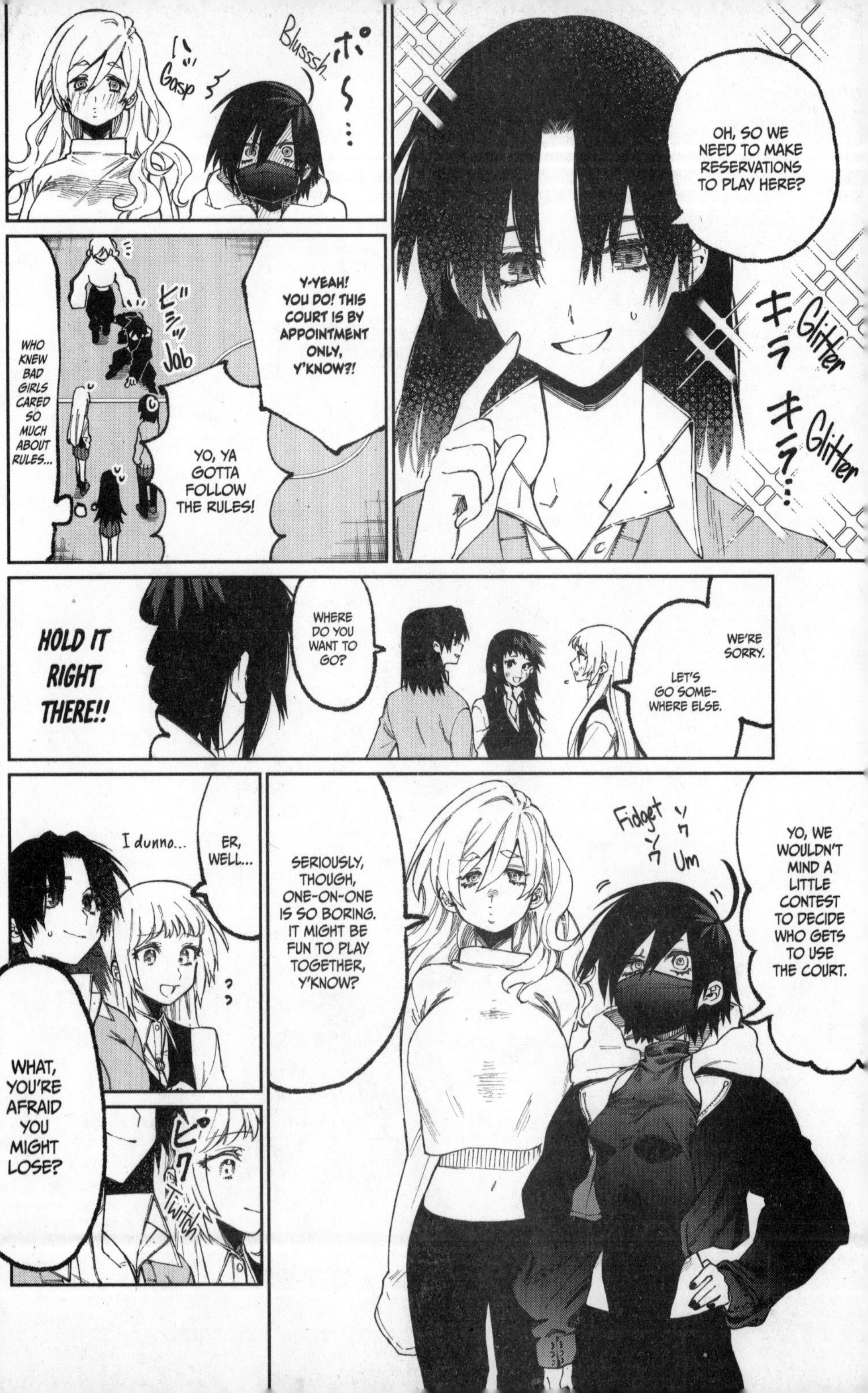
OH, SO WE NEED TO MAKE RESERVATIONS TO PLAY HERE?
キラ Glitter
キラ… Glitter
Blusssh
Gasp
Y-YEAH! YOU DO! THIS COURT IS BY APPOINTMENT ONLY, Y'KNOW?!
Jab
WHO KNEW BAD GIRLS CARED SO MUCH ABOUT RULES...
YO, YA GOTTA FOLLOW THE RULES!
WE'RE SORRY.
LET'S GO SOME-WHERE ELSE.
WHERE DO YOU WANT TO GO?
HOLD IT RIGHT THERE!!
YO, WE WOULDN'T MIND A LITTLE CONTEST TO DECIDE WHO GETS TO USE THE COURT.
Fidget
Um
SERIOUSLY, THOUGH, ONE-ON-ONE IS SO BORING. IT MIGHT BE FUN TO PLAY TOGETHER, Y'KNOW?
ER, WELL...
I dunno...
WHAT, YOU'RE AFRAID YOU MIGHT LOSE?
Twitch

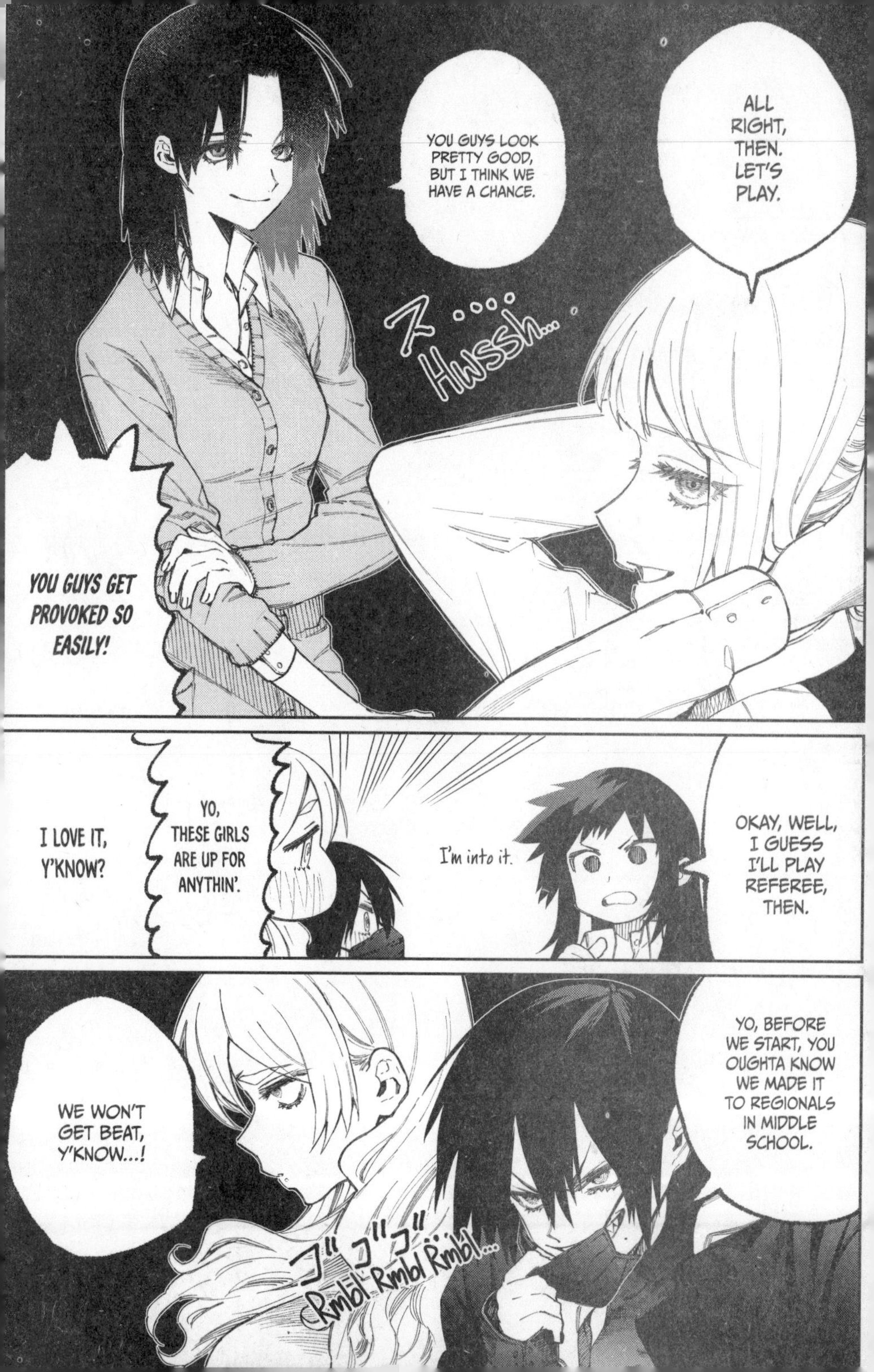
ALL RIGHT, THEN. LET'S PLAY.
YOU GUYS LOOK PRETTY GOOD, BUT I THINK WE HAVE A CHANCE.
ス.... Hwssh...
YOU GUYS GET PROVOKED SO EASILY!
OKAY, WELL, I GUESS I'LL PLAY REFEREE, THEN.
I'm into it.
YO, THESE GIRLS ARE UP FOR ANYTHIN'.
I LOVE IT, Y'KNOW?
YO, BEFORE WE START, YOU OUGHTA KNOW WE MADE IT TO REGIONALS IN MIDDLE SCHOOL.
WE WON'T GET BEAT, Y'KNOW...!
ゴゴゴ... Rmbl Rmbl Rmbl...

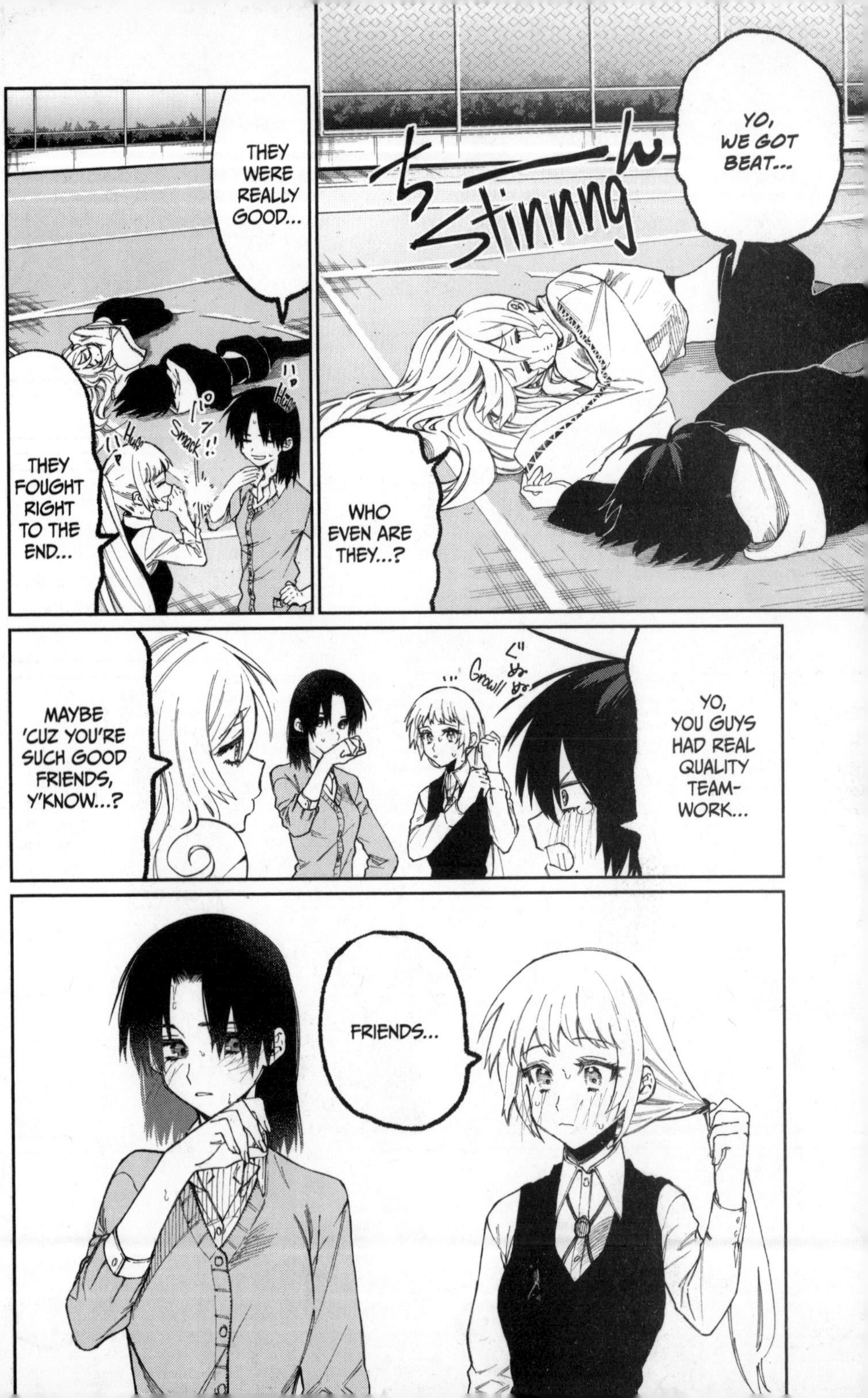
YO, WE GOT BEAT...
Stinnng
WHO EVEN ARE THEY...?
THEY WERE REALLY GOOD...
Smack!!
THEY FOUGHT RIGHT TO THE END...
YO, YOU GUYS HAD REAL QUALITY TEAM-WORK...
Growl
MAYBE 'CUZ YOU'RE SUCH GOOD FRIENDS, Y'KNOW...?
FRIENDS...

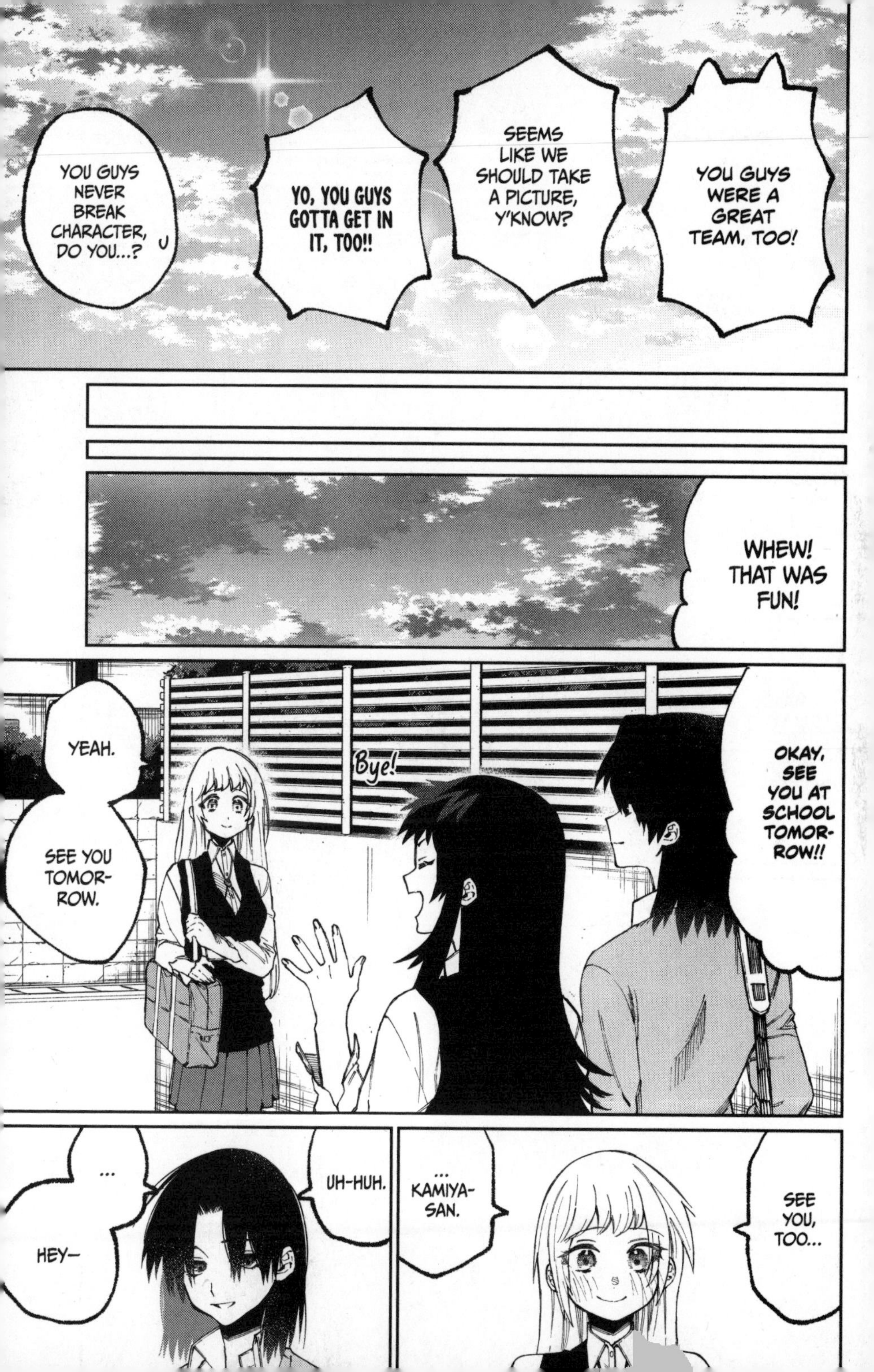
YOU GUYS WERE A GREAT TEAM, TOO!
SEEMS LIKE WE SHOULD TAKE A PICTURE, Y'KNOW?
YO, YOU GUYS GOTTA GET IN IT, TOO!!
YOU GUYS NEVER BREAK CHARACTER, DO YOU...?
WHEW! THAT WAS FUN!
OKAY, SEE YOU AT SCHOOL TOMOR-ROW!!
Bye!
YEAH.
SEE YOU TOMOR-ROW.
SEE YOU, TOO...
... KAMIYA-SAN.
UH-HUH.
...
HEY—

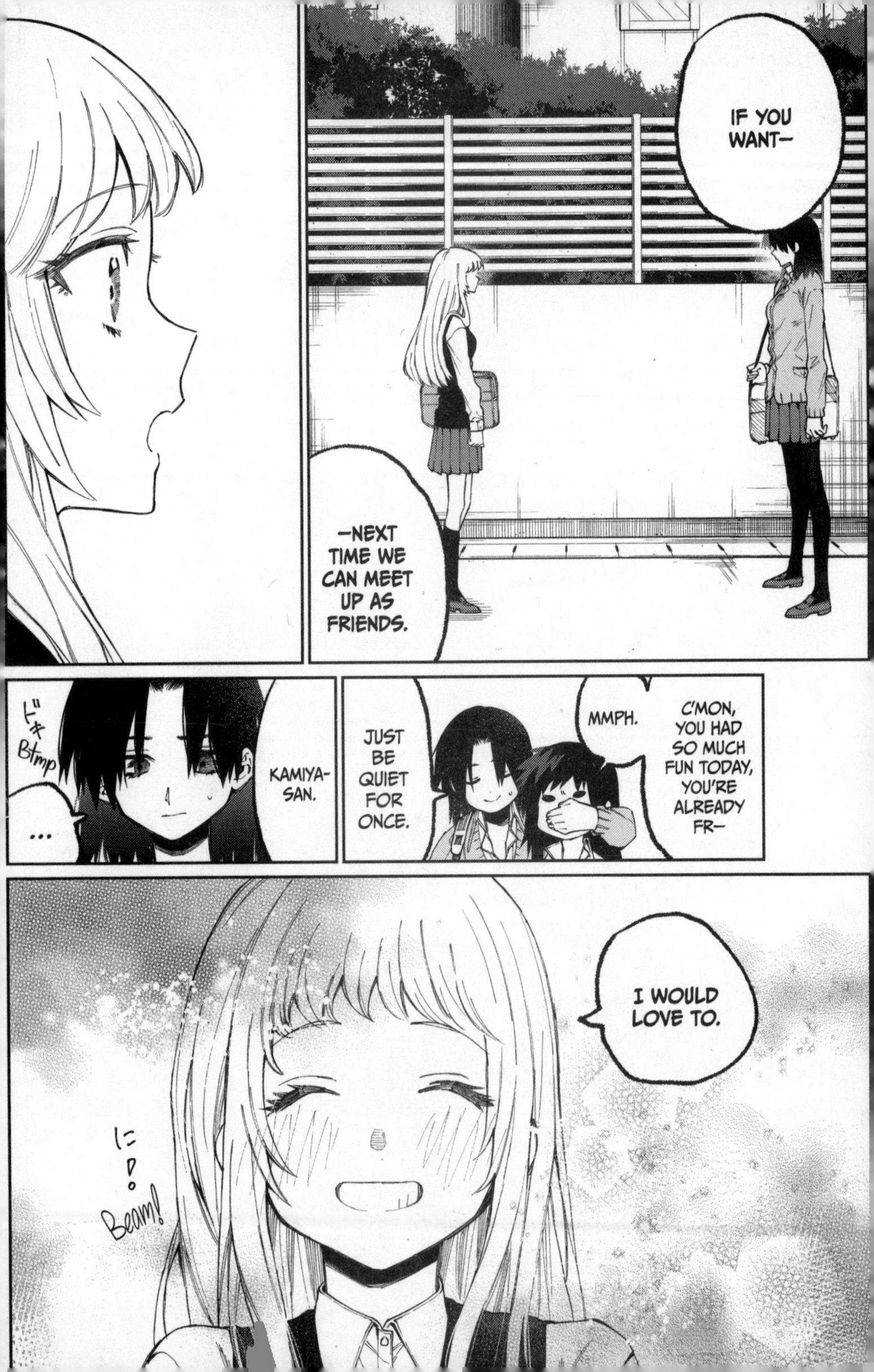
IF YOU WANT—
—NEXT TIME WE CAN MEET UP AS FRIENDS.
C'MON, YOU HAD SO MUCH FUN TODAY, YOU'RE ALREADY FR—
MMPH.
JUST BE QUIET FOR ONCE.
KAMIYA-SAN.
ドキ Btmp
...
I WOULD LOVE TO.
Beam!

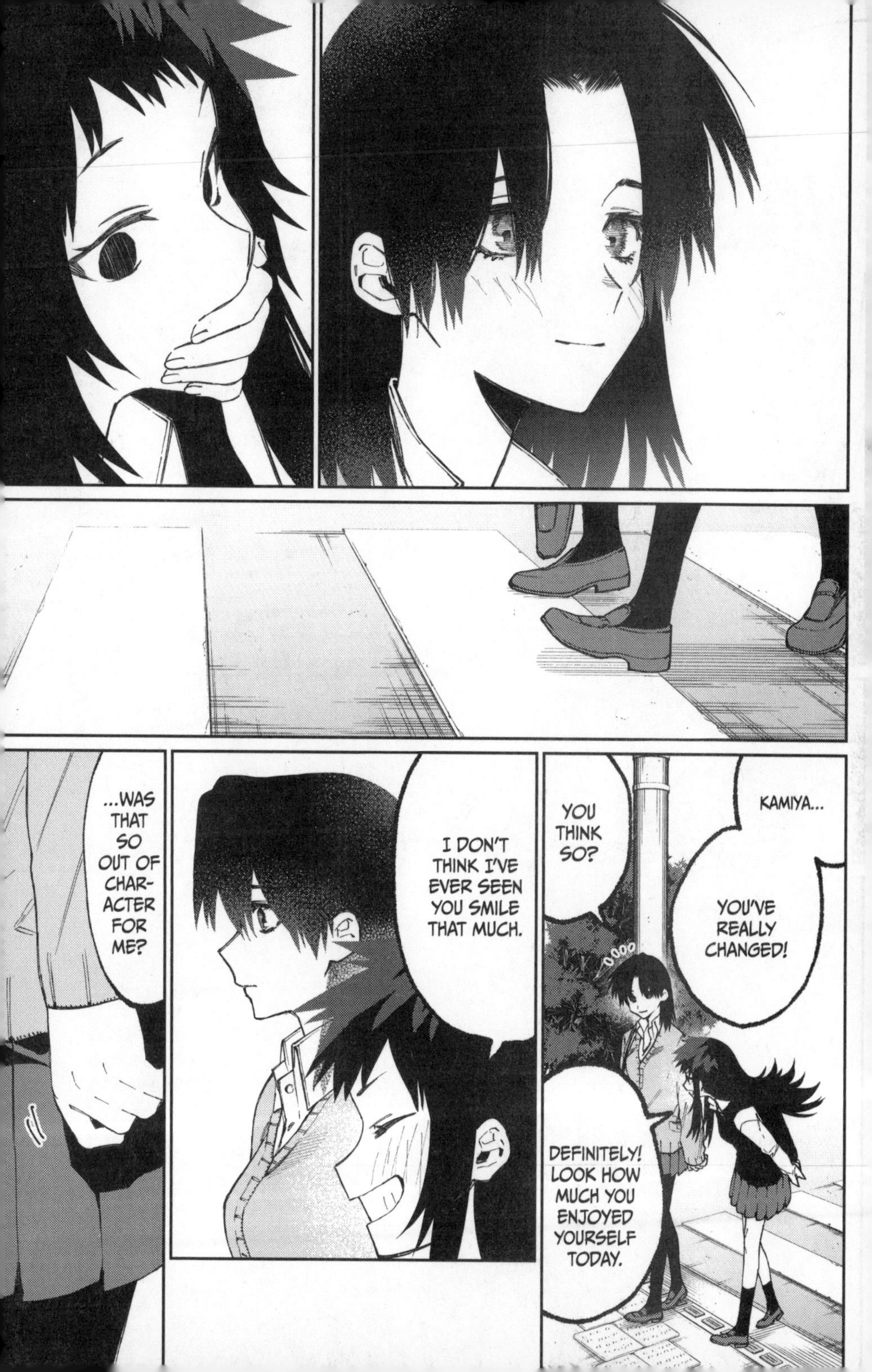
KAMIYA... YOU'VE REALLY CHANGED!
YOU THINK SO?
DEFINITELY! LOOK HOW MUCH YOU ENJOYED YOURSELF TODAY.
I DON'T THINK I'VE EVER SEEN YOU SMILE THAT MUCH.
...WAS THAT SO OUT OF CHARACTER FOR ME?

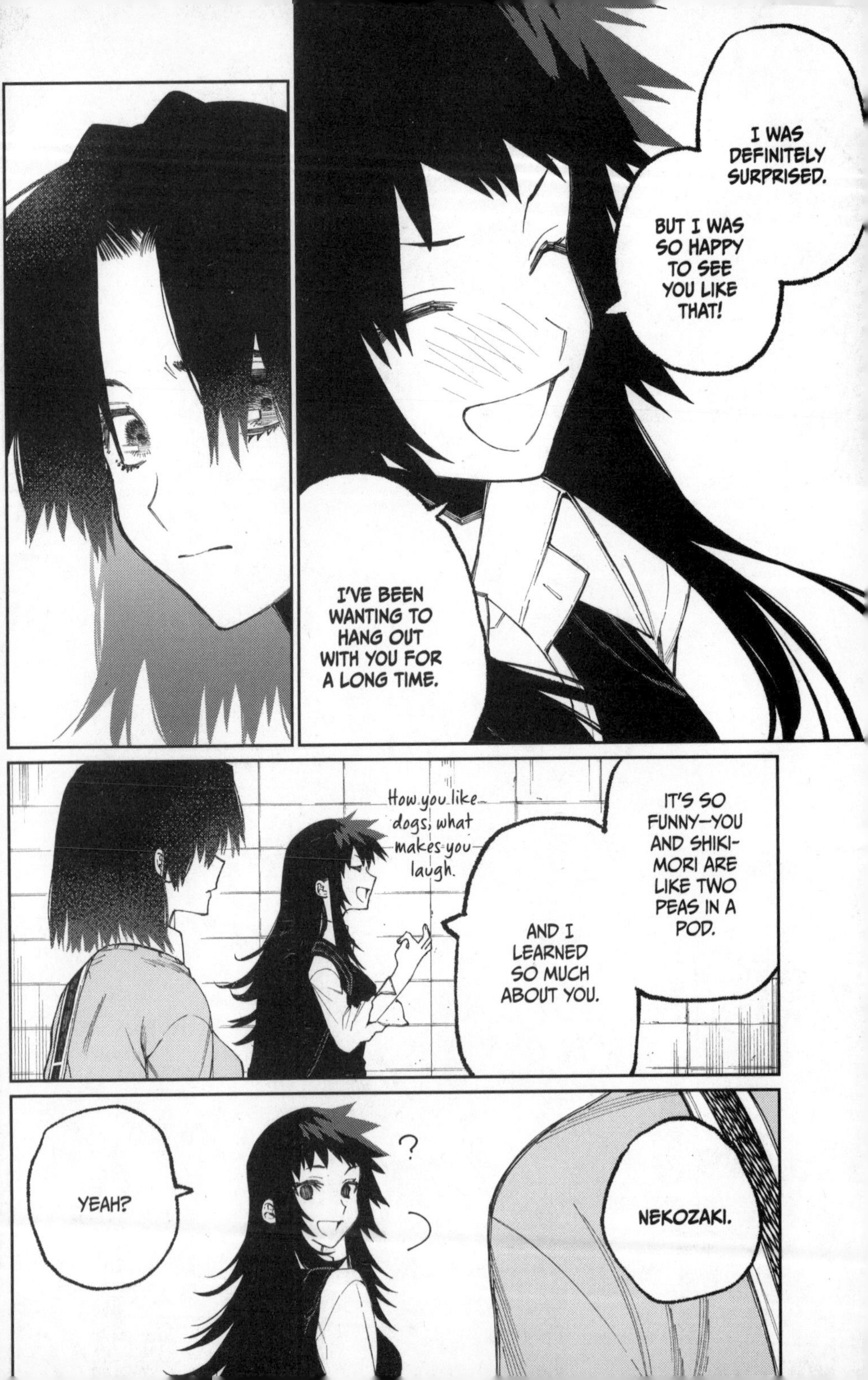
I WAS DEFINITELY SURPRISED.
BUT I WAS SO HAPPY TO SEE YOU LIKE THAT!
I'VE BEEN WANTING TO HANG OUT WITH YOU FOR A LONG TIME.
IT'S SO FUNNY—YOU AND SHIKI-MORI ARE LIKE TWO PEAS IN A POD.
AND I LEARNED SO MUCH ABOUT YOU.
How you like dogs, what makes you laugh.
NEKOZAKI.
?
YEAH?

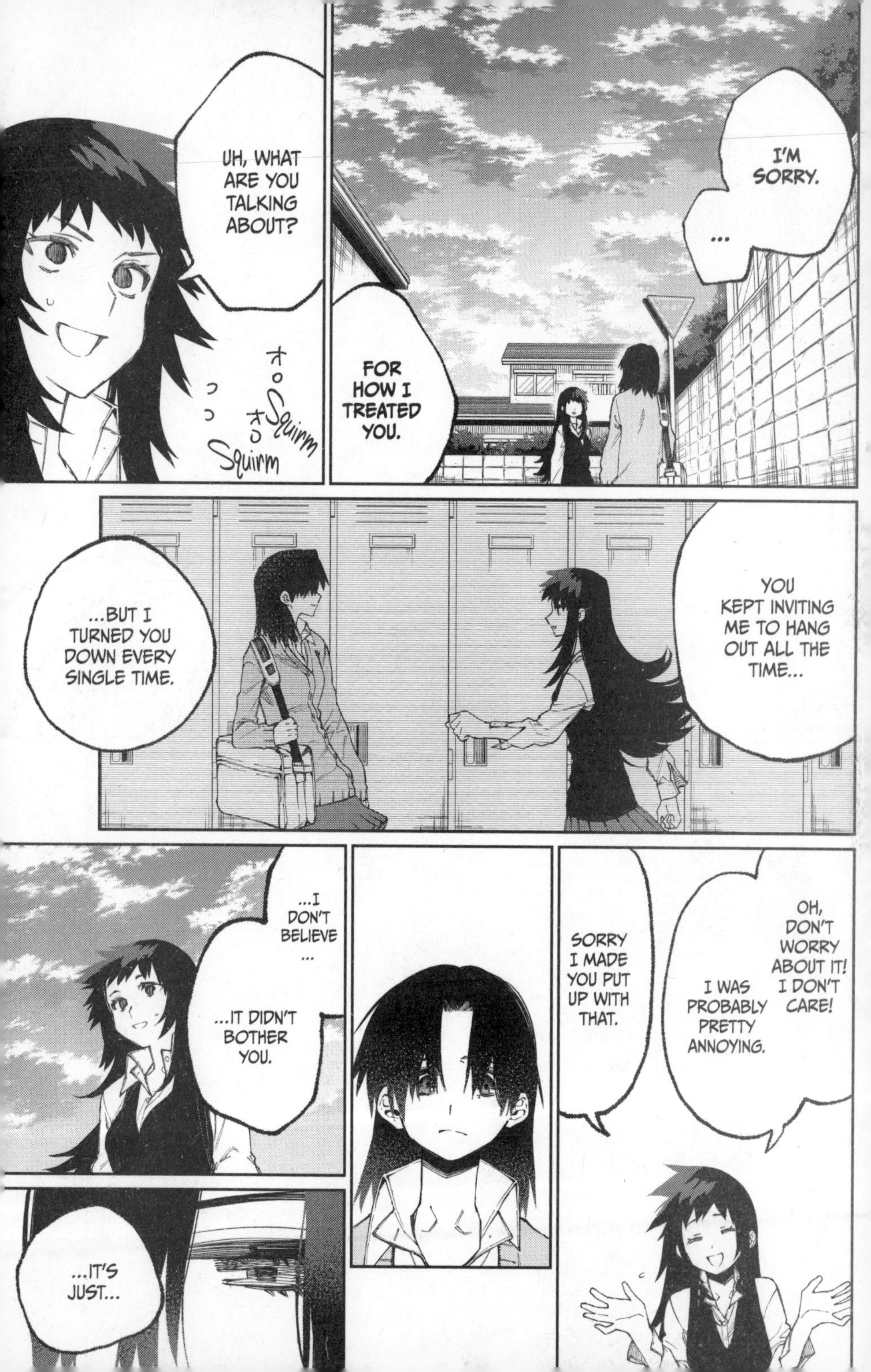
I'M SORRY.
...
FOR HOW I TREATED YOU.
UH, WHAT ARE YOU TALKING ABOUT?
Squirm Squirm
YOU KEPT INVITING ME TO HANG OUT ALL THE TIME...
...BUT I TURNED YOU DOWN EVERY SINGLE TIME.
OH, DON'T WORRY ABOUT IT! I DON'T CARE!
I WAS PROBABLY PRETTY ANNOYING.
SORRY I MADE YOU PUT UP WITH THAT.
...I DON'T BELIEVE ...
...IT DIDN'T BOTHER YOU.
...IT'S JUST...

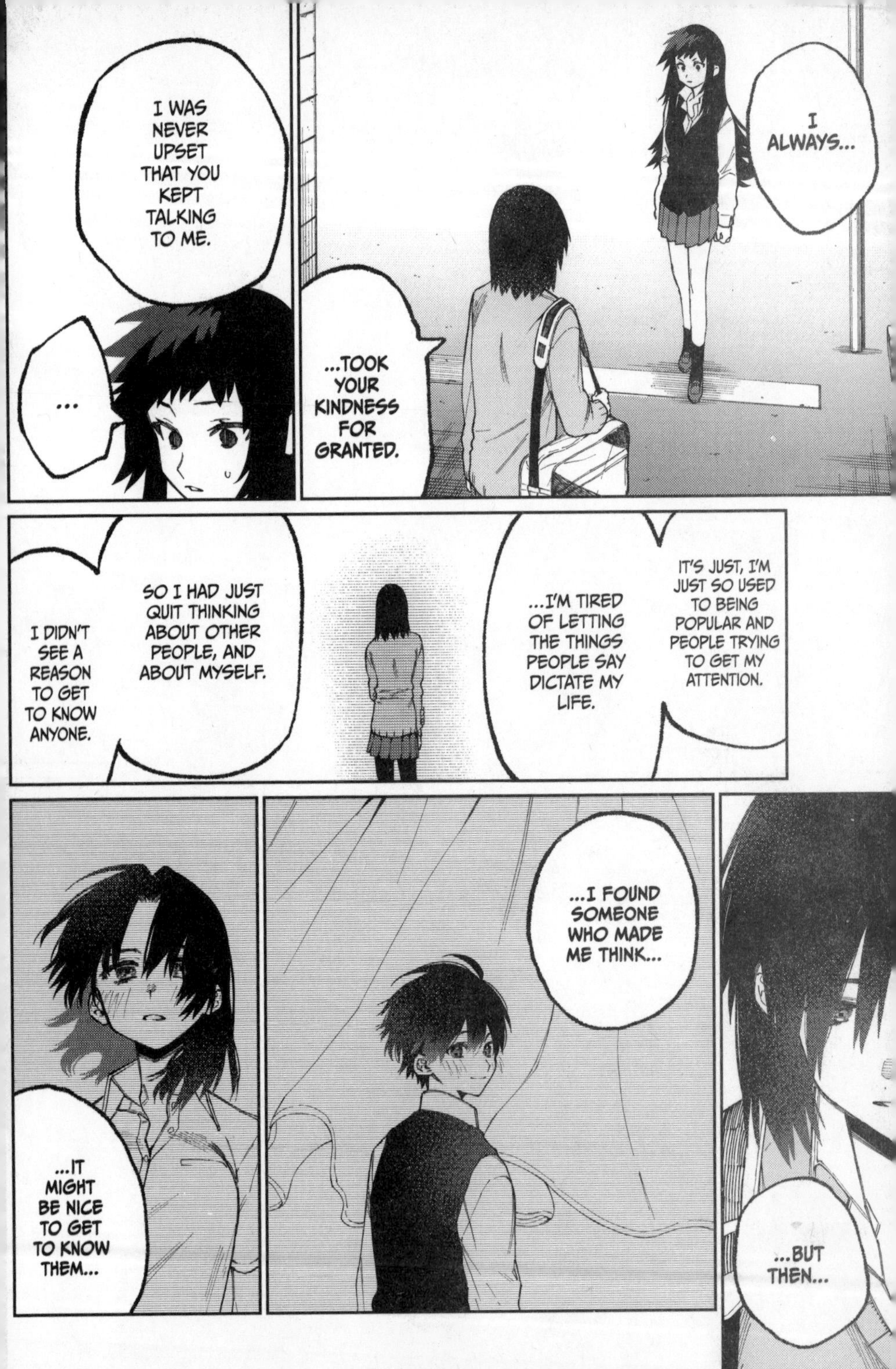
I ALWAYS...
...TOOK YOUR KINDNESS FOR GRANTED.
I WAS NEVER UPSET THAT YOU KEPT TALKING TO ME.
...
IT'S JUST, I'M JUST SO USED TO BEING POPULAR AND PEOPLE TRYING TO GET MY ATTENTION.
...I'M TIRED OF LETTING THE THINGS PEOPLE SAY DICTATE MY LIFE.
SO I HAD JUST QUIT THINKING ABOUT OTHER PEOPLE, AND ABOUT MYSELF.
I DIDN'T SEE A REASON TO GET TO KNOW ANYONE.
...BUT THEN...
...I FOUND SOMEONE WHO MADE ME THINK...
...IT MIGHT BE NICE TO GET TO KNOW THEM...

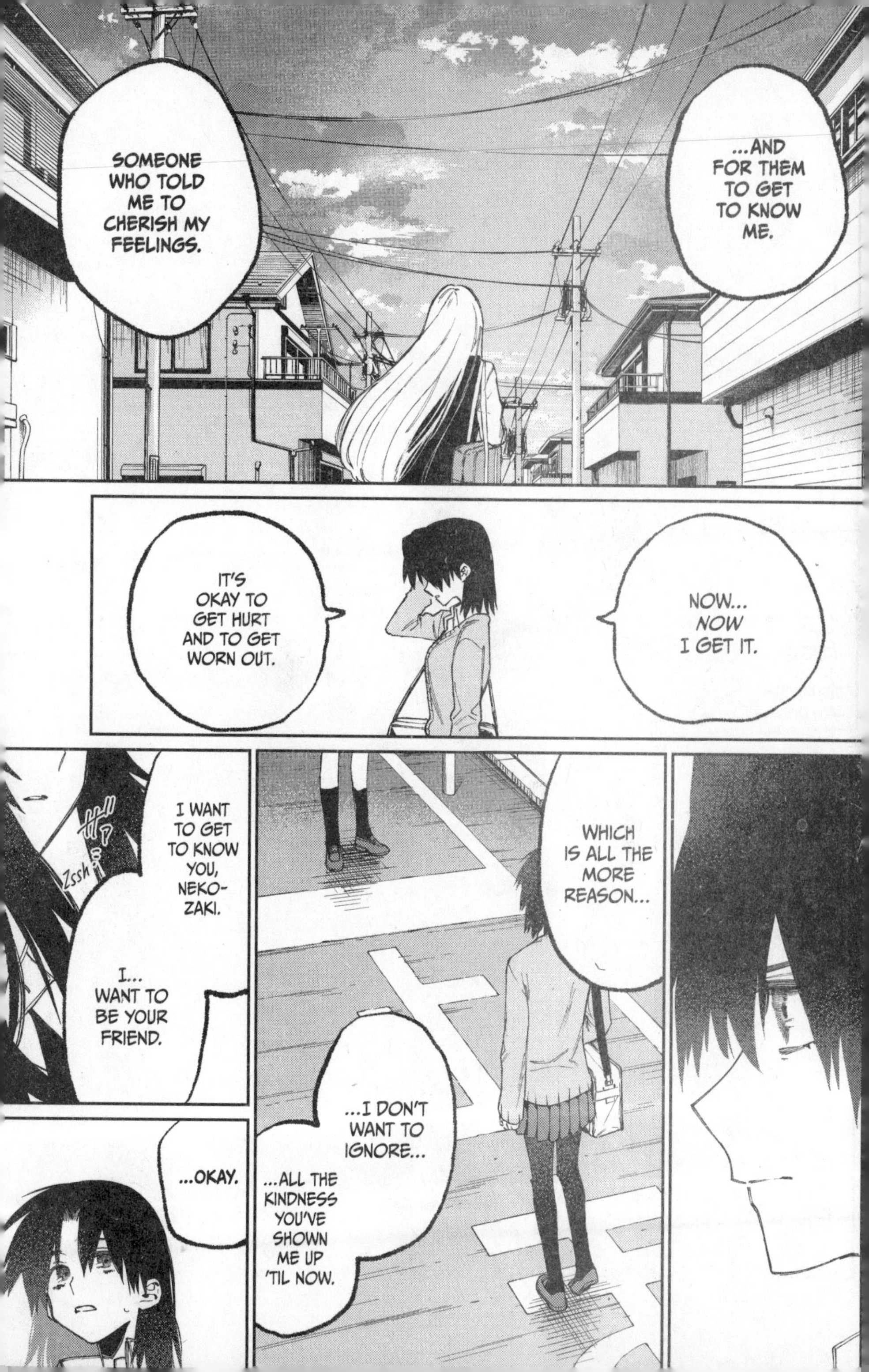
...AND FOR THEM TO GET TO KNOW ME.
SOMEONE WHO TOLD ME TO CHERISH MY FEELINGS.
NOW... *NOW* I GET IT.
IT'S OKAY TO GET HURT AND TO GET WORN OUT.
WHICH IS ALL THE MORE REASON...
...I DON'T WANT TO IGNORE...
...ALL THE KINDNESS YOU'VE SHOWN ME UP 'TIL NOW.
I WANT TO GET TO KNOW YOU, NEKO-ZAKI.
Zssh
I... WANT TO BE YOUR FRIEND.
...OKAY.

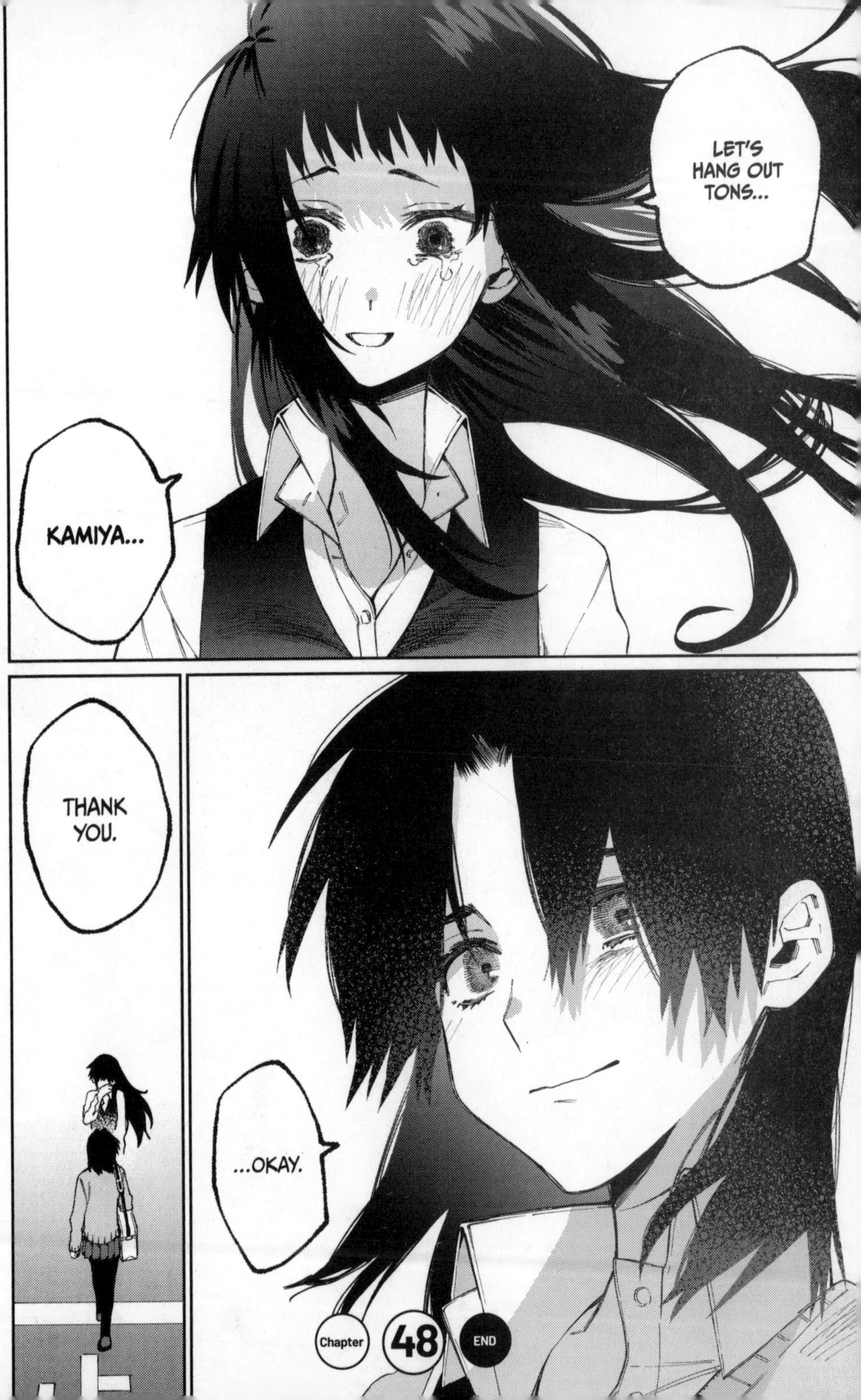
LET'S HANG OUT TONS...
KAMIYA...
...OKAY.
THANK YOU.
Chapter 48 END

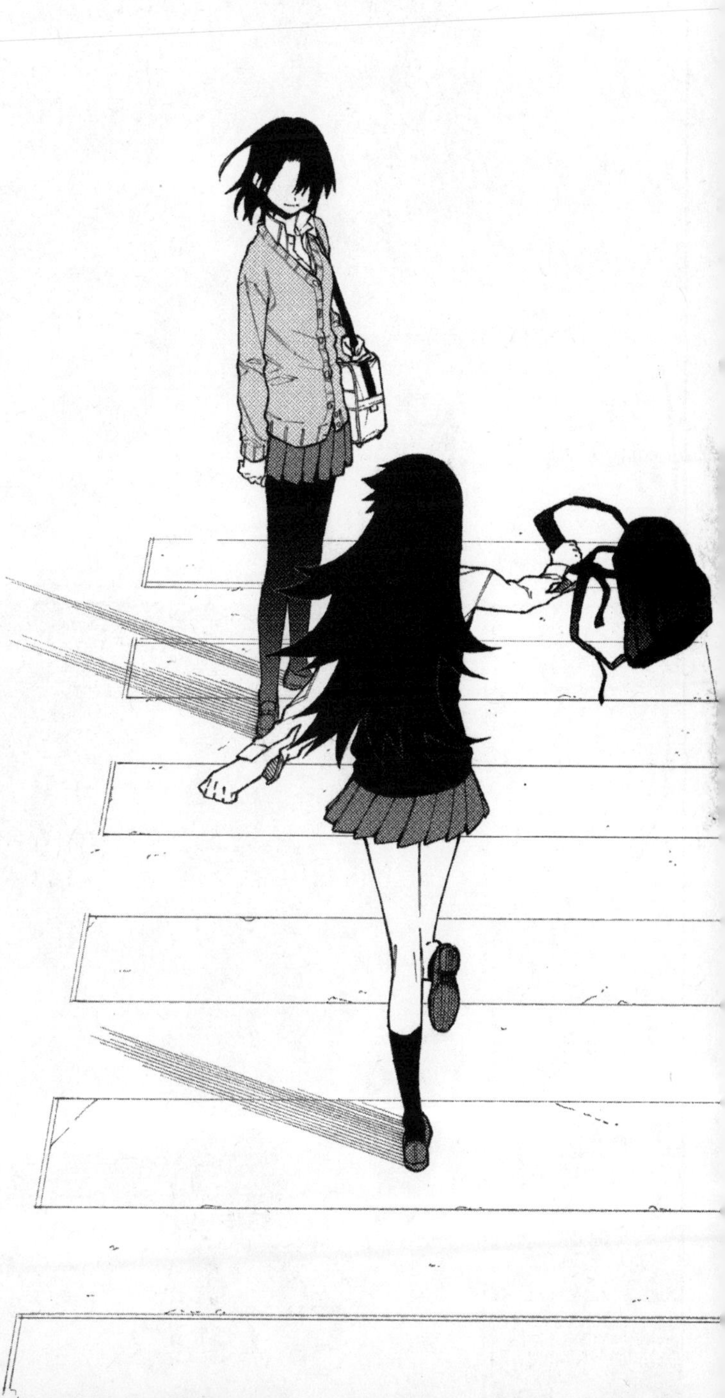

SHIKIMORI'S not just a cutie

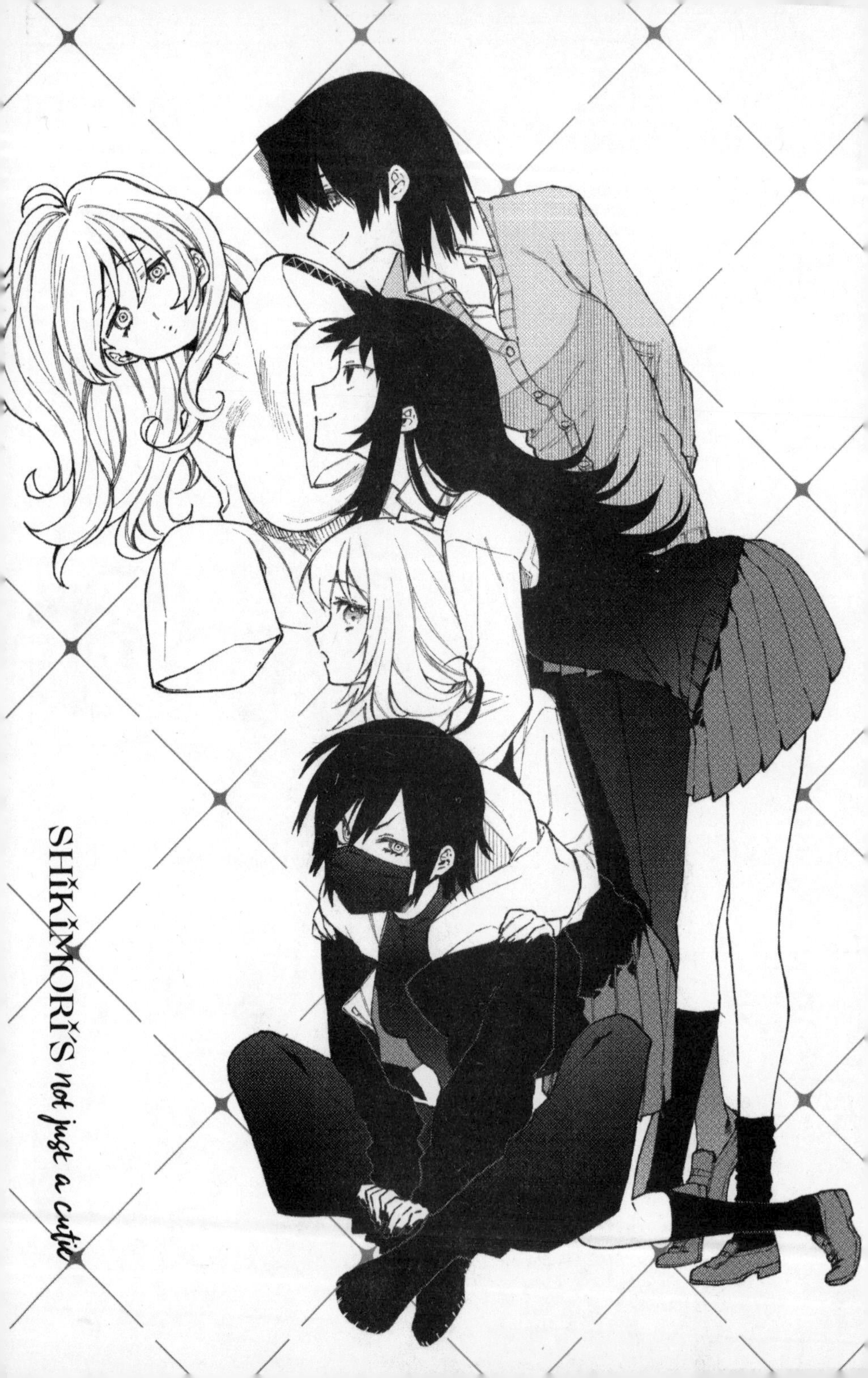
SHIKIMORI'S not just a cutie

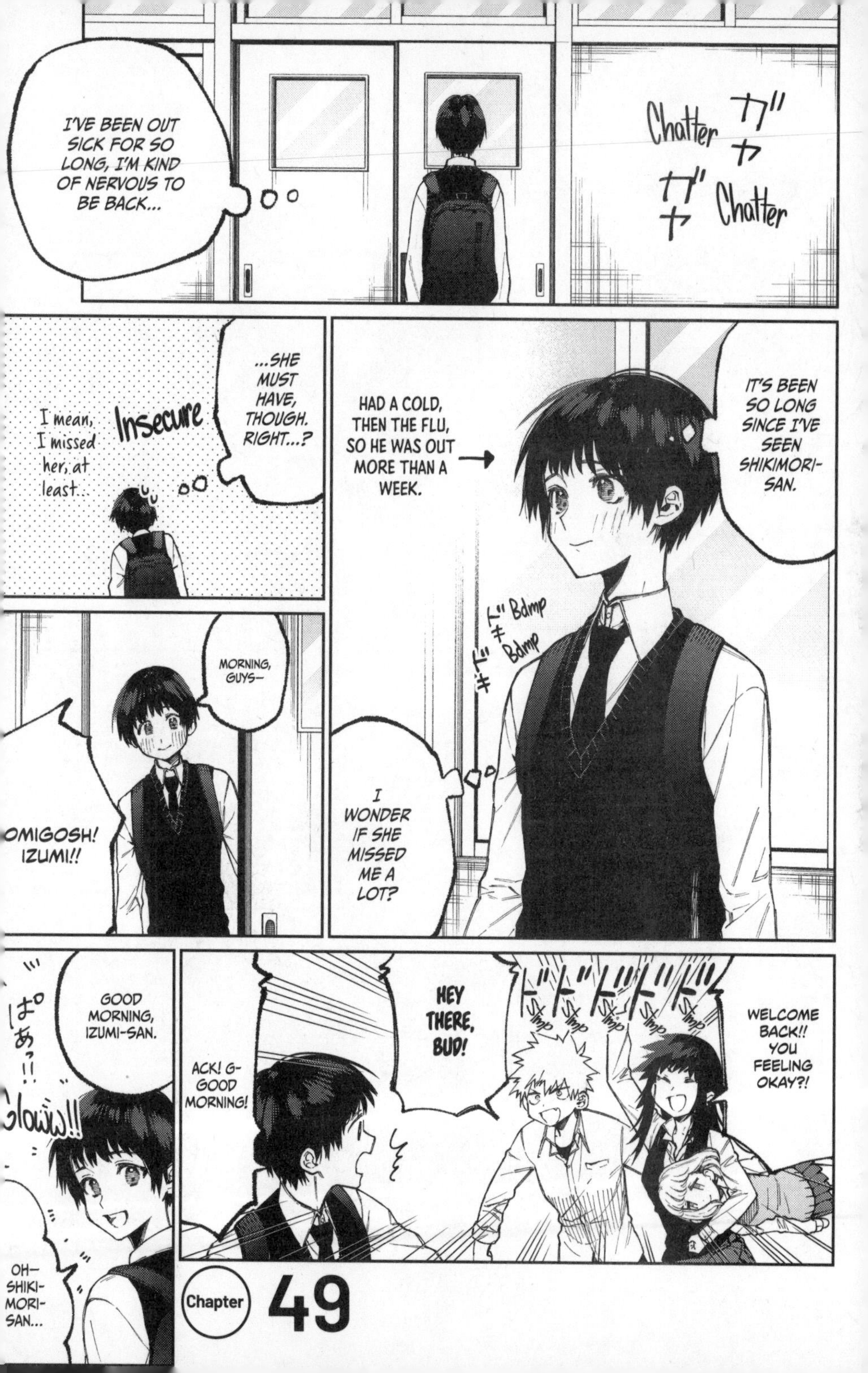
Chatter
Chatter
I'VE BEEN OUT SICK FOR SO LONG, I'M KIND OF NERVOUS TO BE BACK...
IT'S BEEN SO LONG SINCE I'VE SEEN SHIKIMORI-SAN.
HAD A COLD, THEN THE FLU, SO HE WAS OUT MORE THAN A WEEK.
Bdmp Bdmp
I WONDER IF SHE MISSED ME A LOT?
...SHE MUST HAVE, THOUGH. RIGHT...?
Insecure
I mean, I missed her, at least...
MORNING, GUYS–
OMIGOSH! IZUMI!!
WELCOME BACK!! YOU FEELING OKAY?!
HEY THERE, BUD!
ACK! G-GOOD MORNING!
Chapter 49
GOOD MORNING, IZUMI-SAN.
Gloww!!
OH— SHIKIMORI-SAN...

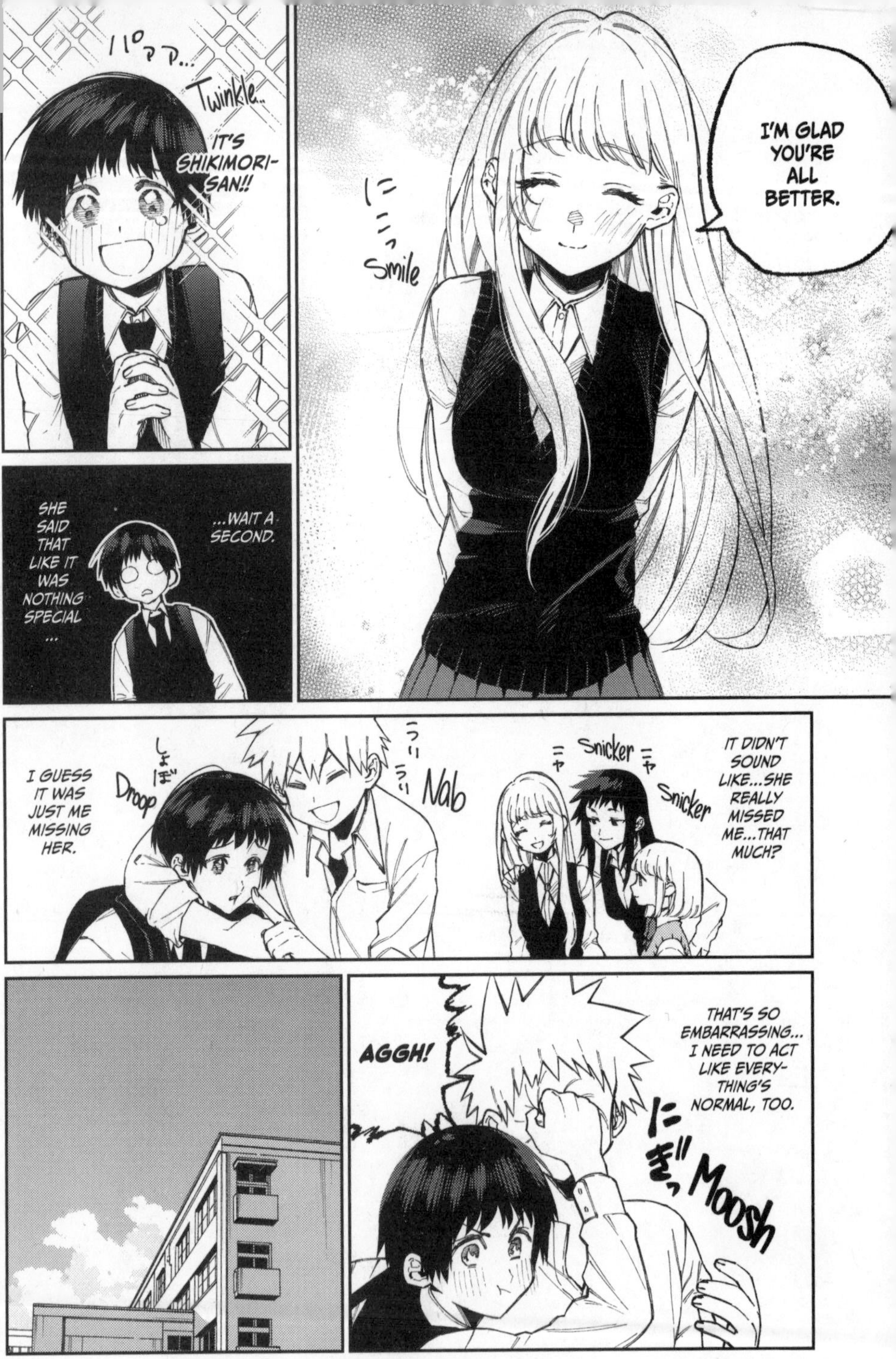
I'M GLAD YOU'RE ALL BETTER.
にこっ
Smile
パァァ...
Twinkle..
IT'S SHIKIMORI-SAN!!
...WAIT A SECOND.
SHE SAID THAT LIKE IT WAS NOTHING SPECIAL...
IT DIDN'T SOUND LIKE...SHE REALLY MISSED ME...THAT MUCH?
ニャ
Snicker
ニャ
Snicker
Nab
しょぼ
Droop
I GUESS IT WAS JUST ME MISSING HER.
THAT'S SO EMBARRASSING... I NEED TO ACT LIKE EVERY-THING'S NORMAL, TOO.
にぎっ
Moosh
AGGH!

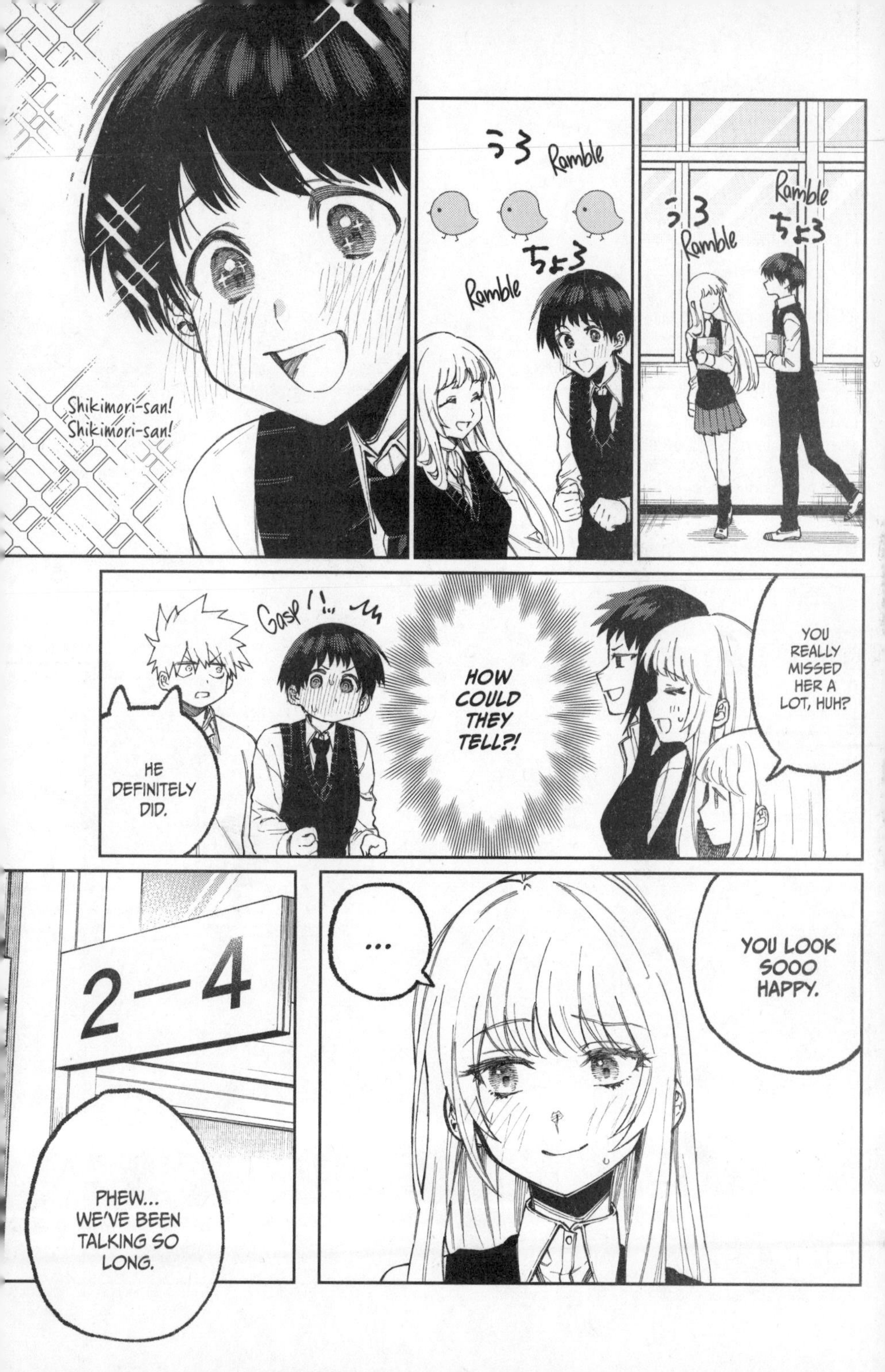
Ramble
うろ
Ramble
ちょろ
うろ
Ramble
ちょろ
Ramble
Shikimori-san! Shikimori-san!
YOU REALLY MISSED HER A LOT, HUH?
HOW COULD THEY TELL?!
Gasp!!...
HE DEFINITELY DID.
YOU LOOK SOOO HAPPY.
...
2-4
PHEW... WE'VE BEEN TALKING SO LONG.

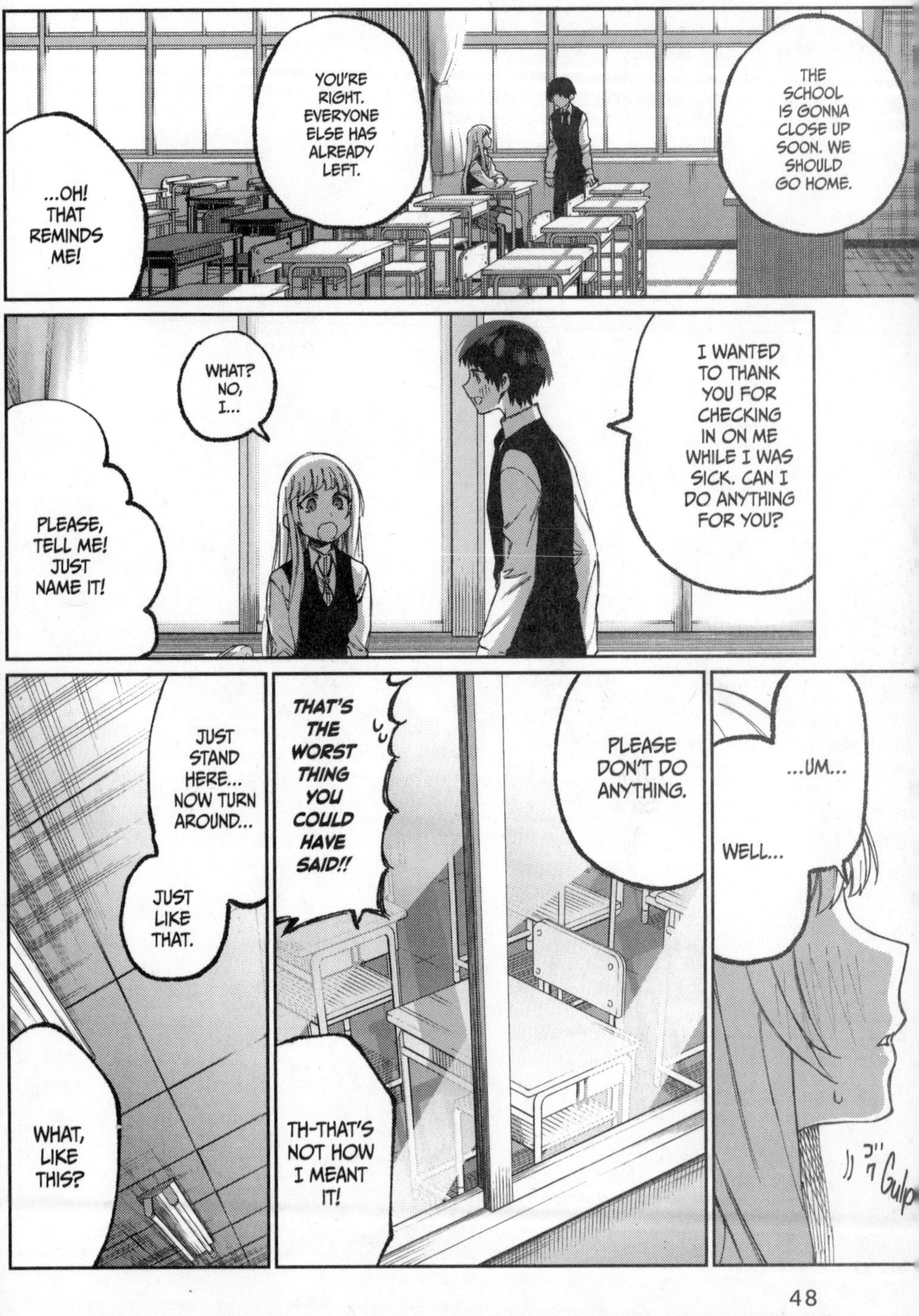
THE SCHOOL IS GONNA CLOSE UP SOON. WE SHOULD GO HOME.
YOU'RE RIGHT. EVERYONE ELSE HAS ALREADY LEFT.
...OH! THAT REMINDS ME!
I WANTED TO THANK YOU FOR CHECKING IN ON ME WHILE I WAS SICK. CAN I DO ANYTHING FOR YOU?
WHAT? NO, I...
PLEASE, TELL ME! JUST NAME IT!
...UM...
WELL...
Gulp
PLEASE DON'T DO ANYTHING.
THAT'S THE WORST THING YOU COULD HAVE SAID!!
TH-THAT'S NOT HOW I MEANT IT!
JUST STAND HERE... NOW TURN AROUND...
JUST LIKE THAT.
WHAT, LIKE THIS?

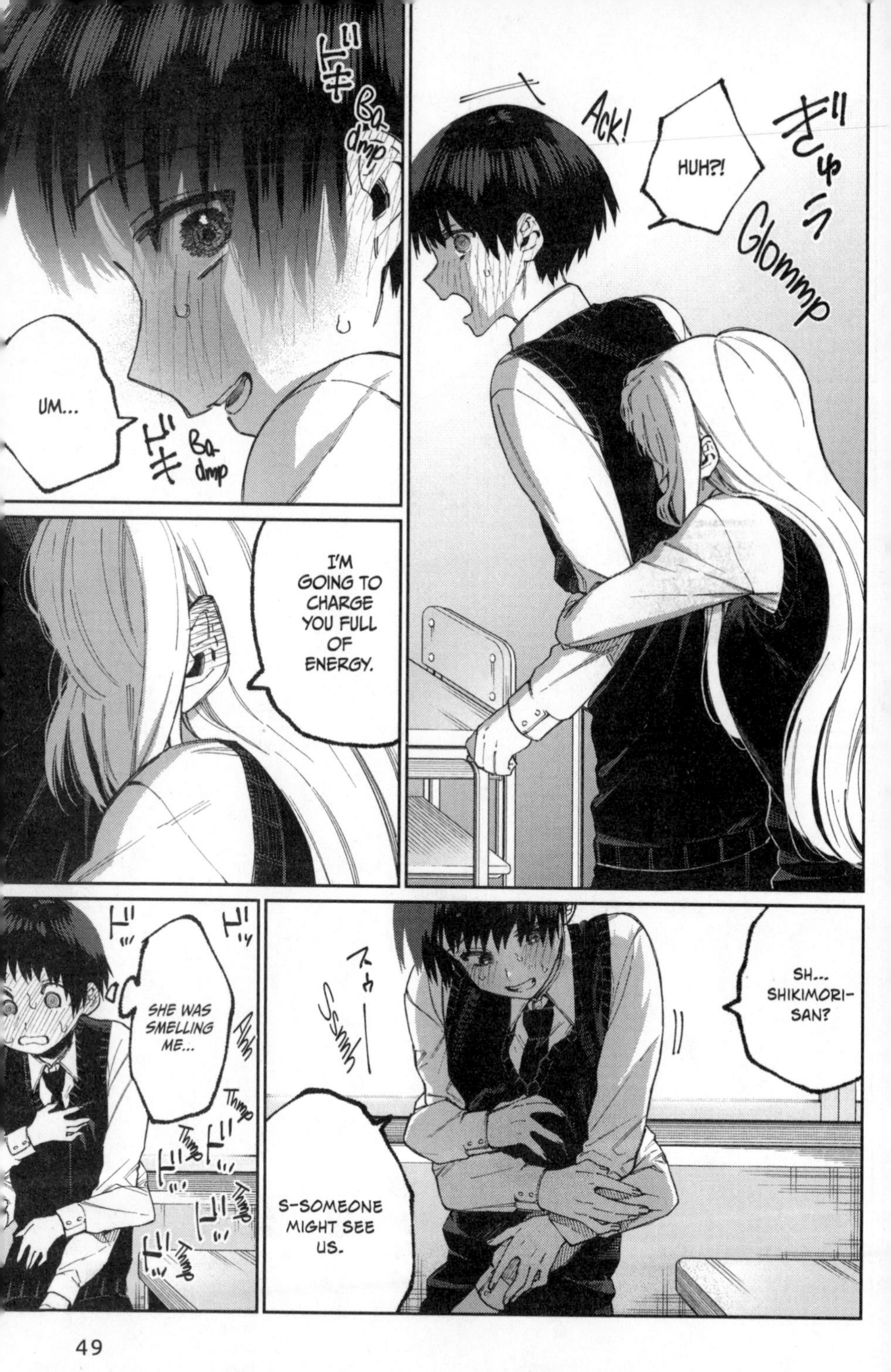
Glommp
HUH?!
Ack!
Ba-dmp
UM...
Ba-dmp
I'M GOING TO CHARGE YOU FULL OF ENERGY.
SH... SHIKIMORI-SAN?
Ssnnf
S-SOMEONE MIGHT SEE US.
SHE WAS SMELLING ME...
Ahh
Thmp
Thmp
Thmp
Thmp

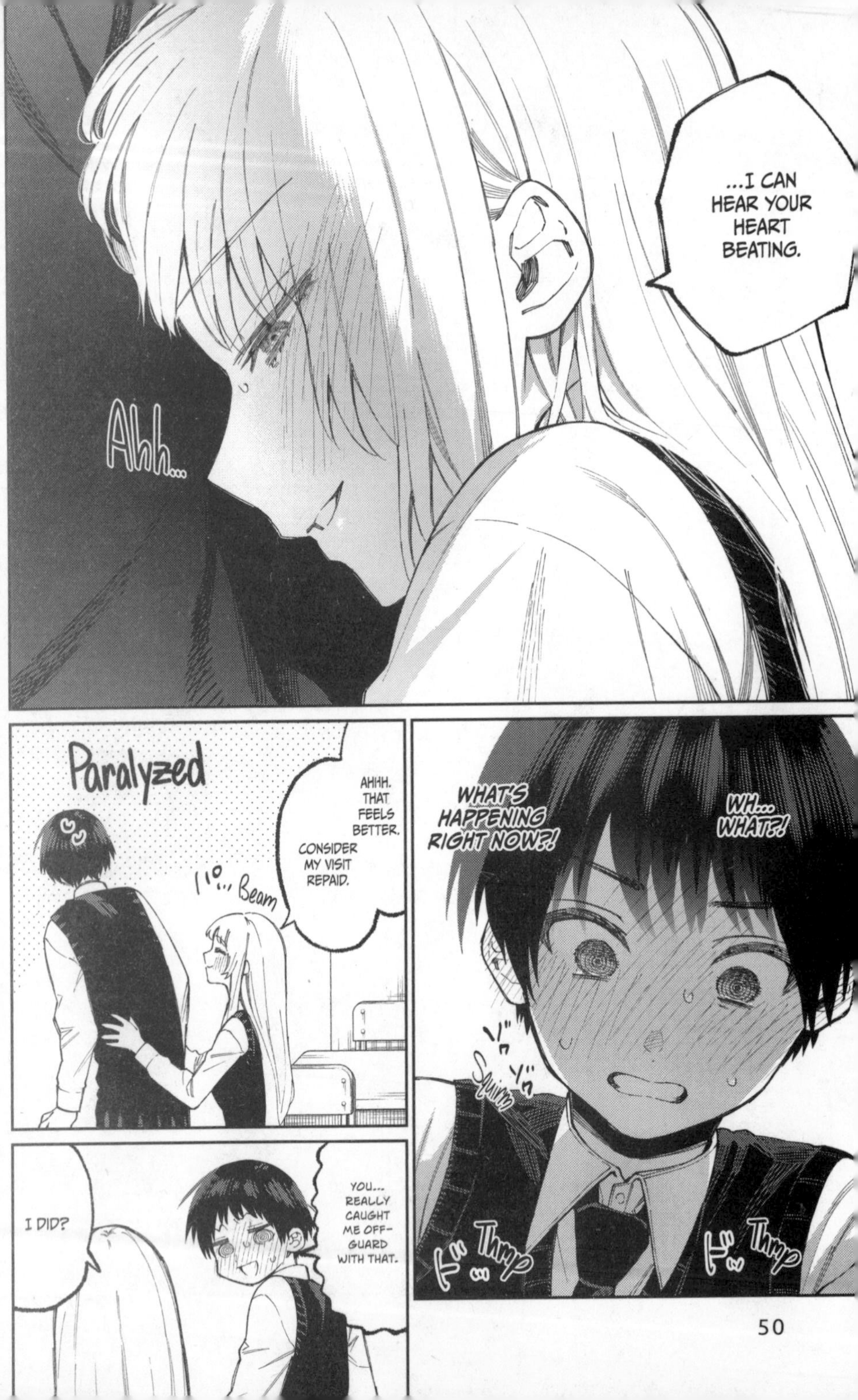
...I CAN HEAR YOUR HEART BEATING.
Ahh...
WH... WHAT?!
WHAT'S HAPPENING RIGHT NOW?!
Squirm
Thmp
Thmp
AHHH. THAT FEELS BETTER.
CONSIDER MY VISIT REPAID.
Beam
Paralyzed
YOU... REALLY CAUGHT ME OFF-GUARD WITH THAT.
I DID?

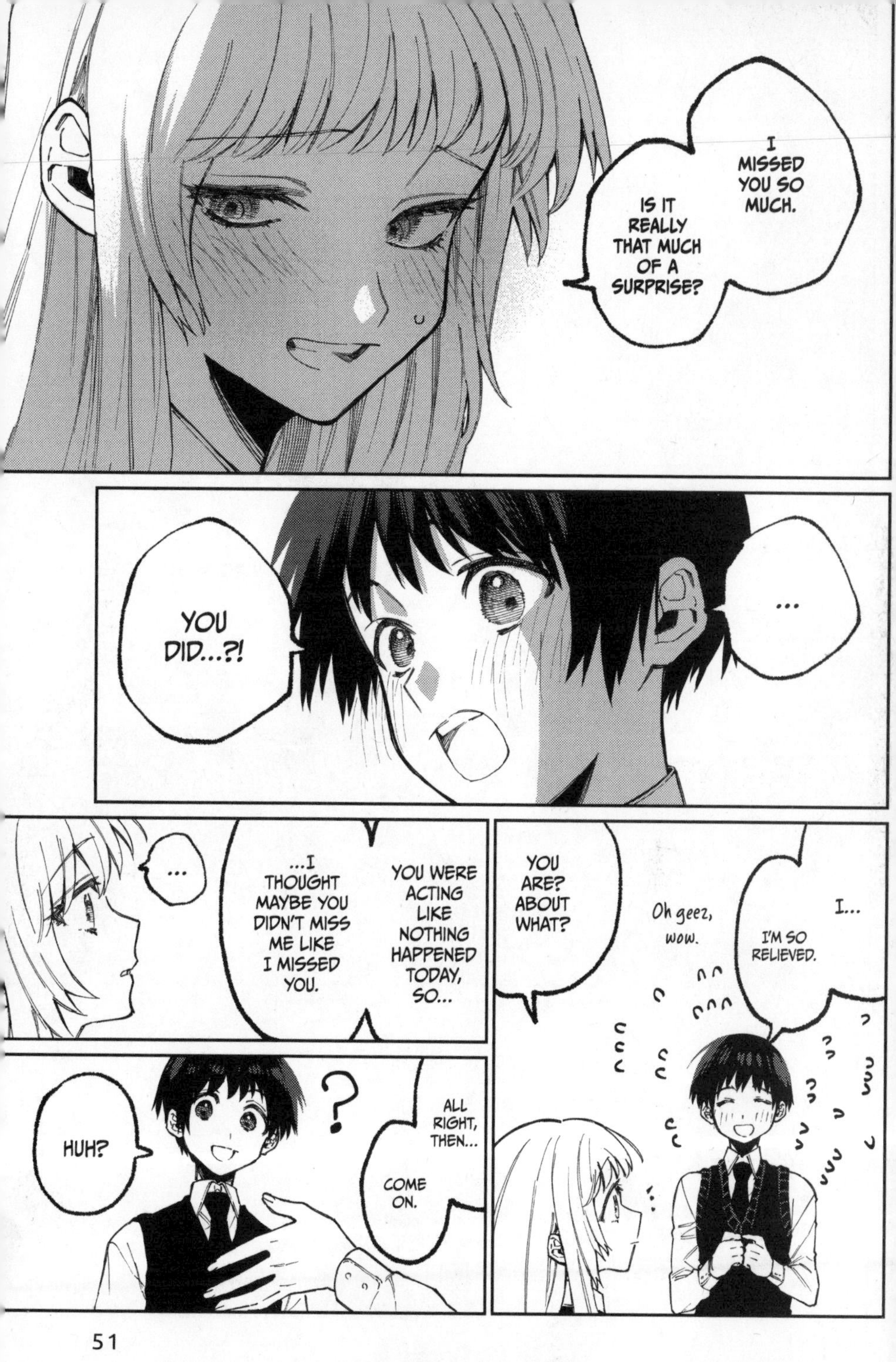

I MISSED YOU SO MUCH.
IS IT REALLY THAT MUCH OF A SURPRISE?
...
YOU DID...?!
I...
I'M SO RELIEVED.
Oh geez, wow.
YOU ARE? ABOUT WHAT?
YOU WERE ACTING LIKE NOTHING HAPPENED TODAY, SO...
...I THOUGHT MAYBE YOU DIDN'T MISS ME LIKE I MISSED YOU.
...
ALL RIGHT, THEN...
COME ON.
HUH?

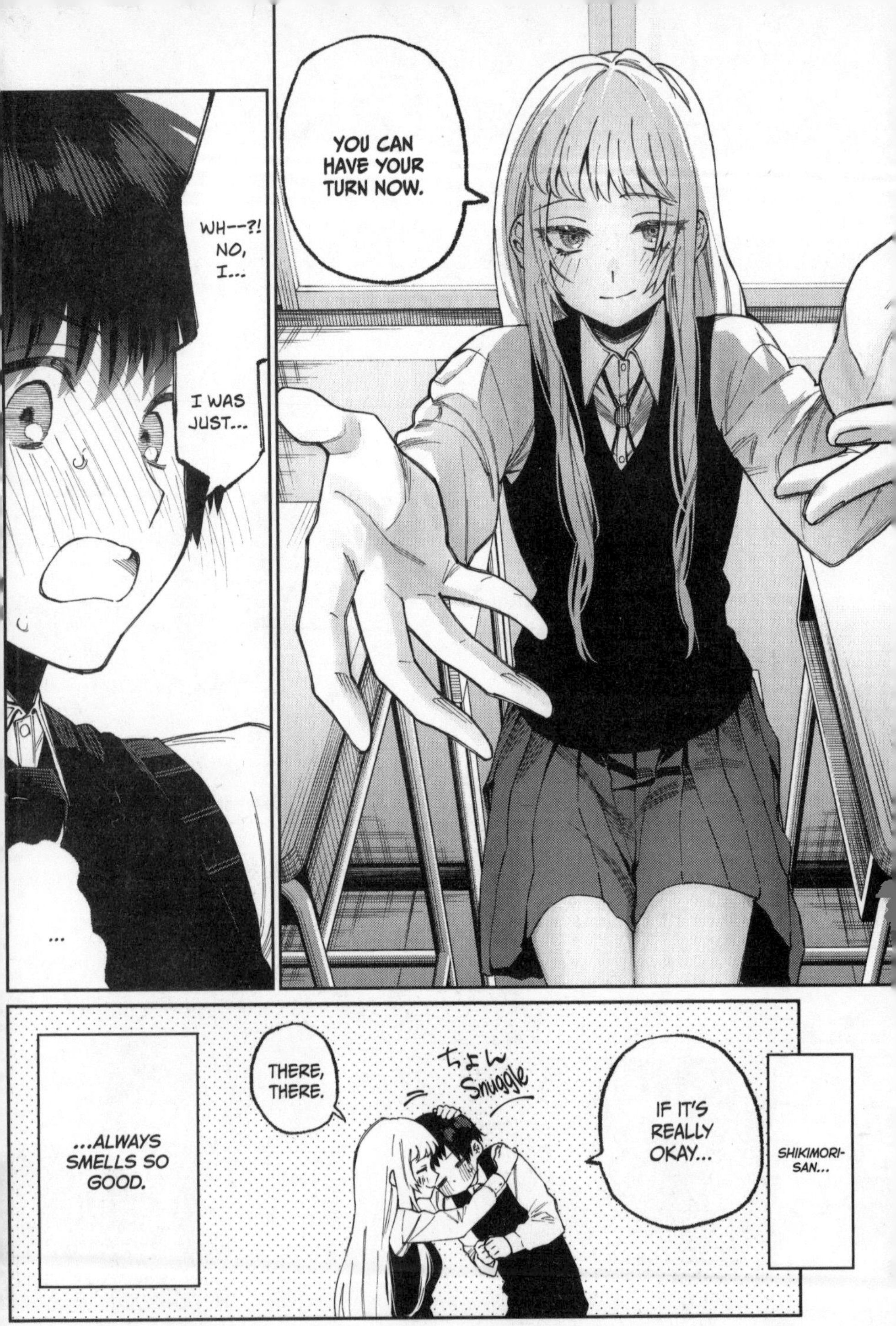
YOU CAN HAVE YOUR TURN NOW.
WH--?! NO, I...
I WAS JUST...
...
SHIKIMORI-SAN...
IF IT'S REALLY OKAY...
ちょん
Snuggle
THERE, THERE.
...ALWAYS SMELLS SO GOOD.

Chapter 49 END

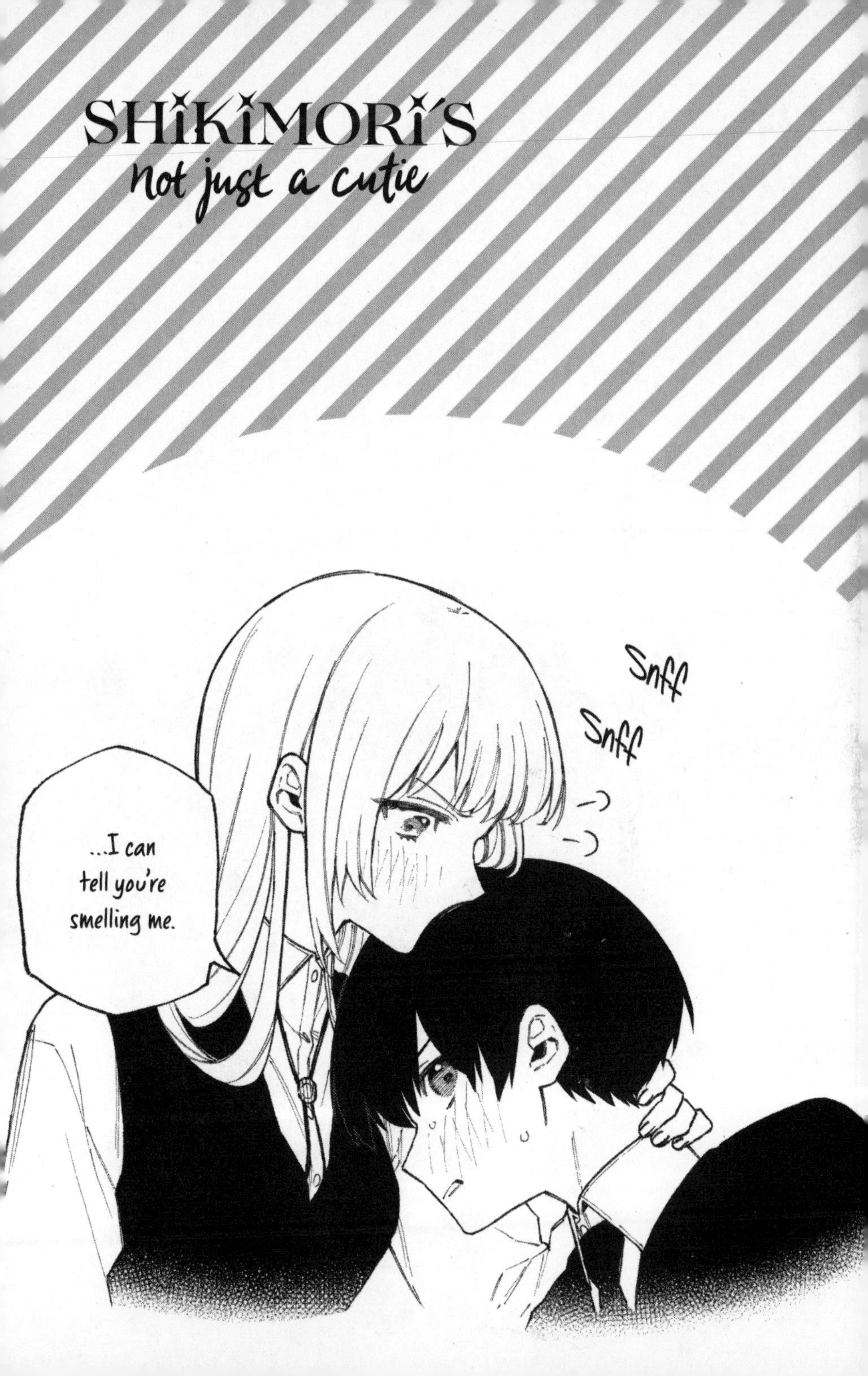
SHIKIMORI'S
not just a cutie
Snff
Snff
...I can tell you're smelling me.

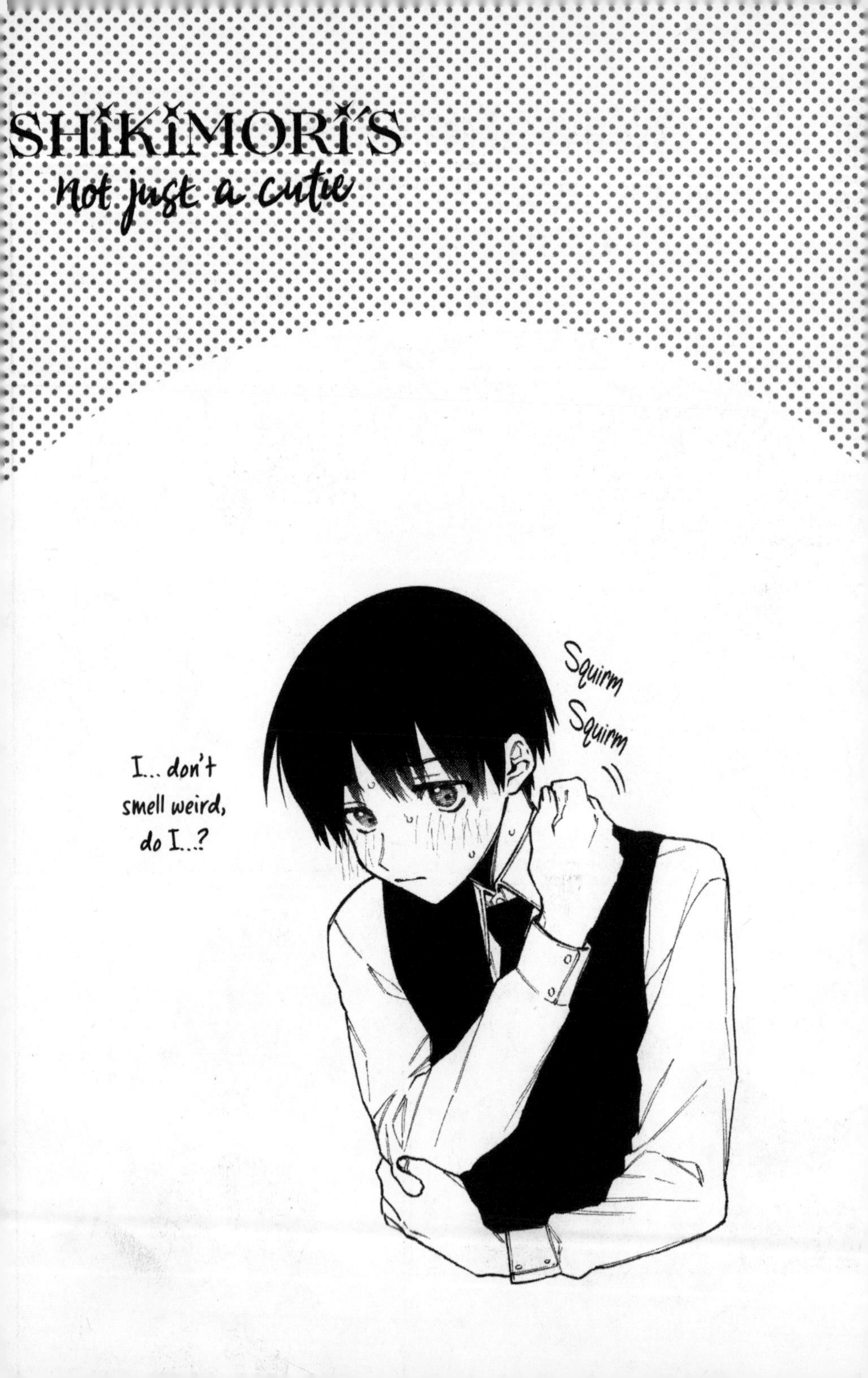
SHIKIMORI'S
Not just a cutie
Squirm Squirm
I... don't smell weird, do I...?

# Chapter 50

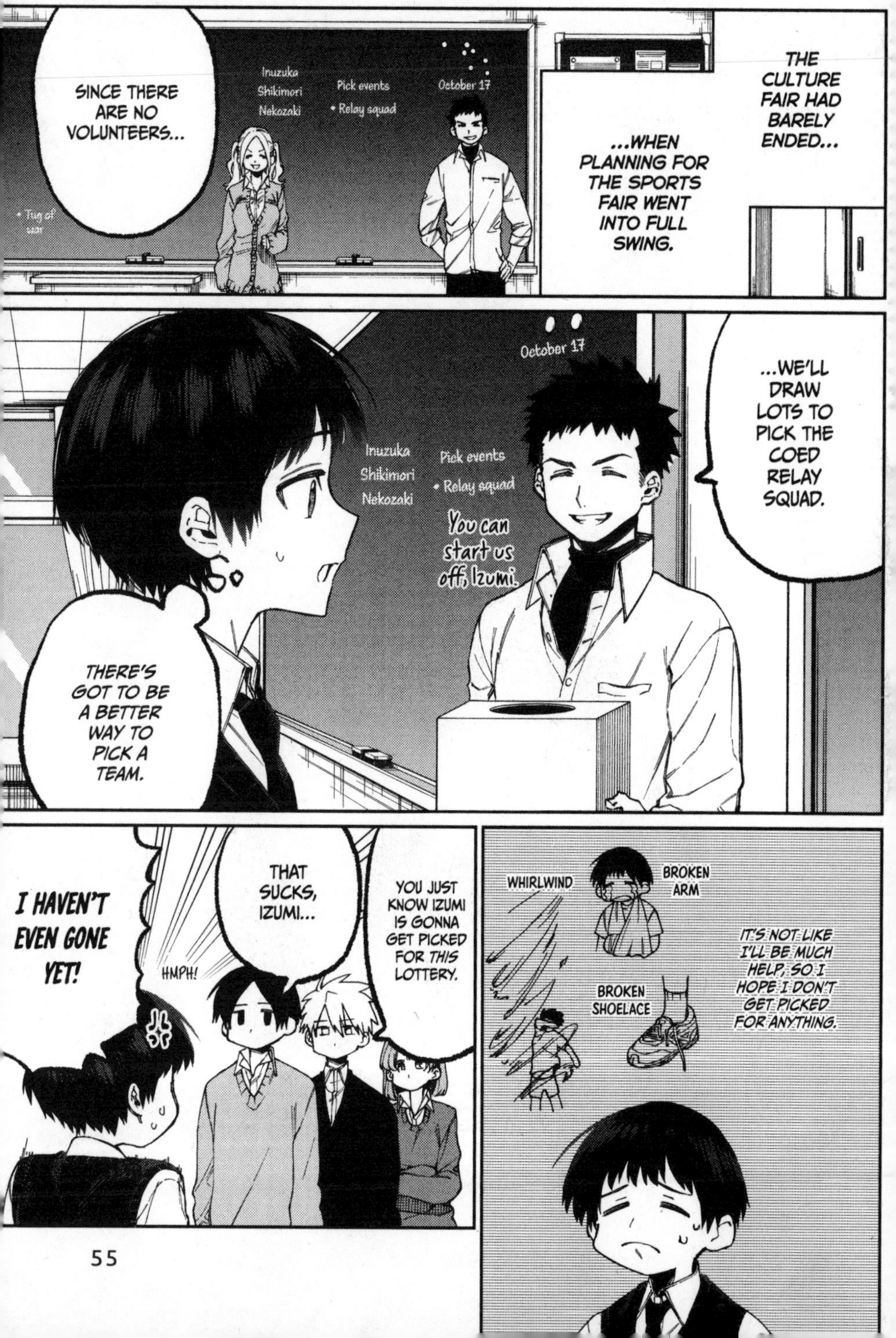
THE CULTURE FAIR HAD BARELY ENDED...
...WHEN PLANNING FOR THE SPORTS FAIR WENT INTO FULL SWING.
October 17
Pick events
+ Relay squad
Inuzuka
Shikimori
Nekozaki
+ Tug of war
SINCE THERE ARE NO VOLUNTEERS...
...WE'LL DRAW LOTS TO PICK THE COED RELAY SQUAD.
October 17
Pick events
+ Relay squad
Inuzuka
Shikimori
Nekozaki
You can start us off, Izumi.
THERE'S GOT TO BE A BETTER WAY TO PICK A TEAM.
BROKEN ARM
WHIRLWIND
IT'S NOT LIKE I'LL BE MUCH HELP, SO I HOPE I DON'T GET PICKED FOR ANYTHING.
BROKEN SHOELACE
YOU JUST KNOW IZUMI IS GONNA GET PICKED FOR *THIS* LOTTERY.
THAT SUCKS, IZUMI...
HMPH!
I HAVEN'T EVEN GONE YET!

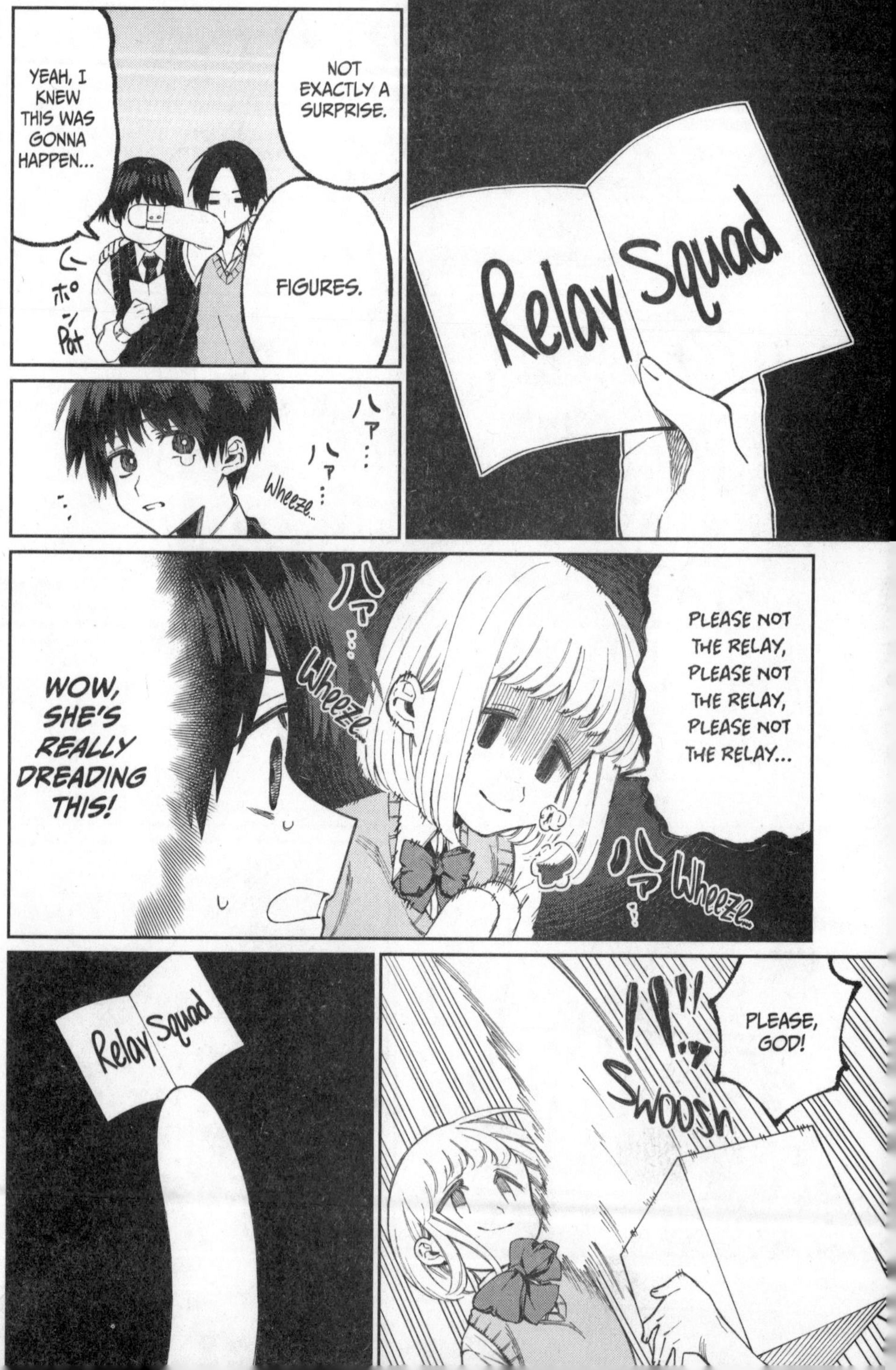
Relay Squad
NOT EXACTLY A SURPRISE.
YEAH, I KNEW THIS WAS GONNA HAPPEN...
FIGURES.
ポン
Pat
ハァ… ハァ…
Wheeze...
PLEASE NOT THE RELAY, PLEASE NOT THE RELAY, PLEASE NOT THE RELAY...
ハァ
Wheeze...
Wheeze...
WOW, SHE'S REALLY DREADING THIS!
PLEASE, GOD!
Swoosh
Relay Squad

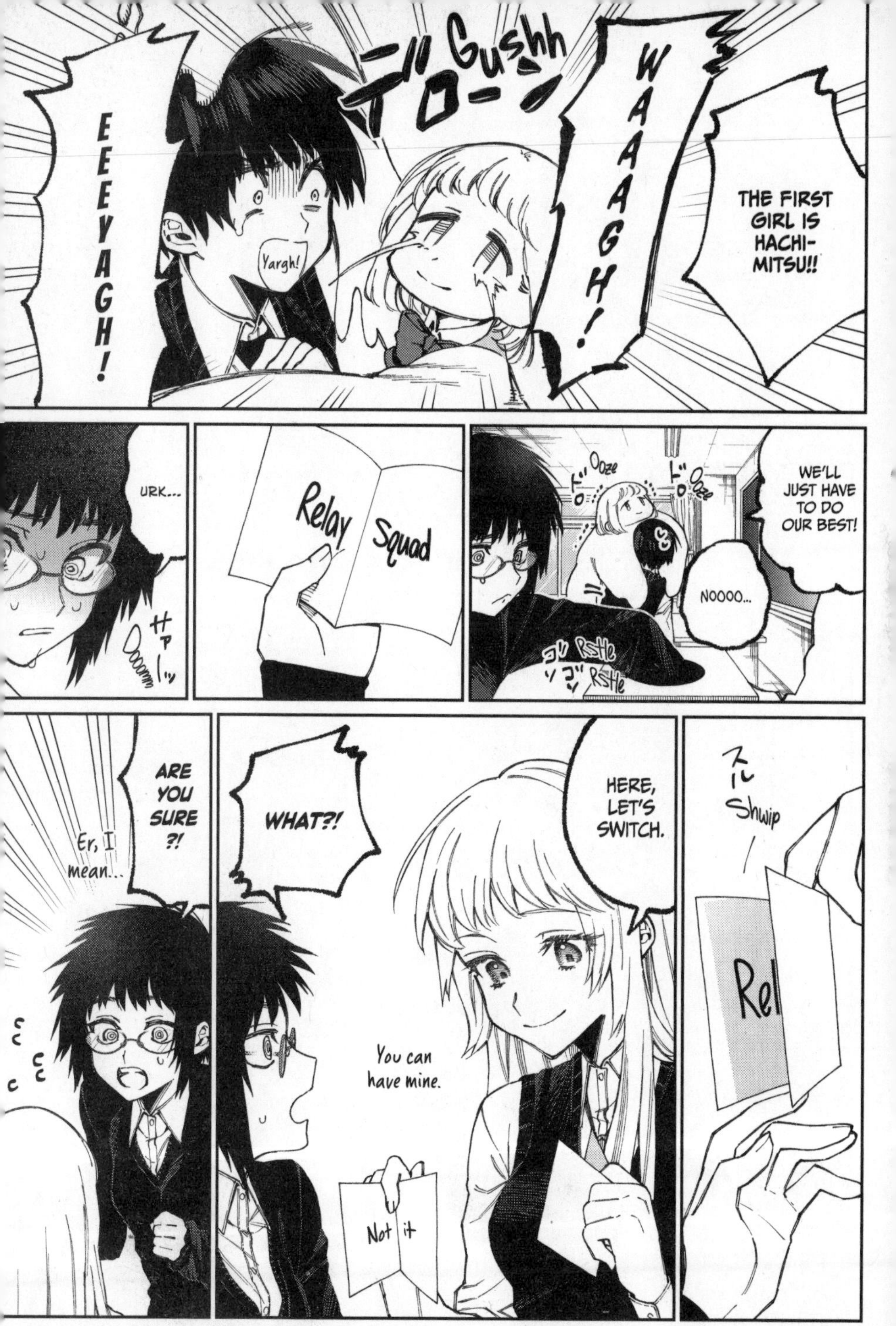
THE FIRST GIRL IS HACHI-MITSU!!
WAAAAGH!
Gushh
Yargh!
EEEYAGH!
WE'LL JUST HAVE TO DO OUR BEST!
NOOOO...
Ooze
Ooze
RStle
RStle
Relay Squad
URK...
Shwip
HERE, LET'S SWITCH.
You can have mine.
Not it
WHAT?!
ARE YOU SURE?!
Er, I mean...

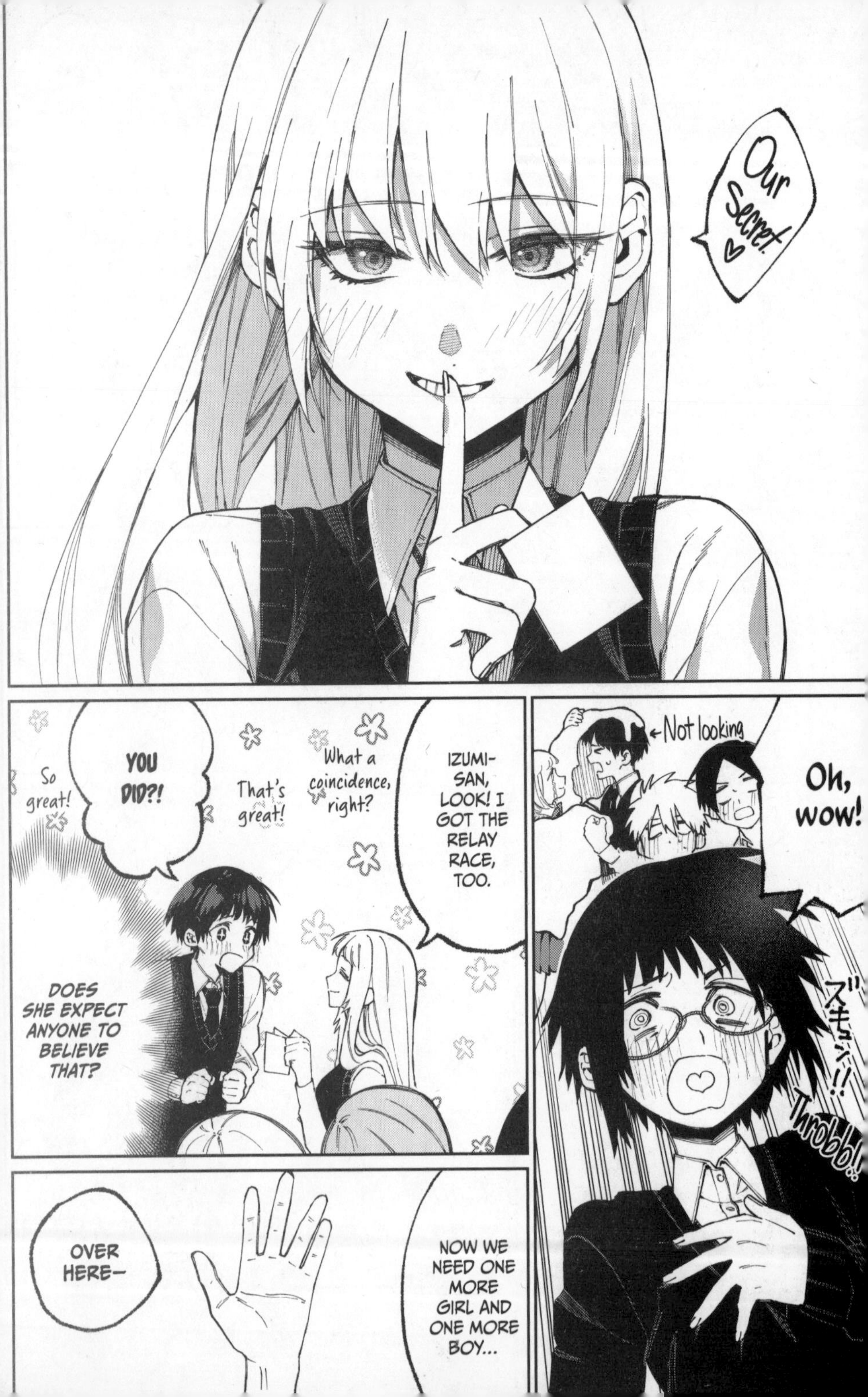
Our Secret ♥
←Not looking
Oh, wow!
ズキュン!!
Throbb!!
IZUMI-SAN, LOOK! I GOT THE RELAY RACE, TOO.
What a coincidence, right?
That's great!
YOU DID?!
So great!
DOES SHE EXPECT ANYONE TO BELIEVE THAT?
NOW WE NEED ONE MORE GIRL AND ONE MORE BOY...
OVER HERE—

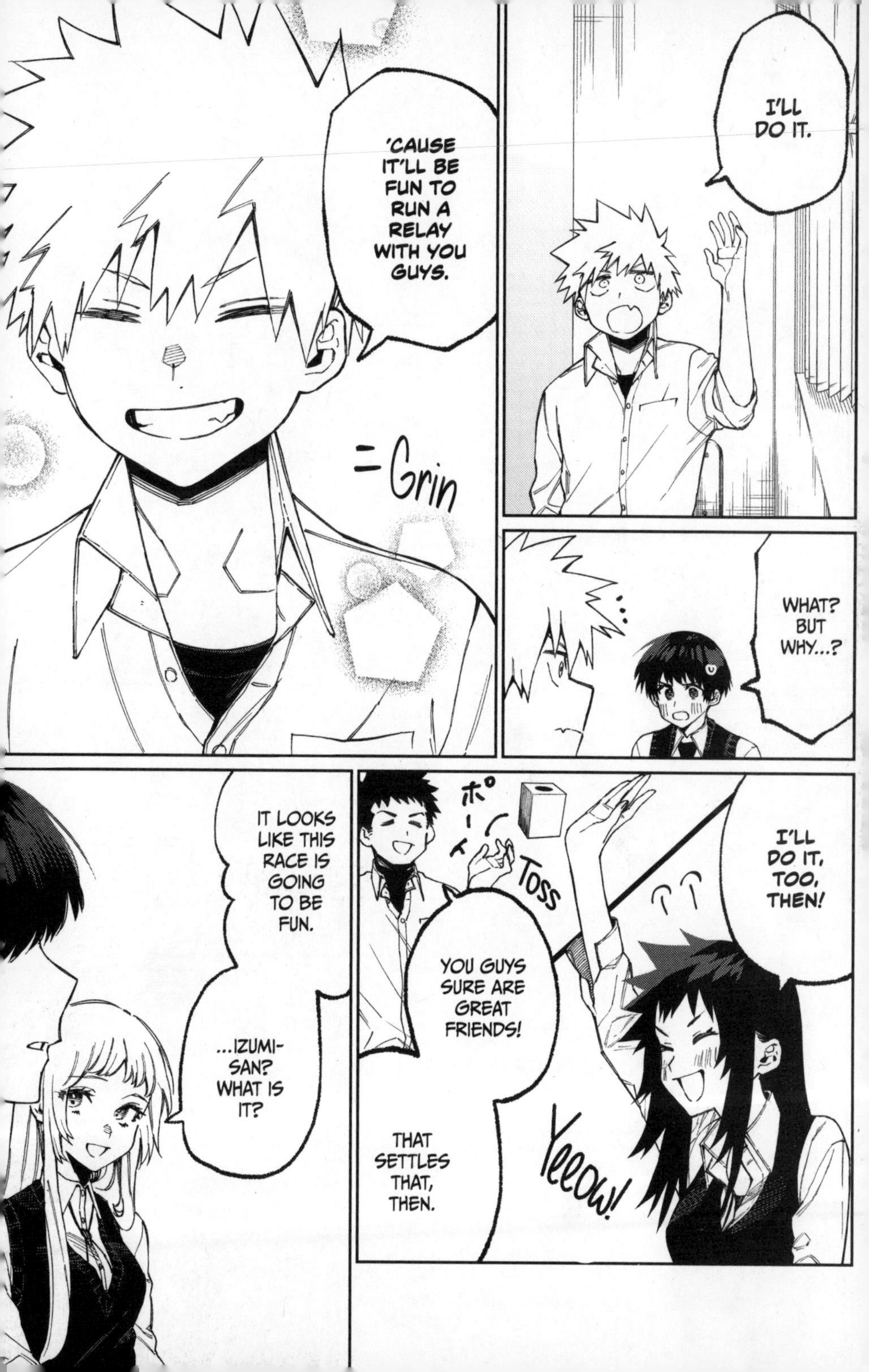
I'LL DO IT.
WHAT? BUT WHY...?
'CAUSE IT'LL BE FUN TO RUN A RELAY WITH YOU GUYS.
Grin
I'LL DO IT, TOO, THEN!
ポイ
Toss
YOU GUYS SURE ARE GREAT FRIENDS!
Yeeow!
THAT SETTLES THAT, THEN.
IT LOOKS LIKE THIS RACE IS GOING TO BE FUN.
...IZUMI-SAN? WHAT IS IT?

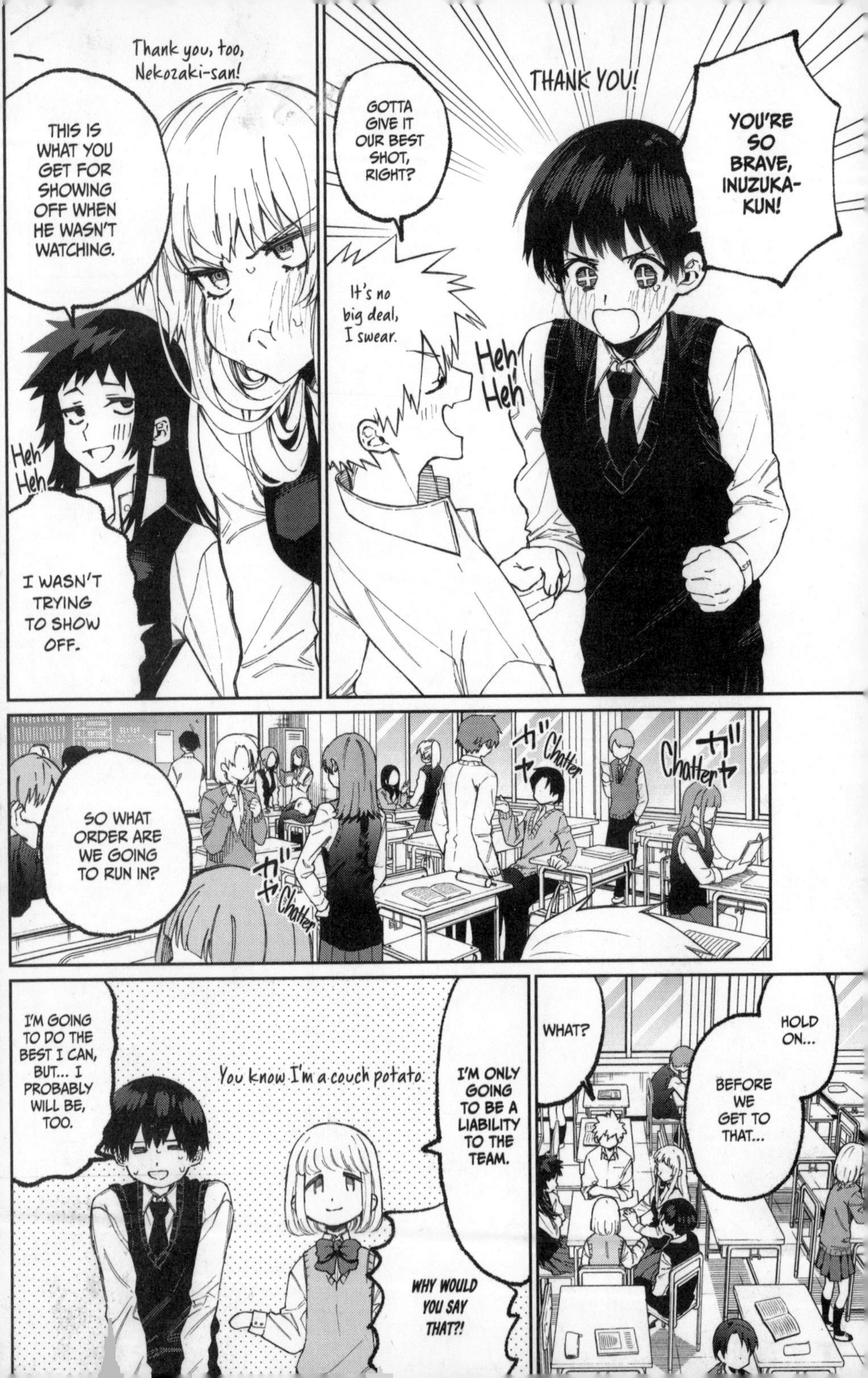
YOU'RE SO BRAVE, INUZUKA-KUN!
THANK YOU!
GOTTA GIVE IT OUR BEST SHOT, RIGHT?
Heh Heh
It's no big deal, I swear.
Thank you, too, Nekozaki-san!
THIS IS WHAT YOU GET FOR SHOWING OFF WHEN HE WASN'T WATCHING.
Heh Heh
I WASN'T TRYING TO SHOW OFF.
Chatter
Chatter
SO WHAT ORDER ARE WE GOING TO RUN IN?
Chatter
HOLD ON...
BEFORE WE GET TO THAT...
WHAT?
I'M ONLY GOING TO BE A LIABILITY TO THE TEAM.
You know I'm a couch potato.
I'M GOING TO DO THE BEST I CAN, BUT... I PROBABLY WILL BE, TOO.
WHY WOULD YOU SAY THAT?!

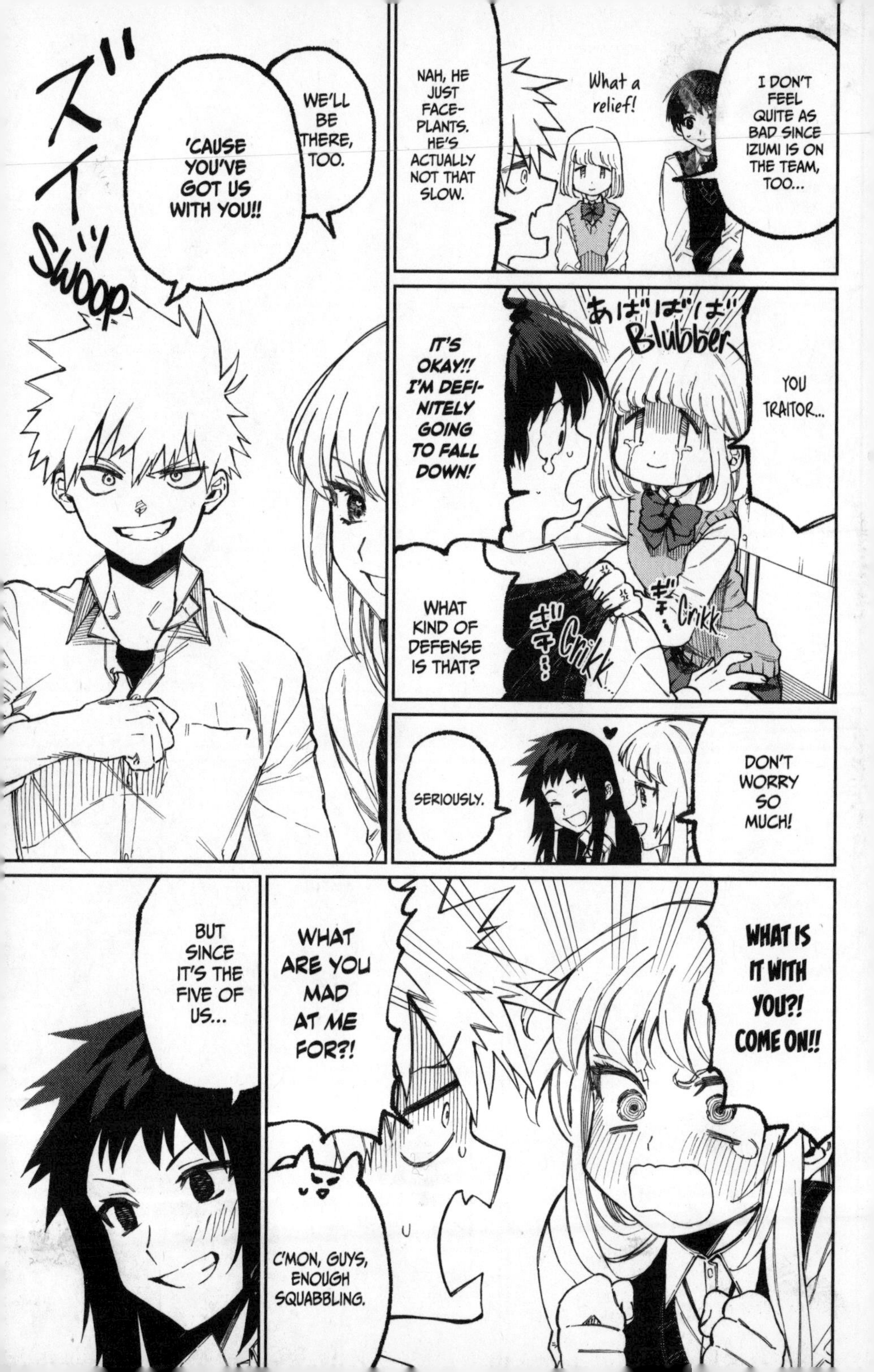

I DON'T FEEL QUITE AS BAD SINCE IZUMI IS ON THE TEAM, TOO...
What a relief!
NAH, HE JUST FACE-PLANTS. HE'S ACTUALLY NOT THAT SLOW.
あばばば
Blubber
YOU TRAITOR...
IT'S OKAY!! I'M DEFI-NITELY GOING TO FALL DOWN!
ギチ…
Crikk
ギチ…
Crikk
WHAT KIND OF DEFENSE IS THAT?
DON'T WORRY SO MUCH!
SERIOUSLY.
ズイッ
SWOOP
WE'LL BE THERE, TOO.
'CAUSE YOU'VE GOT US WITH YOU!!
WHAT IS IT WITH YOU?! COME ON!!
WHAT ARE YOU MAD AT ME FOR?!
C'MON, GUYS, ENOUGH SQUABBLING.
BUT SINCE IT'S THE FIVE OF US...

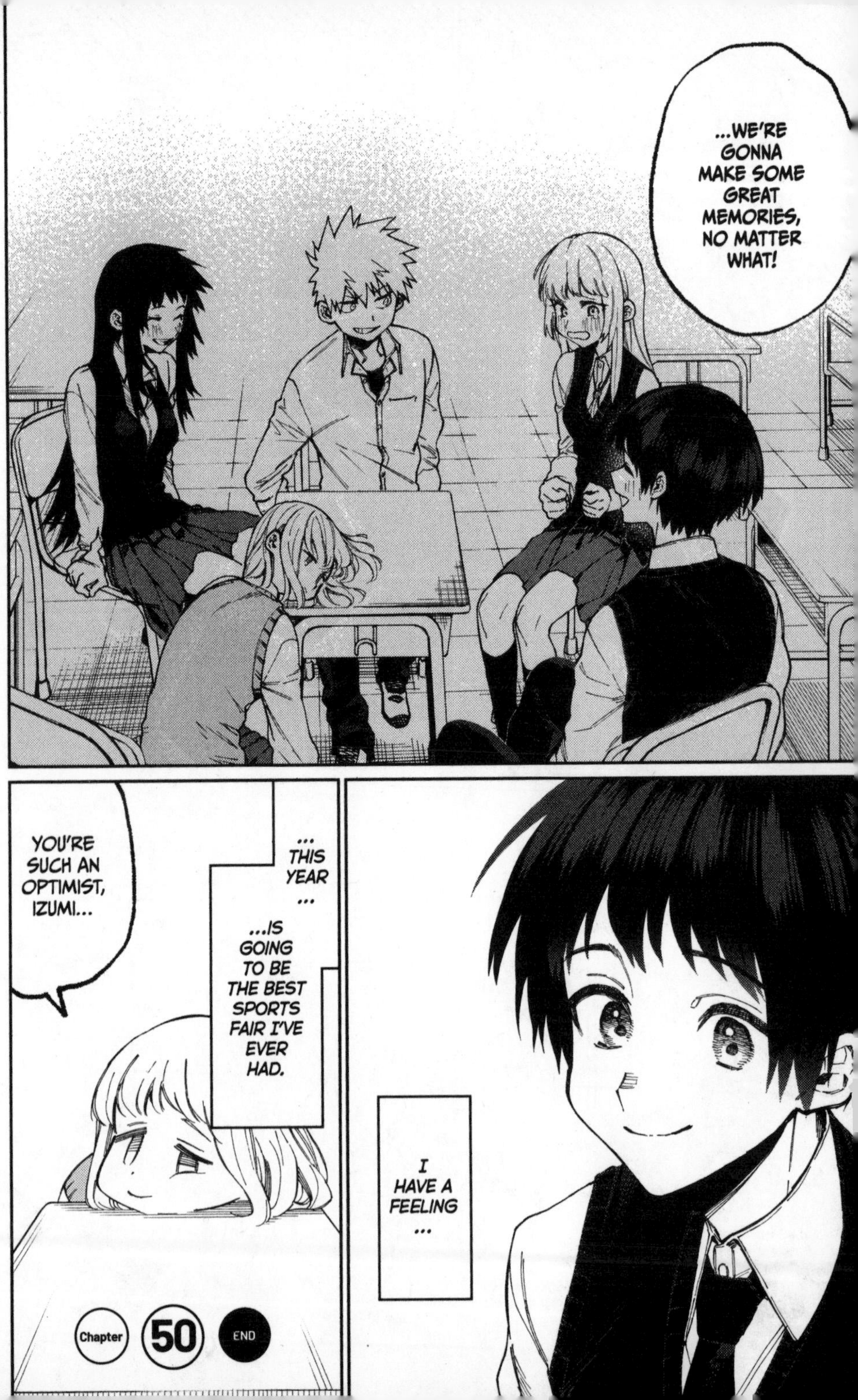
...WE'RE GONNA MAKE SOME GREAT MEMORIES, NO MATTER WHAT!
I HAVE A FEELING ...
... THIS YEAR ...
...IS GOING TO BE THE BEST SPORTS FAIR I'VE EVER HAD.
YOU'RE SUCH AN OPTIMIST, IZUMI...
Chapter 50 END

# SHIKIMORI'S Not just a cutie

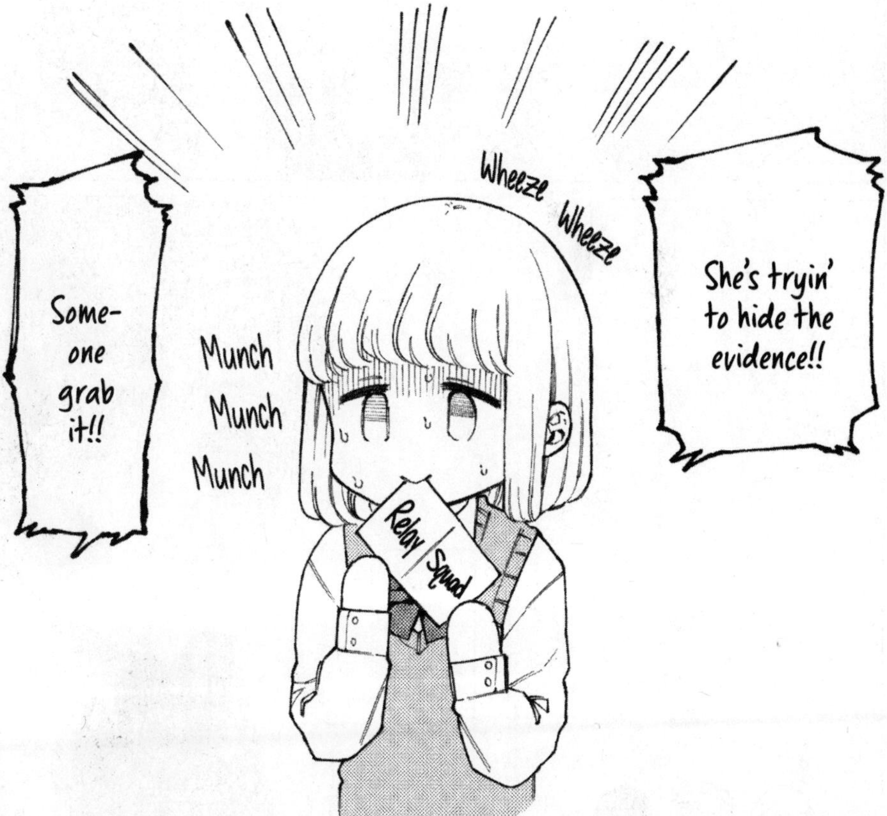
She's tryin' to hide the evidence!!
Wheeze Wheeze
Munch Munch Munch
Some-one grab it!!
Relay Squad

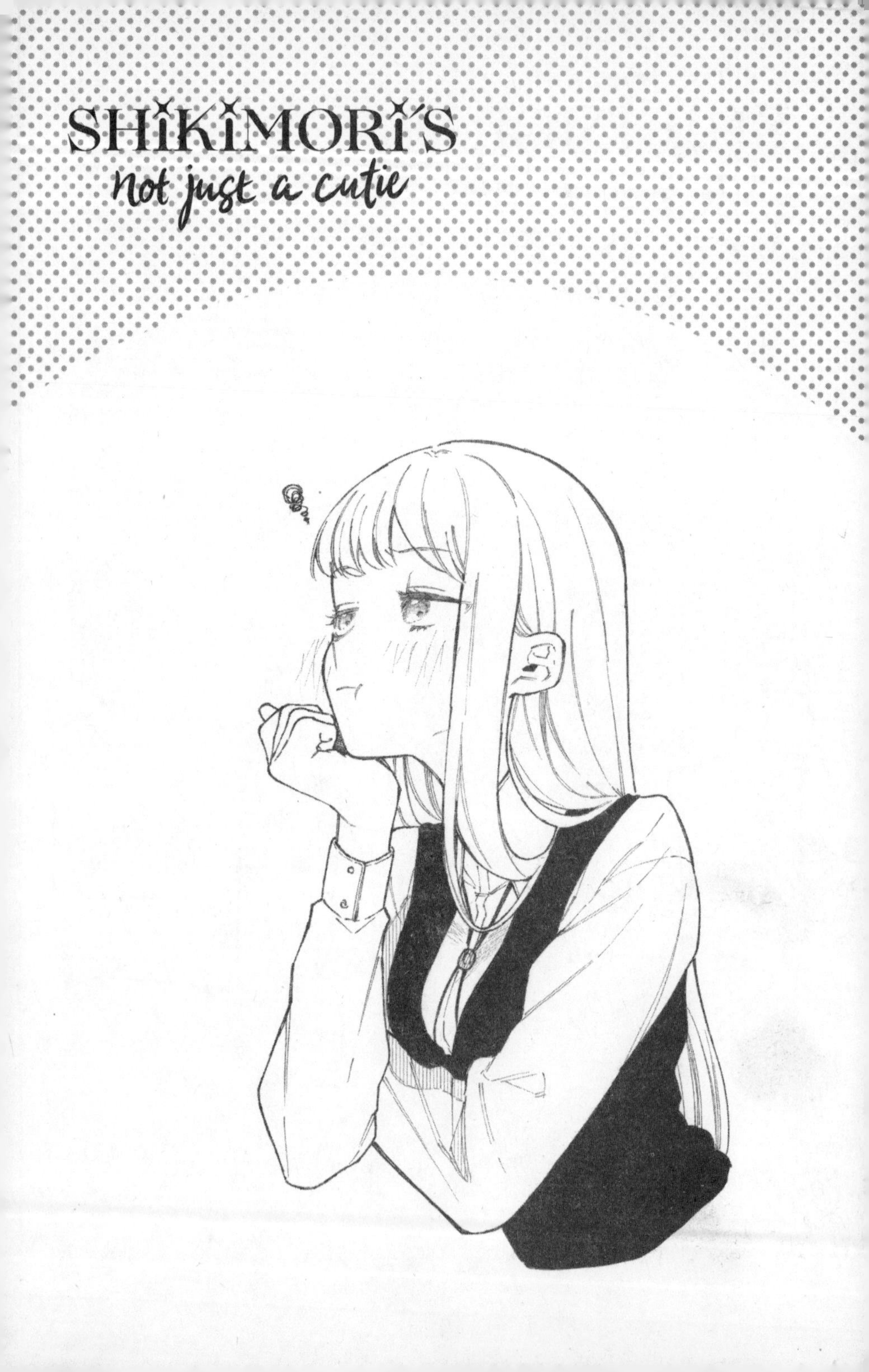
SHIKIMORI'S
not just a cutie

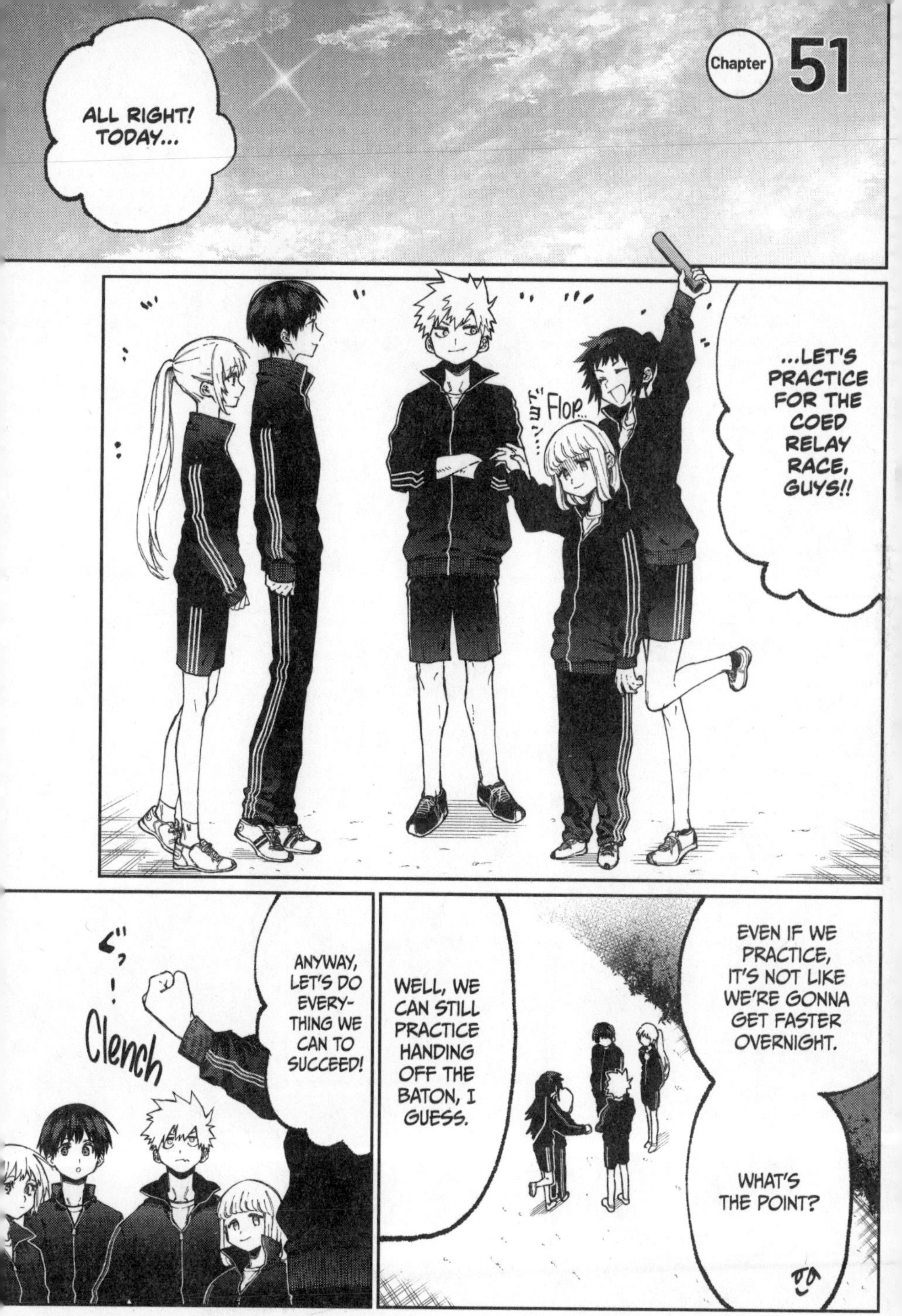
Chapter 51
ALL RIGHT! TODAY...
...LET'S PRACTICE FOR THE COED RELAY RACE, GUYS!!
Flop...
EVEN IF WE PRACTICE, IT'S NOT LIKE WE'RE GONNA GET FASTER OVERNIGHT.
WHAT'S THE POINT?
WELL, WE CAN STILL PRACTICE HANDING OFF THE BATON, I GUESS.
ANYWAY, LET'S DO EVERY-THING WE CAN TO SUCCEED!
Clench

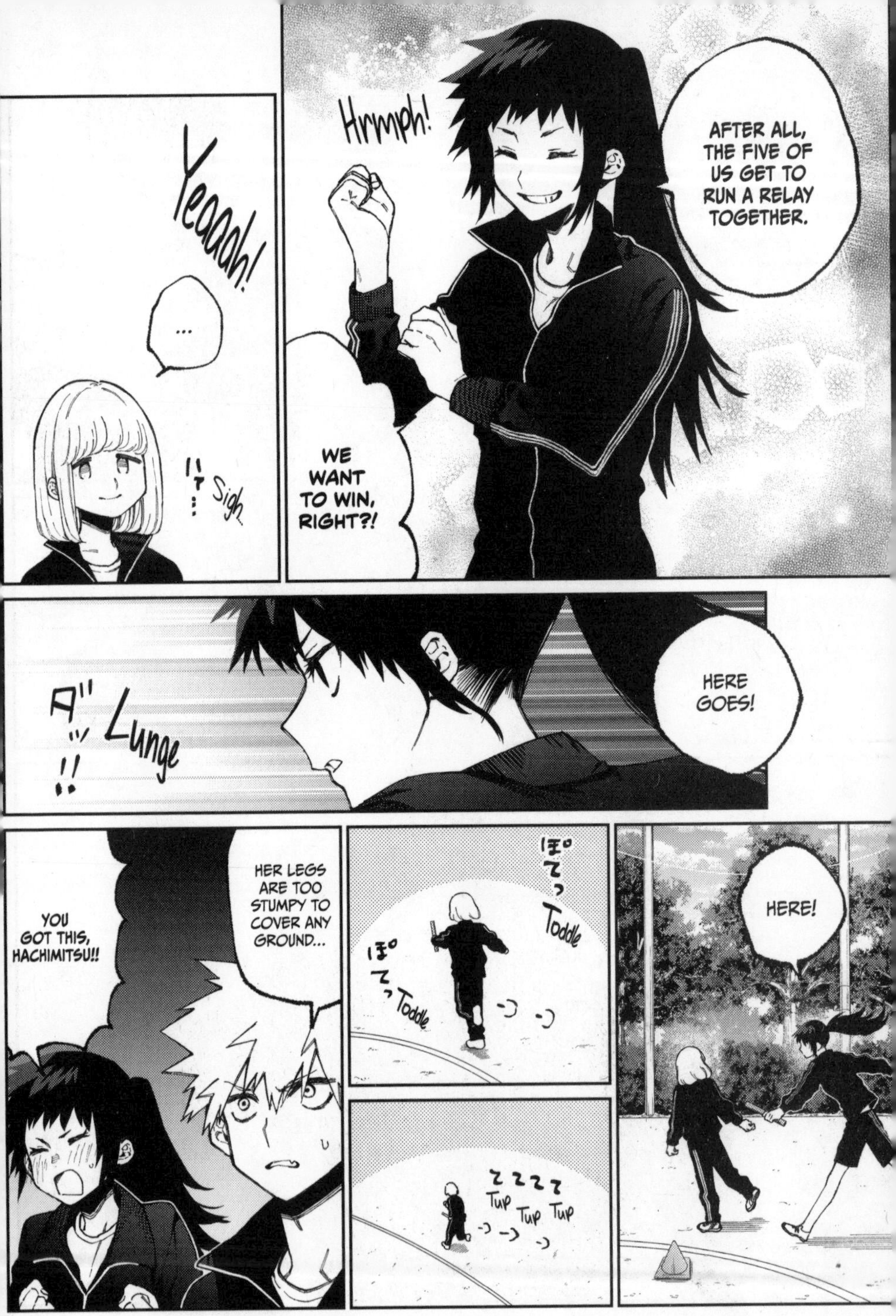
AFTER ALL, THE FIVE OF US GET TO RUN A RELAY TOGETHER.
Hrmph!
WE WANT TO WIN, RIGHT?!
Yeaaah!
...
ハァ…
Sigh
HERE GOES!
ダッ!!
Lunge
HERE!
ぽてっ
Toddle
ぽてっ
Toddle
てててて
Tup Tup Tup
HER LEGS ARE TOO STUMPY TO COVER ANY GROUND...
YOU GOT THIS, HACHIMITSU!!

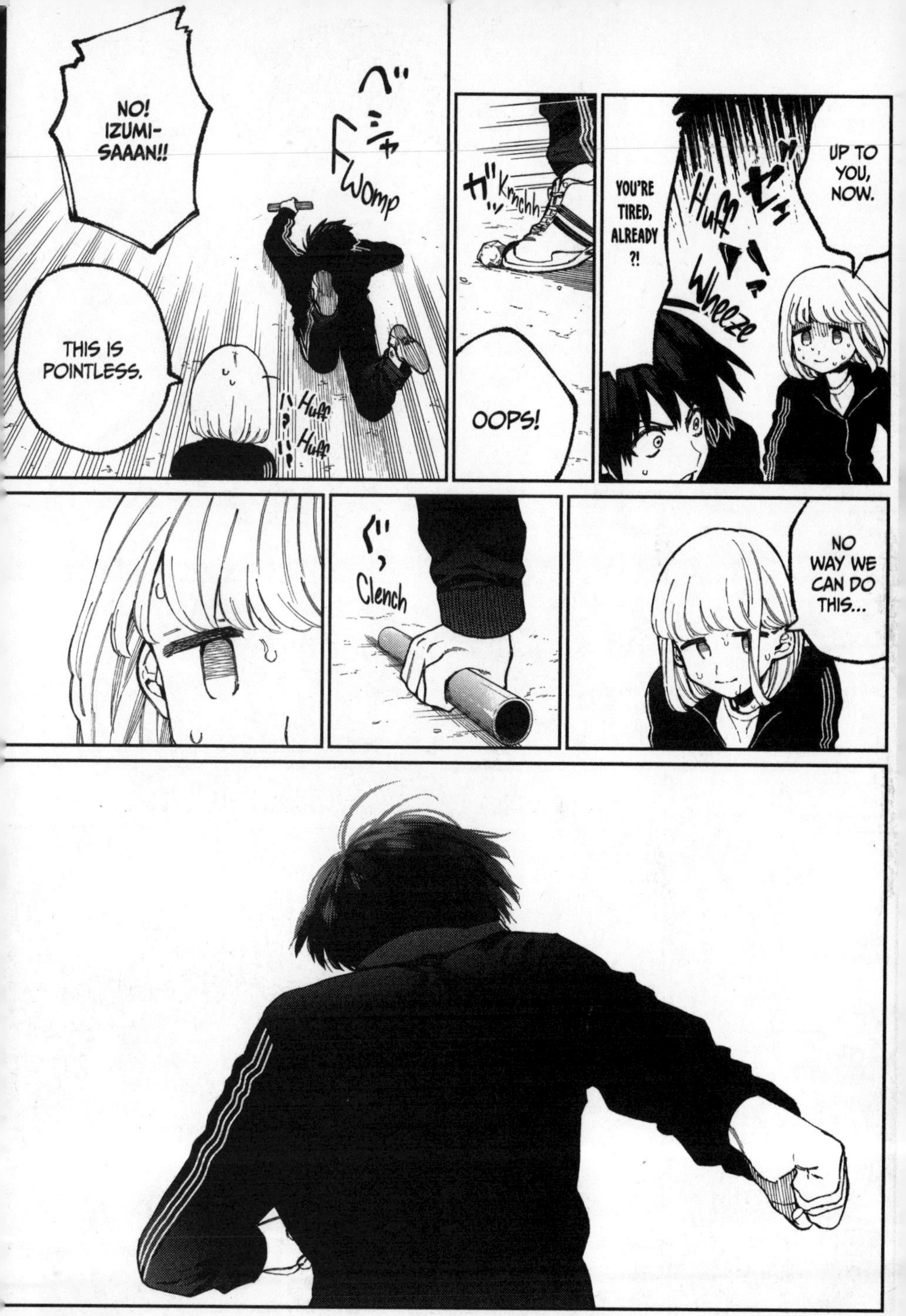
UP TO YOU, NOW.
Huff
Wheeze
YOU'RE TIRED, ALREADY ?!
ガッ
Krnchh
OOPS!
NO! IZUMI-SAAAN!!
ベシャ
Fwomp
THIS IS POINTLESS.
Huff
Huff
NO WAY WE CAN DO THIS...
ぐっ
Clench

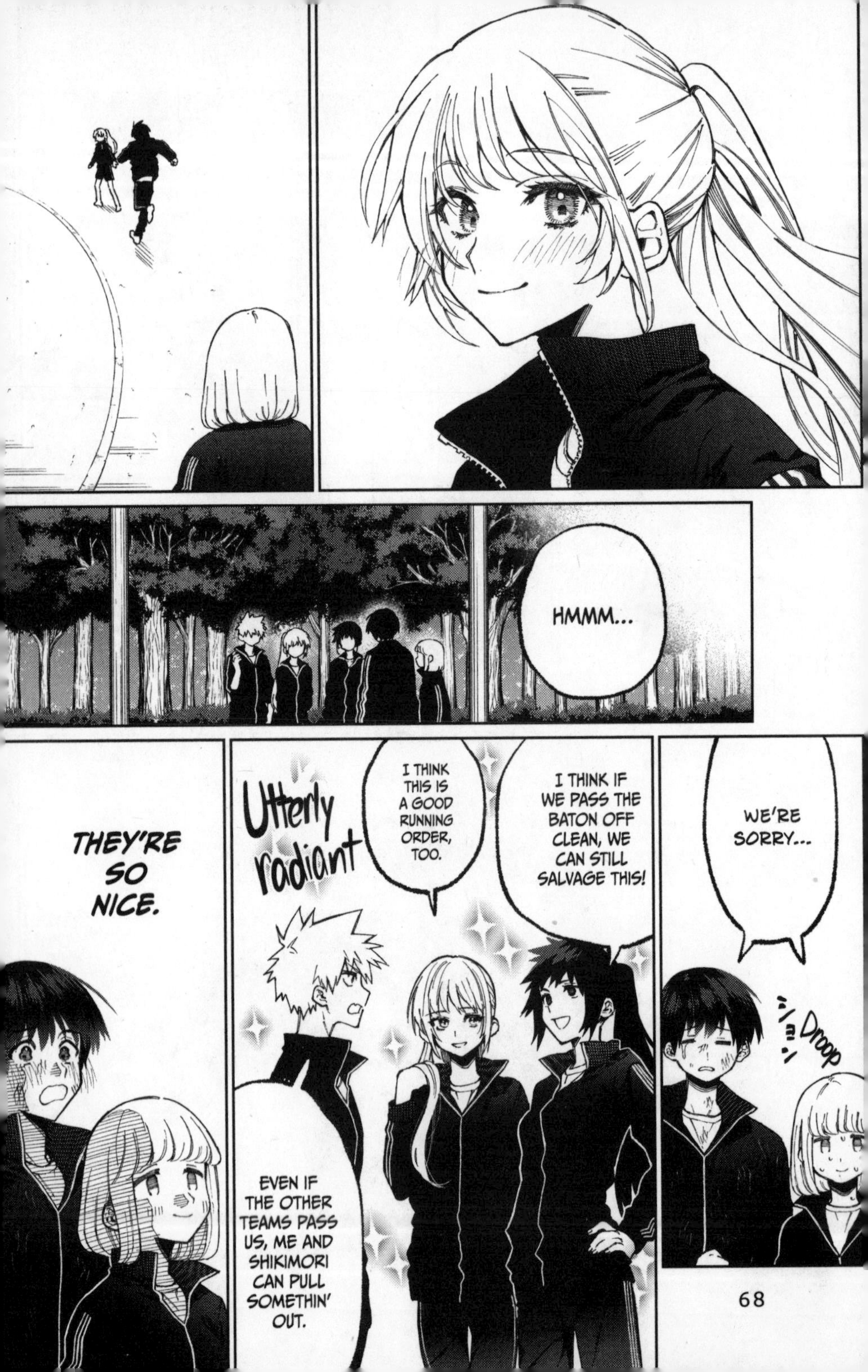
HMMM...
WE'RE SORRY...
Droop
I THINK IF WE PASS THE BATON OFF CLEAN, WE CAN STILL SALVAGE THIS!
I THINK THIS IS A GOOD RUNNING ORDER, TOO.
Utterly radiant
EVEN IF THE OTHER TEAMS PASS US, ME AND SHIKIMORI CAN PULL SOMETHIN' OUT.
THEY'RE SO NICE.

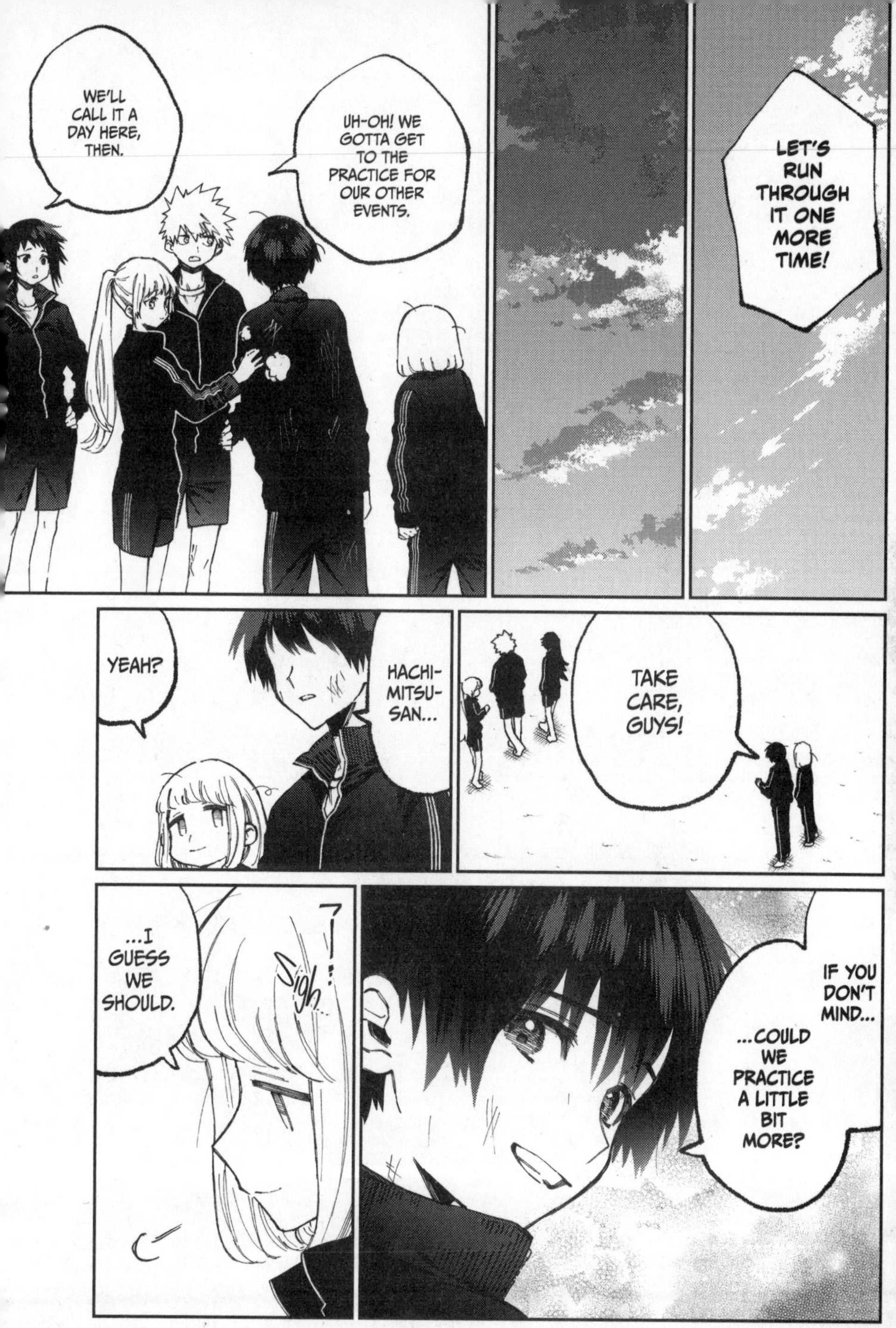
LET'S RUN THROUGH IT ONE MORE TIME!
UH-OH! WE GOTTA GET TO THE PRACTICE FOR OUR OTHER EVENTS.
WE'LL CALL IT A DAY HERE, THEN.
TAKE CARE, GUYS!
HACHI-MITSU-SAN...
YEAH?
IF YOU DON'T MIND...
...COULD WE PRACTICE A LITTLE BIT MORE?
Sigh...
...I GUESS WE SHOULD.

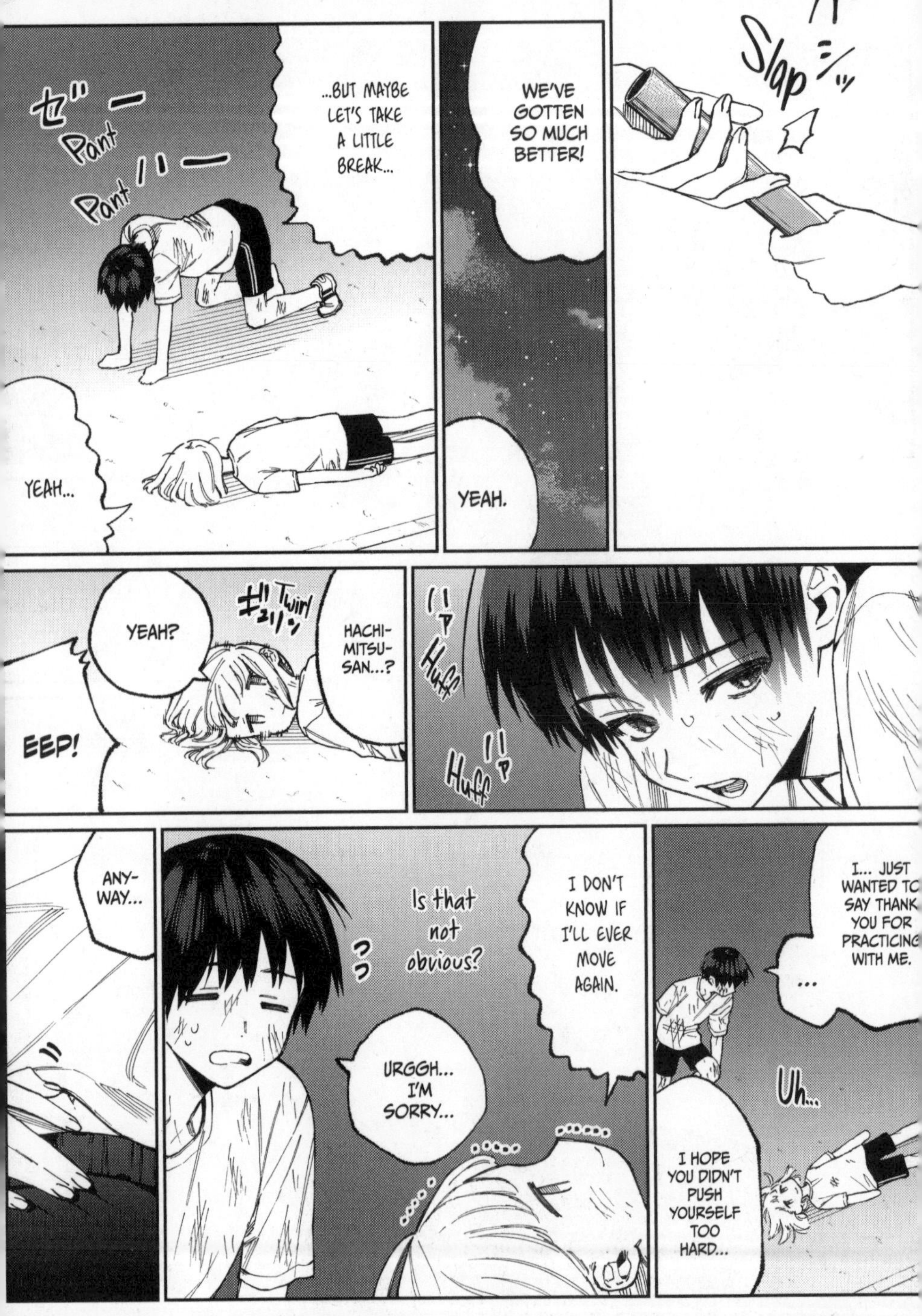
Slap
WE'VE GOTTEN SO MUCH BETTER!
YEAH.
...BUT MAYBE LET'S TAKE A LITTLE BREAK...
Pant
Pant
YEAH...
Huff
Huff
HACHI-MITSU-SAN...?
Twirl
YEAH?
EEP!
I... JUST WANTED TO SAY THANK YOU FOR PRACTICING WITH ME.
...
Uh...
I HOPE YOU DIDN'T PUSH YOURSELF TOO HARD...
I DON'T KNOW IF I'LL EVER MOVE AGAIN.
Is that not obvious?
URGGH... I'M SORRY...
ANY-WAY...

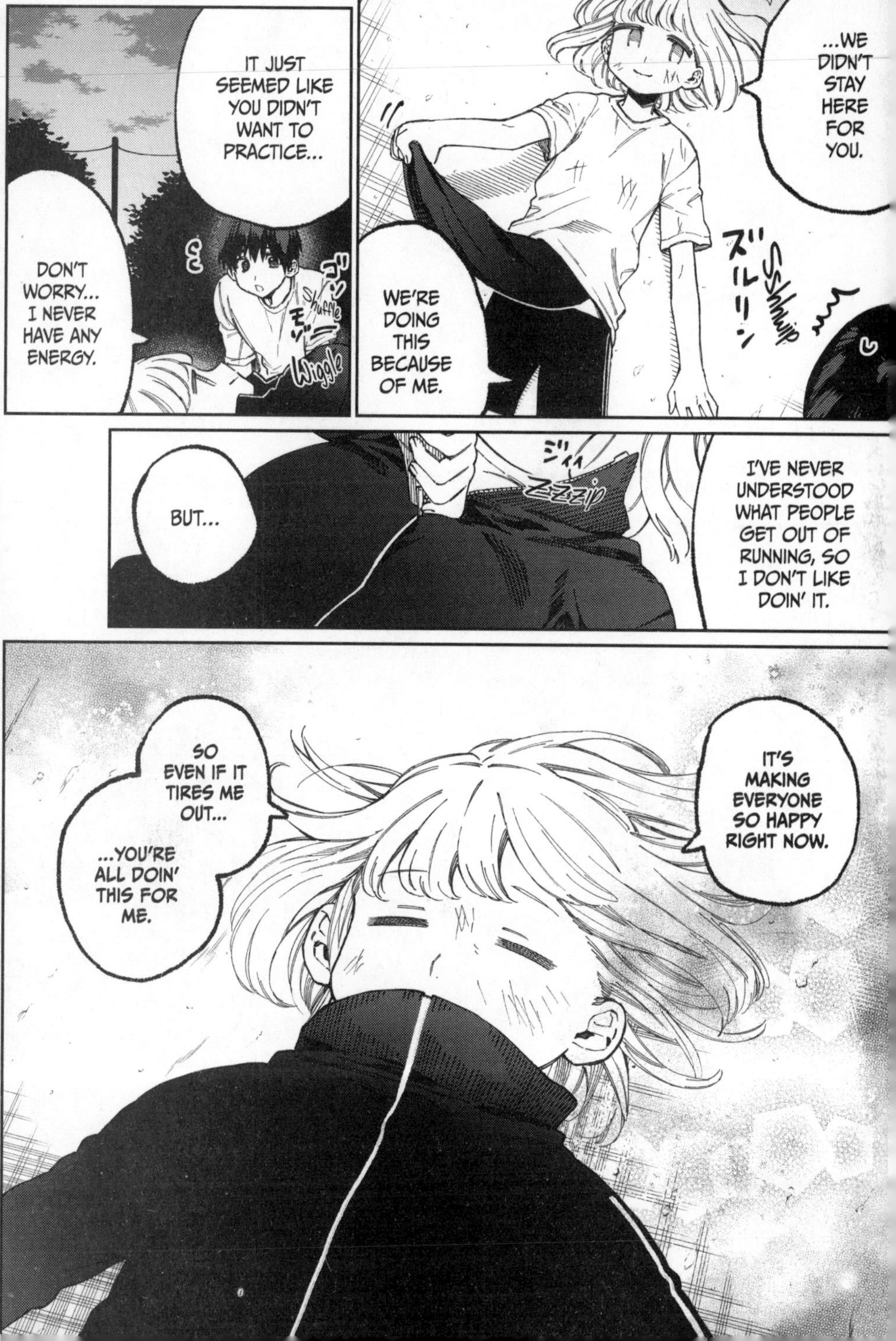
...WE DIDN'T STAY HERE FOR YOU.
ズルリッ
Sshhuip
WE'RE DOING THIS BECAUSE OF ME.
IT JUST SEEMED LIKE YOU DIDN'T WANT TO PRACTICE...
DON'T WORRY... I NEVER HAVE ANY ENERGY.
Shuffle
Wiggle
I'VE NEVER UNDERSTOOD WHAT PEOPLE GET OUT OF RUNNING, SO I DON'T LIKE DOIN' IT.
Zzzip
BUT...
IT'S MAKING EVERYONE SO HAPPY RIGHT NOW.
SO EVEN IF IT TIRES ME OUT...
...YOU'RE ALL DOIN' THIS FOR ME.

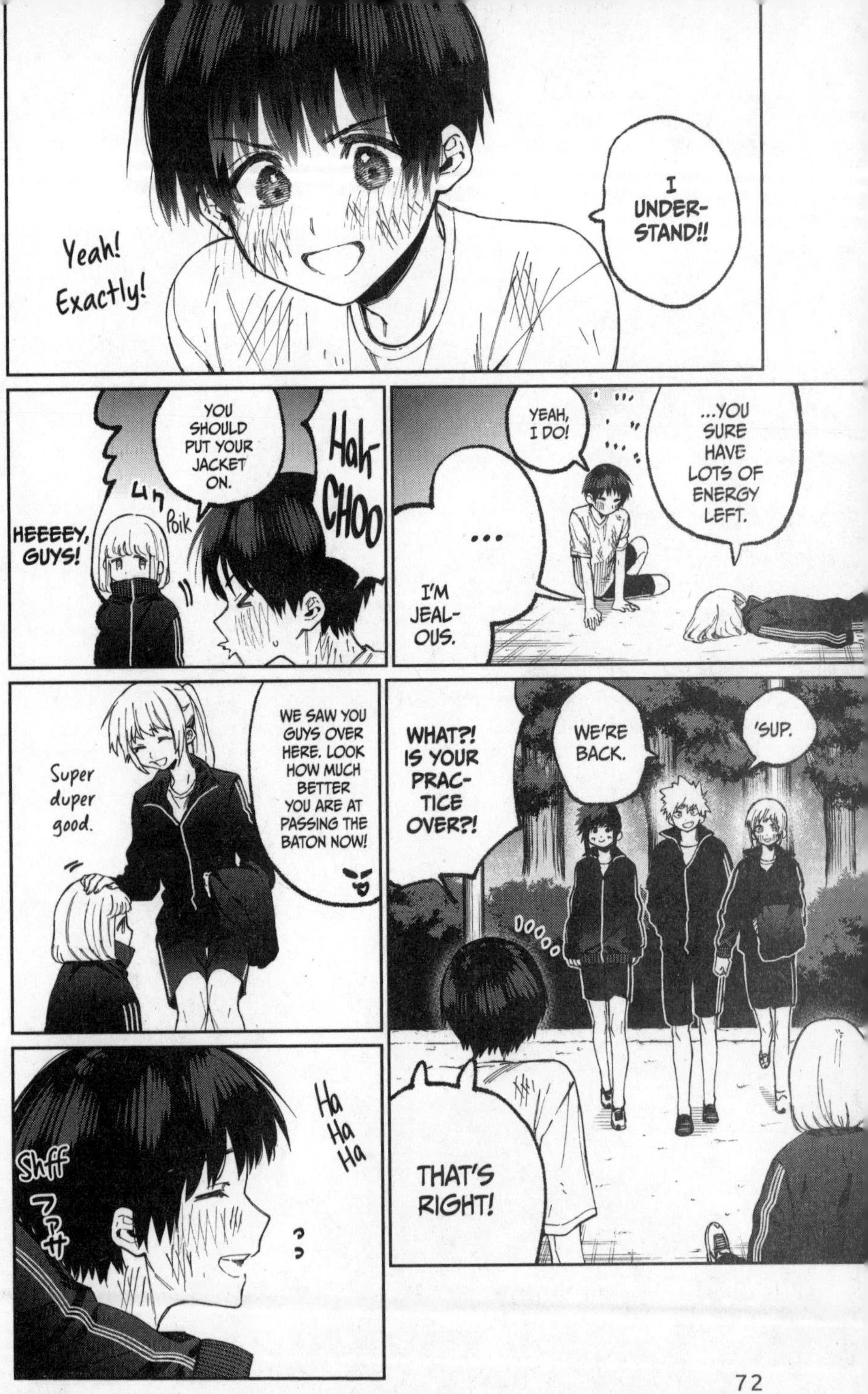
I UNDER-STAND!!
Yeah! Exactly!
...YOU SURE HAVE LOTS OF ENERGY LEFT.
YEAH, I DO!
...
I'M JEAL-OUS.
Hak CHOO
YOU SHOULD PUT YOUR JACKET ON.
Poik
HEEEEY, GUYS!
'SUP.
WE'RE BACK.
WHAT?! IS YOUR PRAC-TICE OVER?!
OOOOO
WE SAW YOU GUYS OVER HERE. LOOK HOW MUCH BETTER YOU ARE AT PASSING THE BATON NOW!
Super duper good.
THAT'S RIGHT!
Ha Ha Ha
Shff

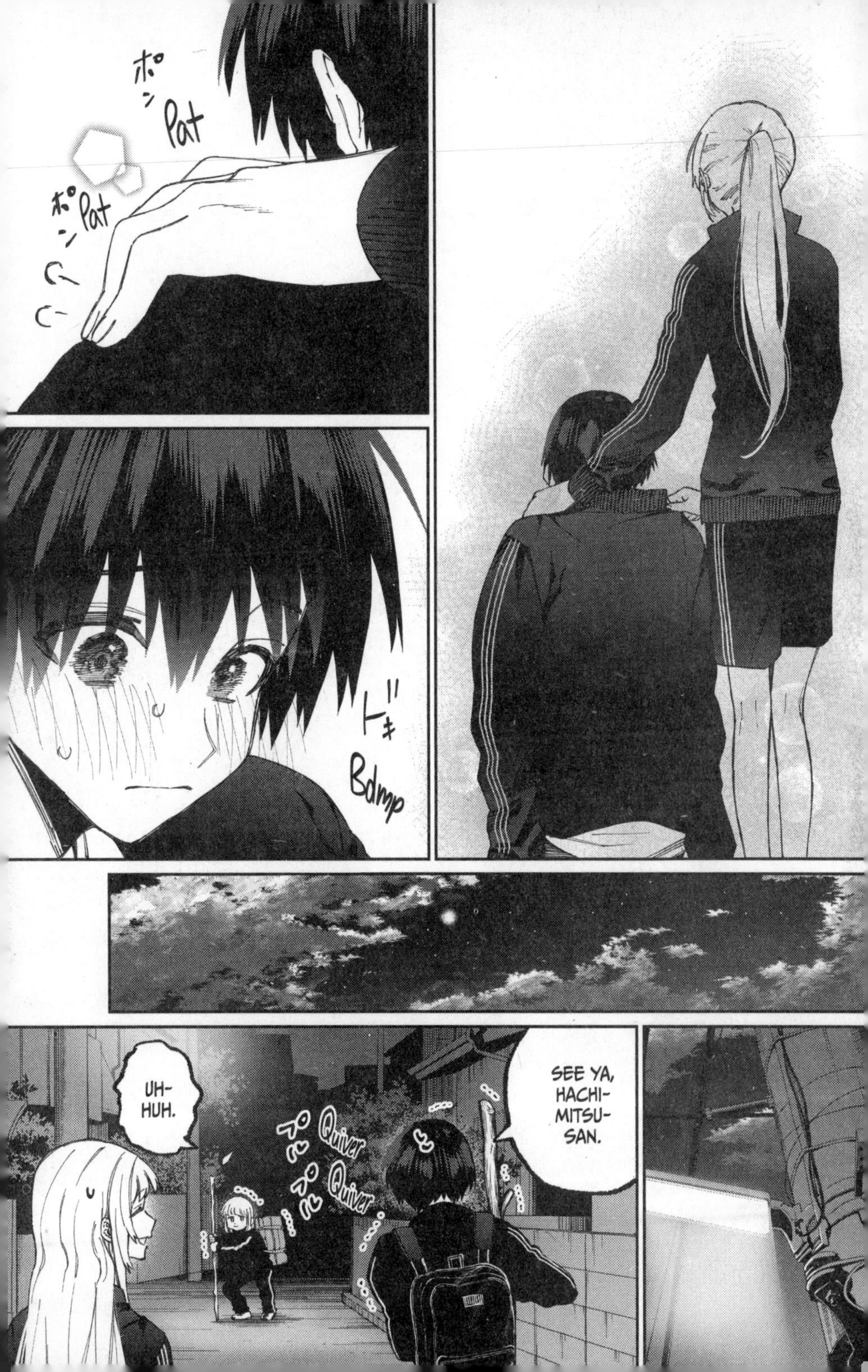
ポン Pat
ポン Pat
ドキ Bdmp
SEE YA, HACHI-MITSU-SAN.
Quiver Quiver
UH-HUH.

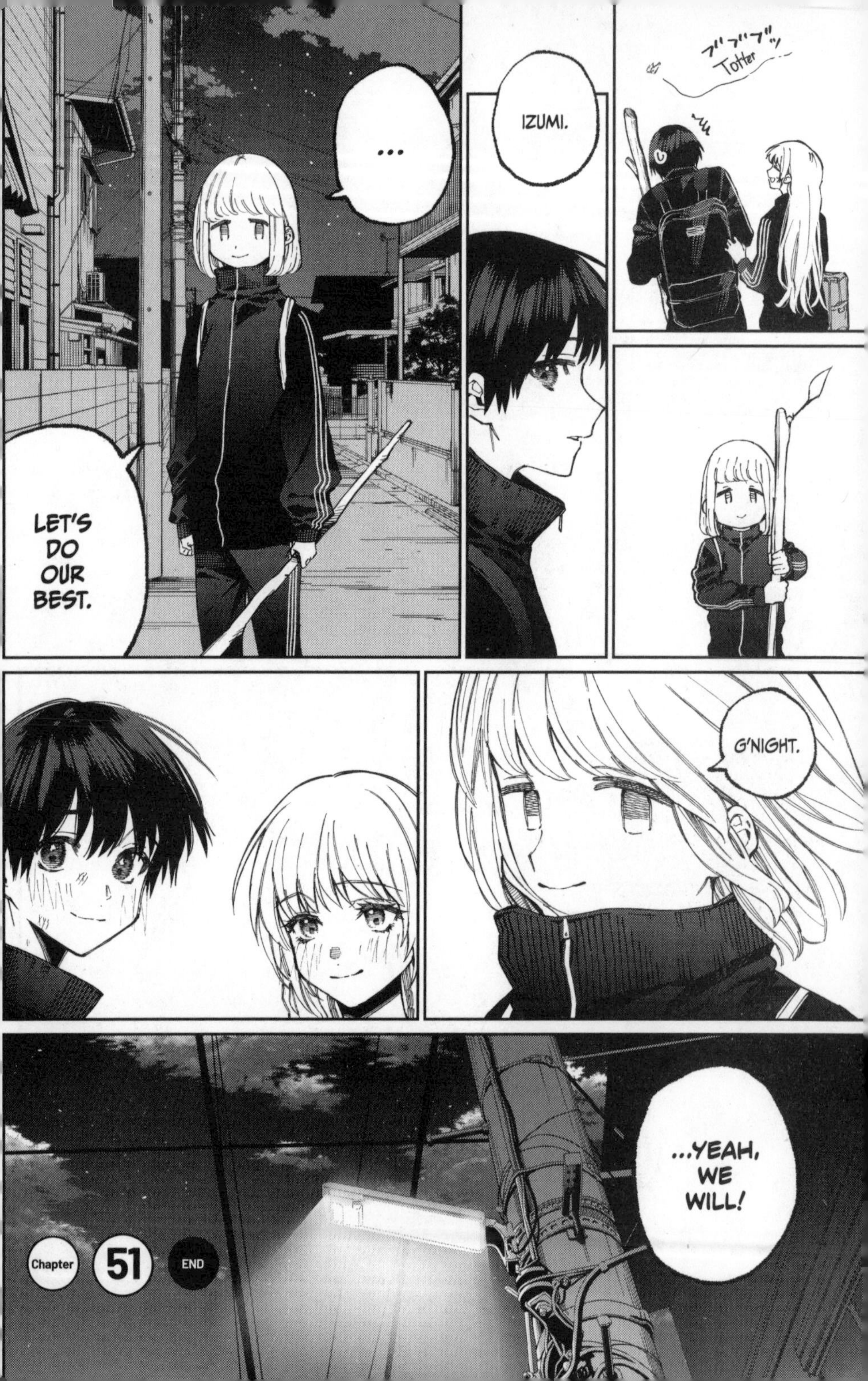
ブブブッ
Totter
IZUMI.
...
LET'S DO OUR BEST.
G'NIGHT.
...YEAH, WE WILL!
Chapter 51 END

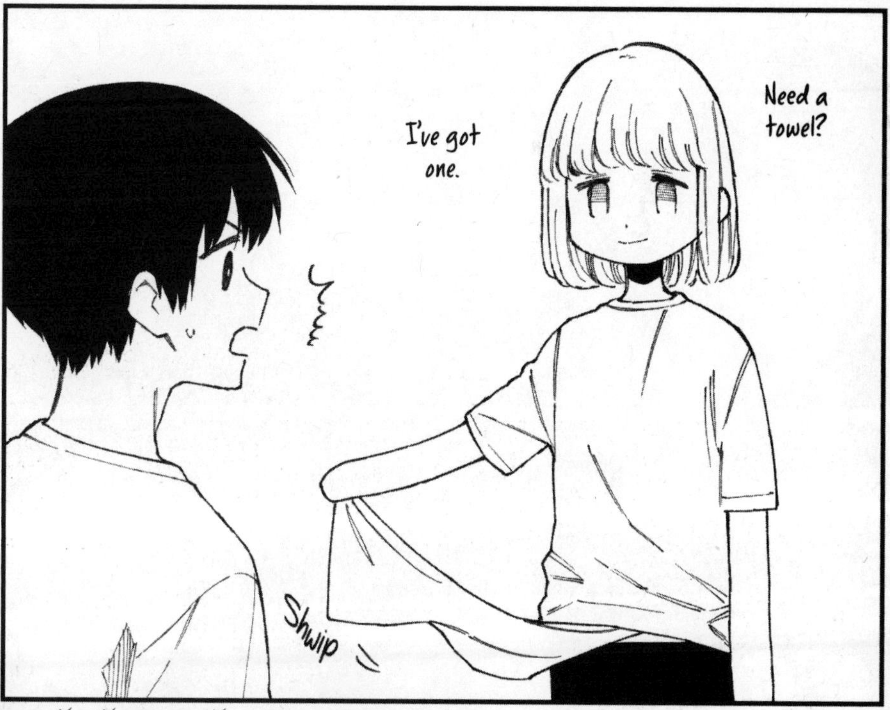
Need a towel?
I've got one.
Shwip

SHIKIMORI'S not just a cutie

# SHIKIMORI'S not just a cutie

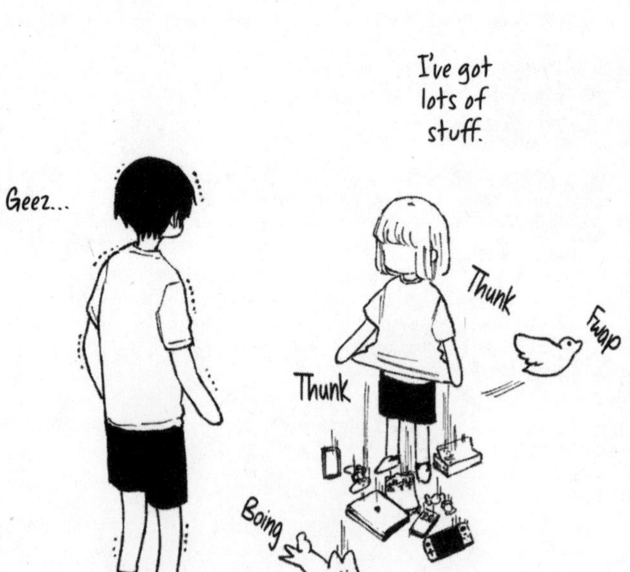
I've got lots of stuff.
Geez...
Thunk
Fwap
Thunk
Boing

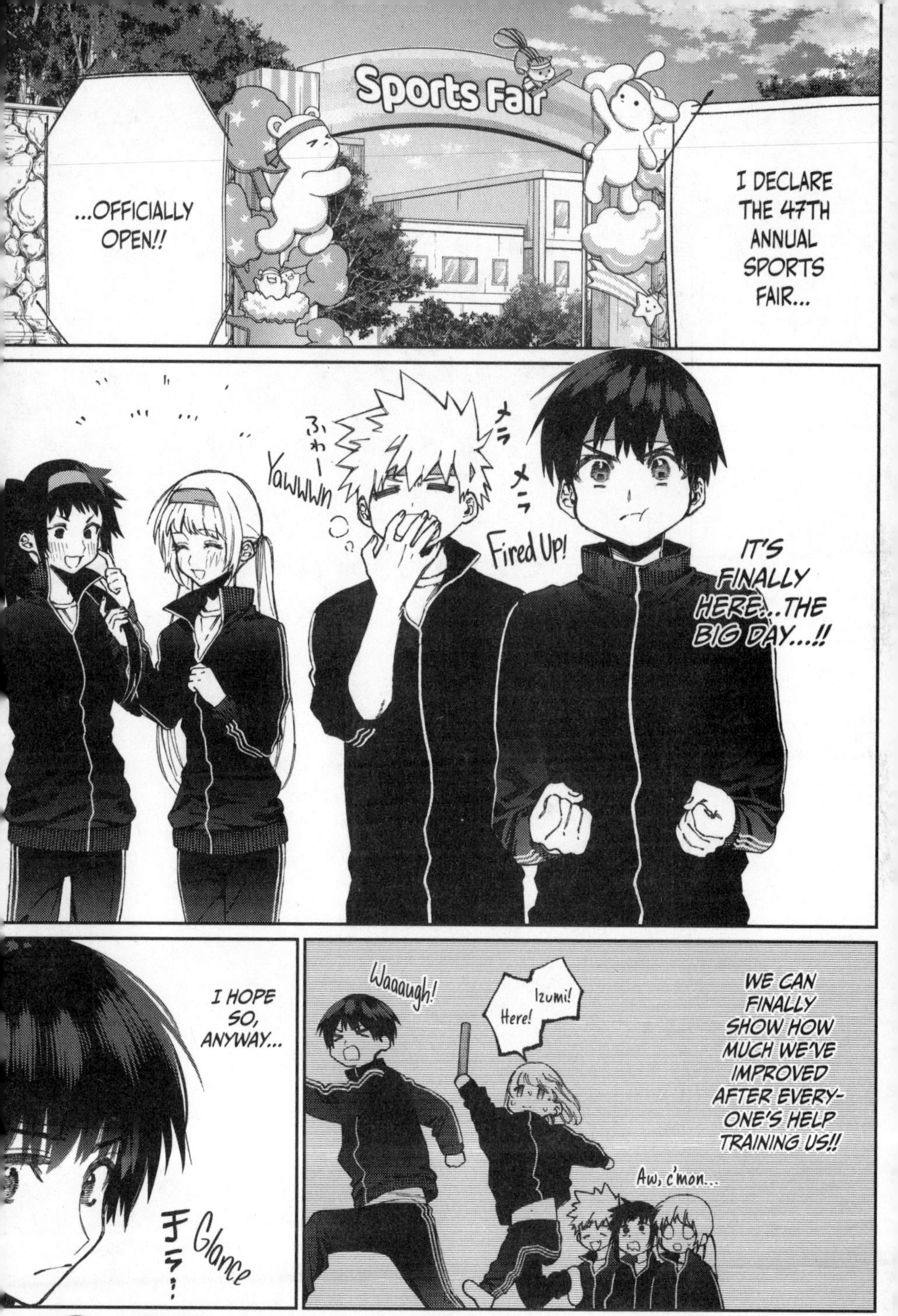
Sports Fair
I DECLARE THE 47TH ANNUAL SPORTS FAIR...
...OFFICIALLY OPEN!!
IT'S FINALLY HERE...THE BIG DAY...!!
メラ メラ
Fired Up!
ふわ〜
Yawwwn
WE CAN FINALLY SHOW HOW MUCH WE'VE IMPROVED AFTER EVERY-ONE'S HELP TRAINING US!!
Izumi!
Here!
Waaaugh!
Aw, c'mon...
I HOPE SO, ANYWAY...
チラ
Glance

Chapter 52

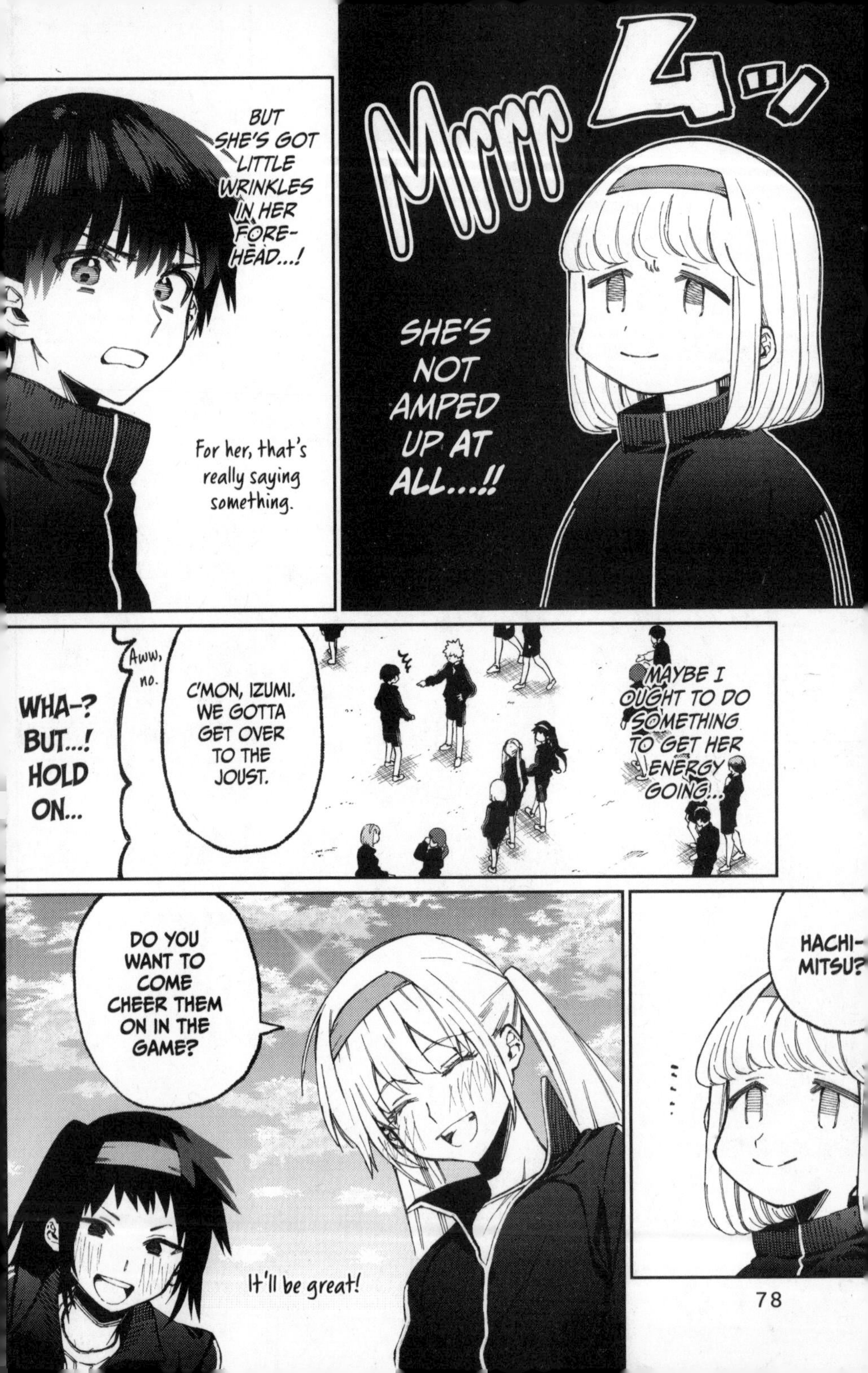
Mrrr ムッ
SHE'S NOT AMPED UP AT ALL...!!
BUT SHE'S GOT LITTLE WRINKLES IN HER FORE-HEAD...!
For her, that's really saying something.
MAYBE I OUGHT TO DO SOMETHING TO GET HER ENERGY GOING...
C'MON, IZUMI. WE GOTTA GET OVER TO THE JOUST.
Aww, no.
WHA-? BUT...! HOLD ON...
HACHI-MITSU?
....
DO YOU WANT TO COME CHEER THEM ON IN THE GAME?
It'll be great!

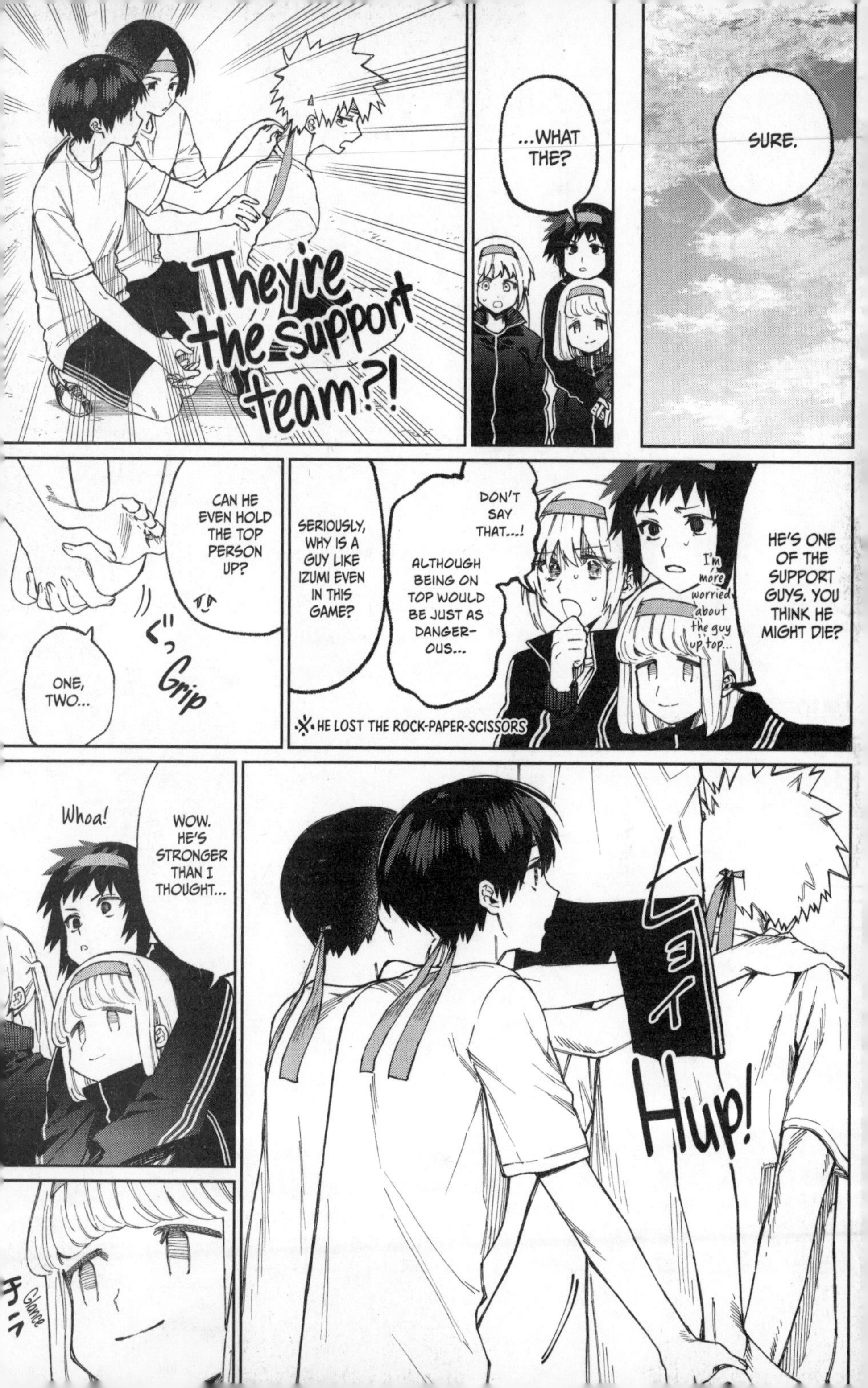
SURE.
...WHAT THE?
They're the support team?!
HE'S ONE OF THE SUPPORT GUYS. YOU THINK HE MIGHT DIE?
I'm more worried about the guy up top...
DON'T SAY THAT...!
ALTHOUGH BEING ON TOP WOULD BE JUST AS DANGER-OUS...
SERIOUSLY, WHY IS A GUY LIKE IZUMI EVEN IN THIS GAME?
※ HE LOST THE ROCK-PAPER-SCISSORS
CAN HE EVEN HOLD THE TOP PERSON UP?
ぐっ
Grip
ONE, TWO...
ヒョイ
Hup!
WOW. HE'S STRONGER THAN I THOUGHT...
Whoa!
チラ
Glance

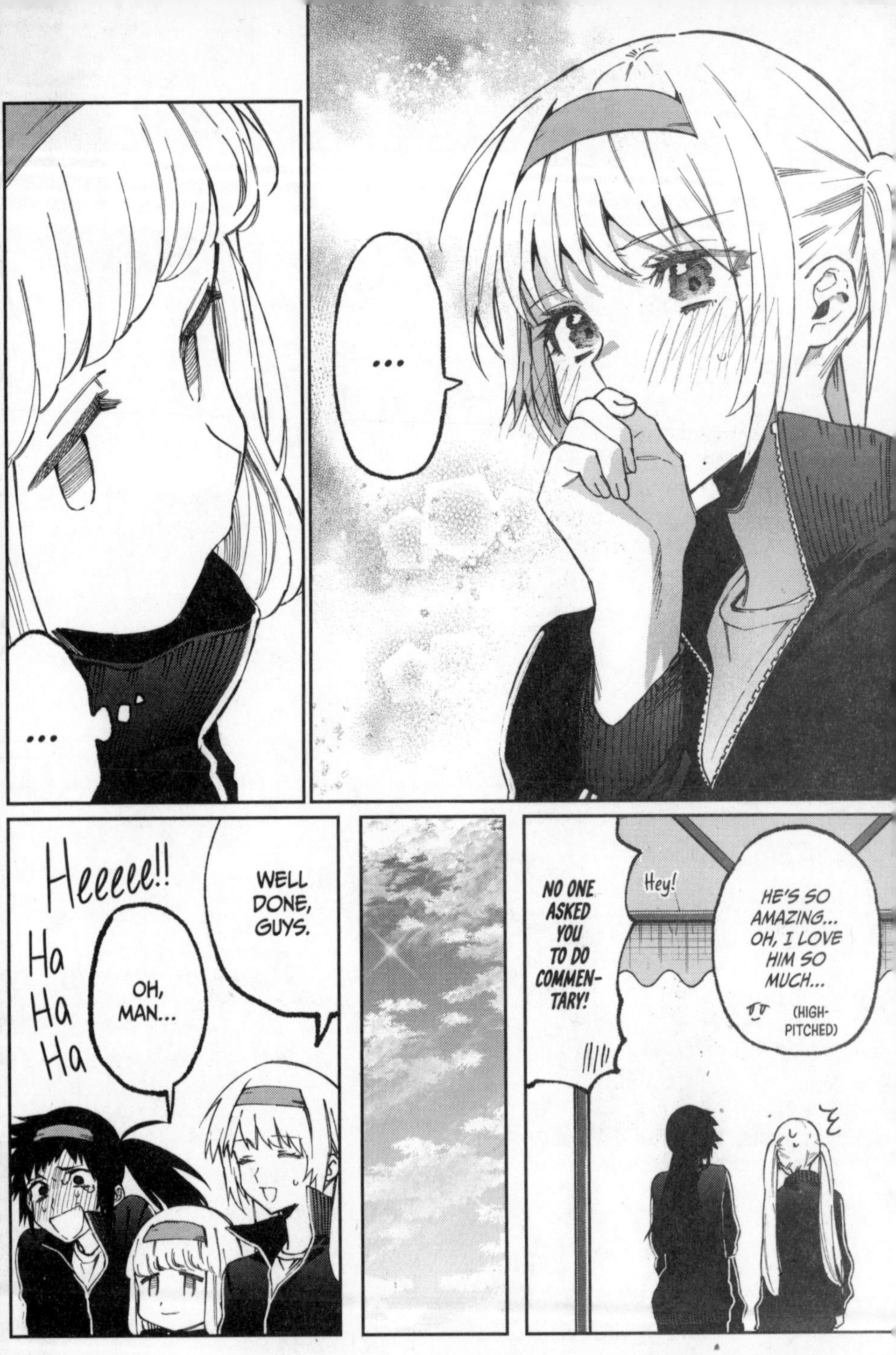
...
...
HE'S SO AMAZING... OH, I LOVE HIM SO MUCH...
(HIGH-PITCHED)
Hey!
NO ONE ASKED YOU TO DO COMMENTARY!
WELL DONE, GUYS.
OH, MAN...
Heeeee!!
Ha Ha Ha

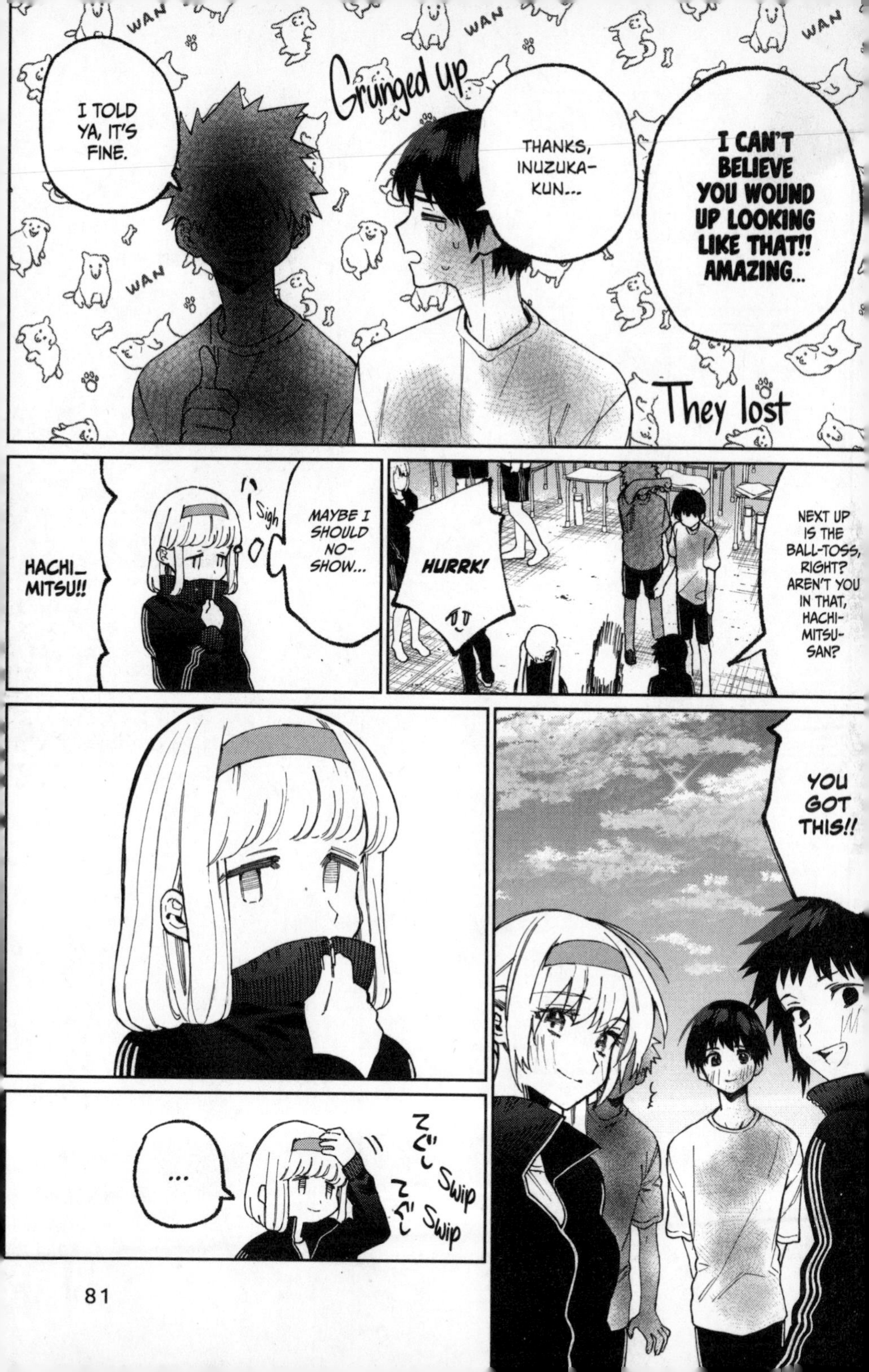
WAN
I CAN'T BELIEVE YOU WOUND UP LOOKING LIKE THAT!! AMAZING...
THANKS, INUZUKA-KUN...
Grunged up
I TOLD YA, IT'S FINE.
They lost
NEXT UP IS THE BALL-TOSS, RIGHT? AREN'T YOU IN THAT, HACHI-MITSU-SAN?
HURRK!
MAYBE I SHOULD NO-SHOW...
Sigh
HACHI_MITSU!!
YOU GOT THIS!!
...
Swip
Swip

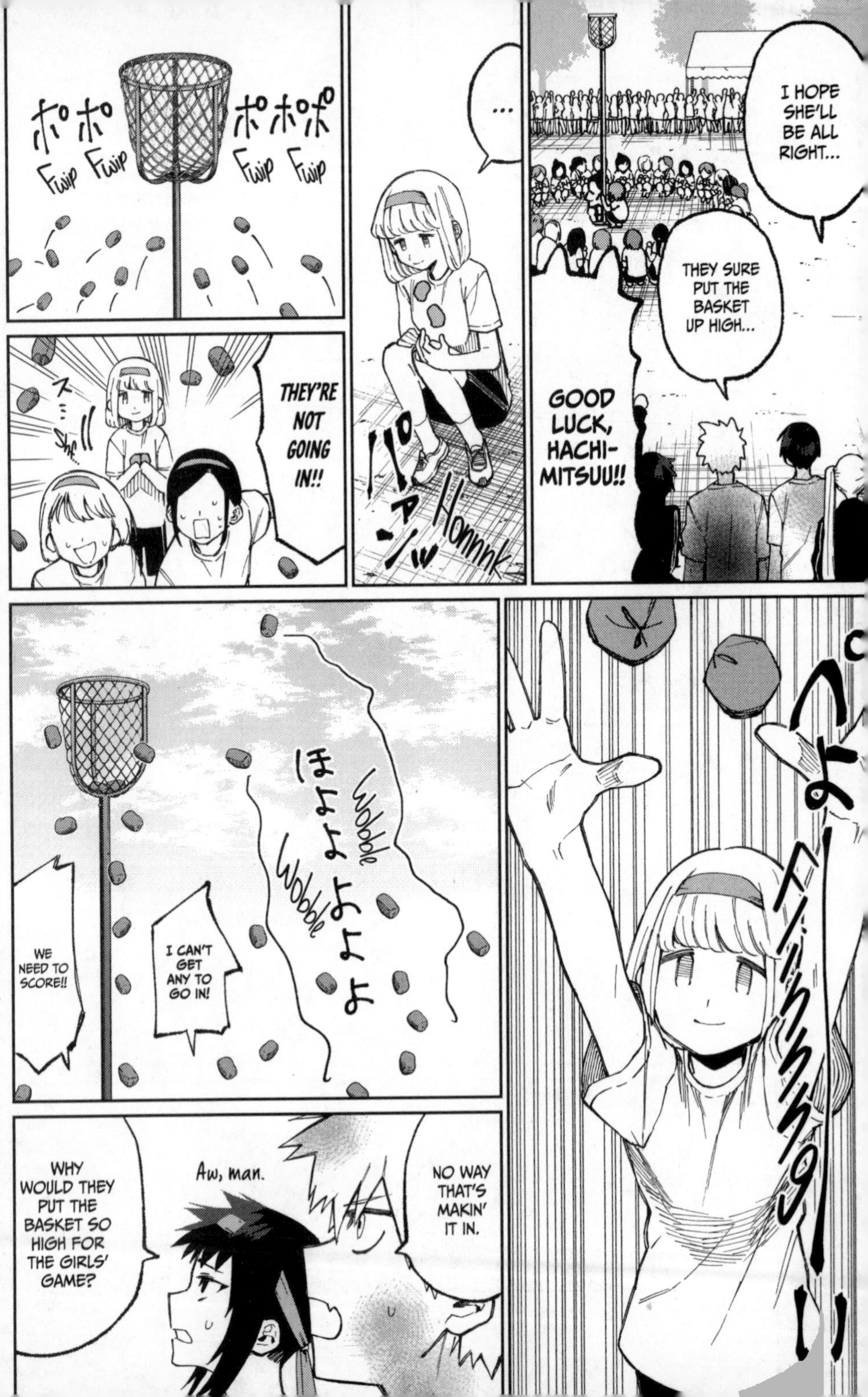
I HOPE SHE'LL BE ALL RIGHT...
THEY SURE PUT THE BASKET UP HIGH...
GOOD LUCK, HACHI-MITSUU!!
...
Honnnk
ポポ
Fwip Fwip
ポポポ
Fwip Fwip
Shf...
THEY'RE NOT GOING IN!!
ほよよよよ
Wobble Wobble
I CAN'T GET ANY TO GO IN!
WE NEED TO SCORE!!
NO WAY THAT'S MAKIN' IT IN.
Aw, man.
WHY WOULD THEY PUT THE BASKET SO HIGH FOR THE GIRLS' GAME?

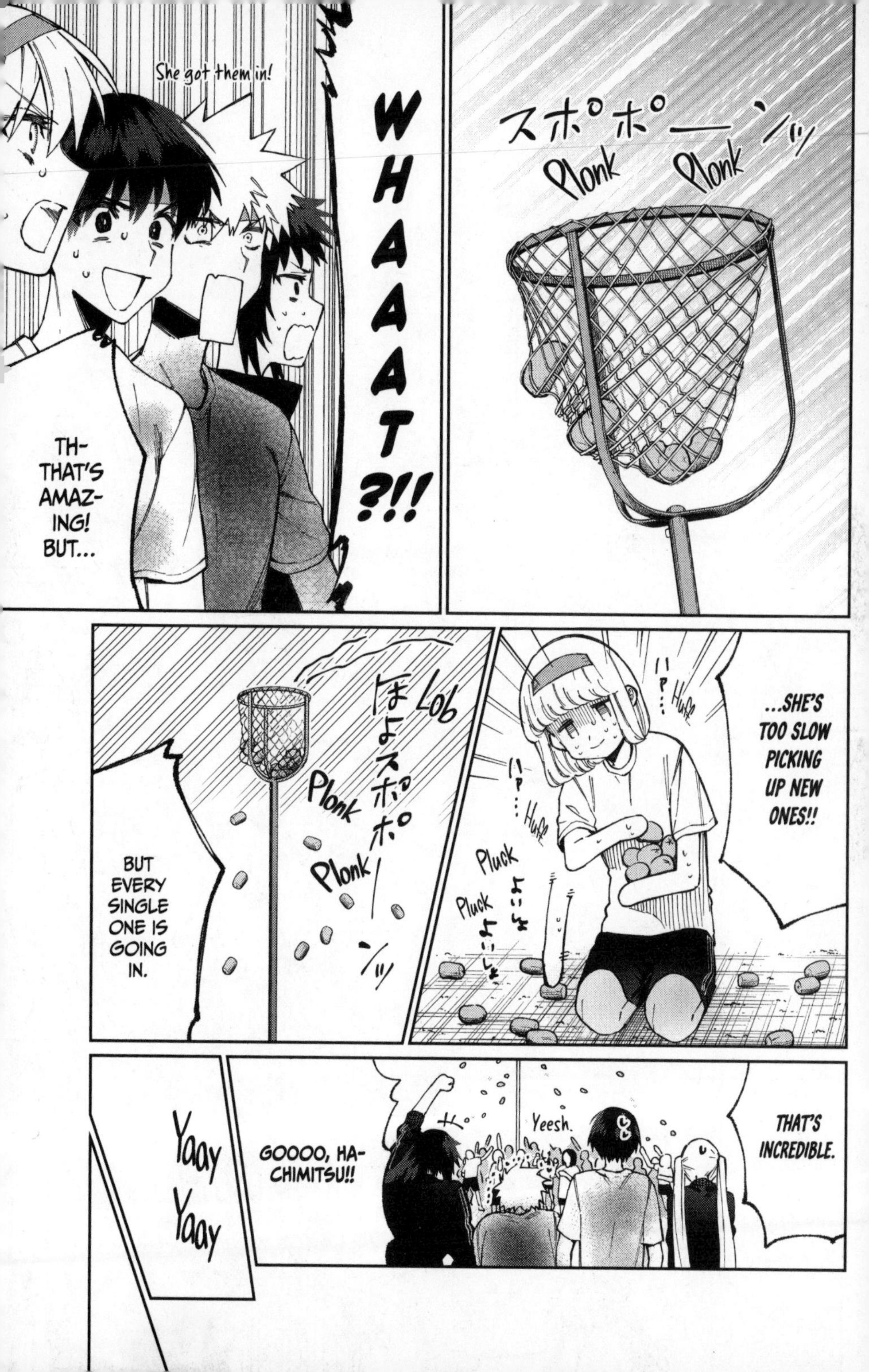

スポポーンッ
Plonk Plonk
She got them in!
WHAAAAT?!!
TH-THAT'S AMAZ-ING! BUT...
...SHE'S TOO SLOW PICKING UP NEW ONES!!
ハァ… Huff
ハァ… Huff
Pluck よいしょ
Pluck よいしょ
Lob
ほよスポポンッ
Plonk
Plonk
BUT EVERY SINGLE ONE IS GOING IN.
THAT'S INCREDIBLE.
Yeesh.
GOOOO, HA-CHIMITSU!!
Yaay Yaay

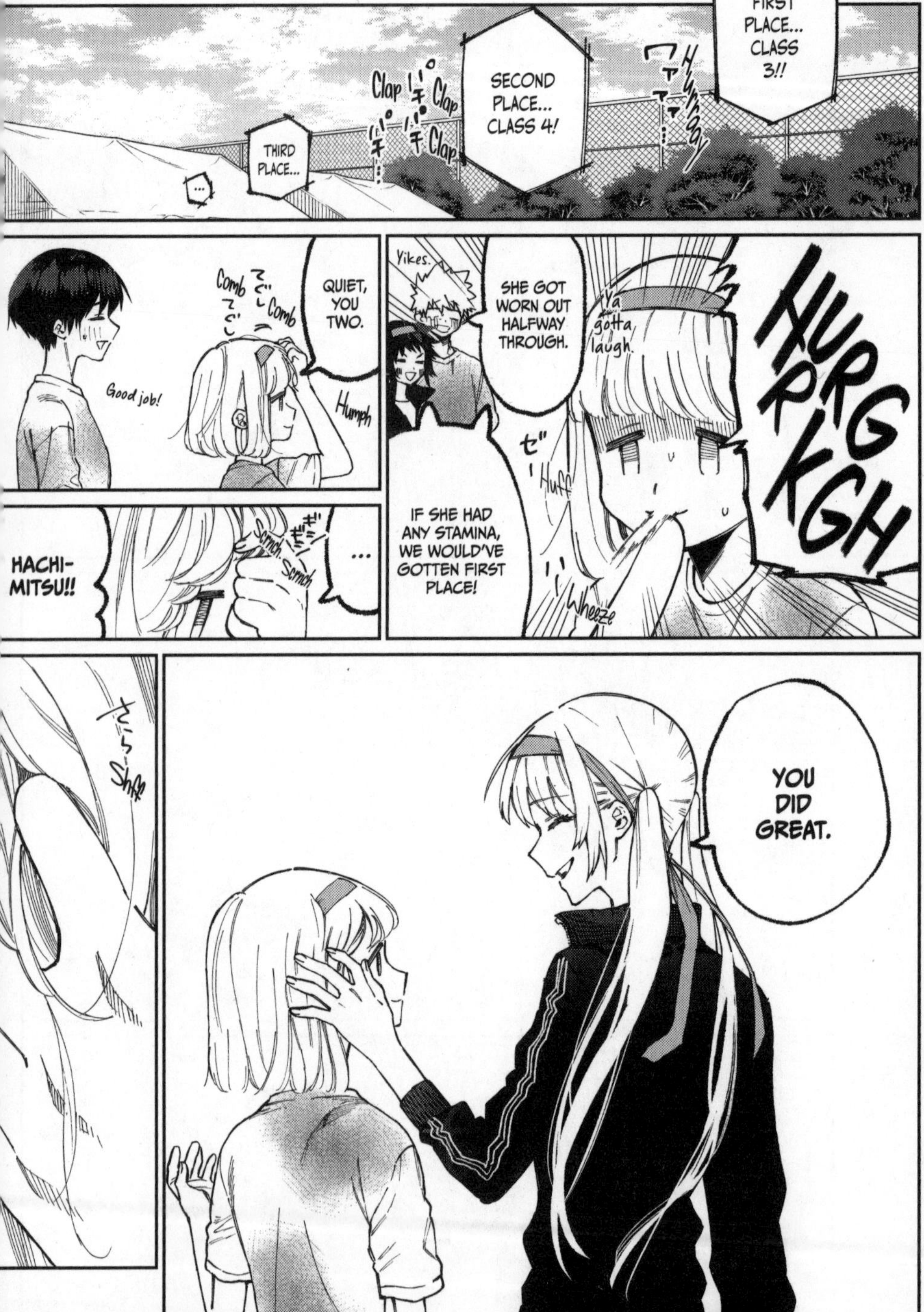
FIRST PLACE... CLASS 3!!
Hurraay
SECOND PLACE... CLASS 4!
Clap Clap Clap
THIRD PLACE...
...
HURG KGH
Ya gotta laugh.
SHE GOT WORN OUT HALFWAY THROUGH.
Yikes.
Huff
Wheeze
IF SHE HAD ANY STAMINA, WE WOULD'VE GOTTEN FIRST PLACE!
QUIET, YOU TWO.
Comb Comb
Humph
Good job!
...
Scrtch Scrtch
HACHI-MITSU!!
YOU DID GREAT.
Shff

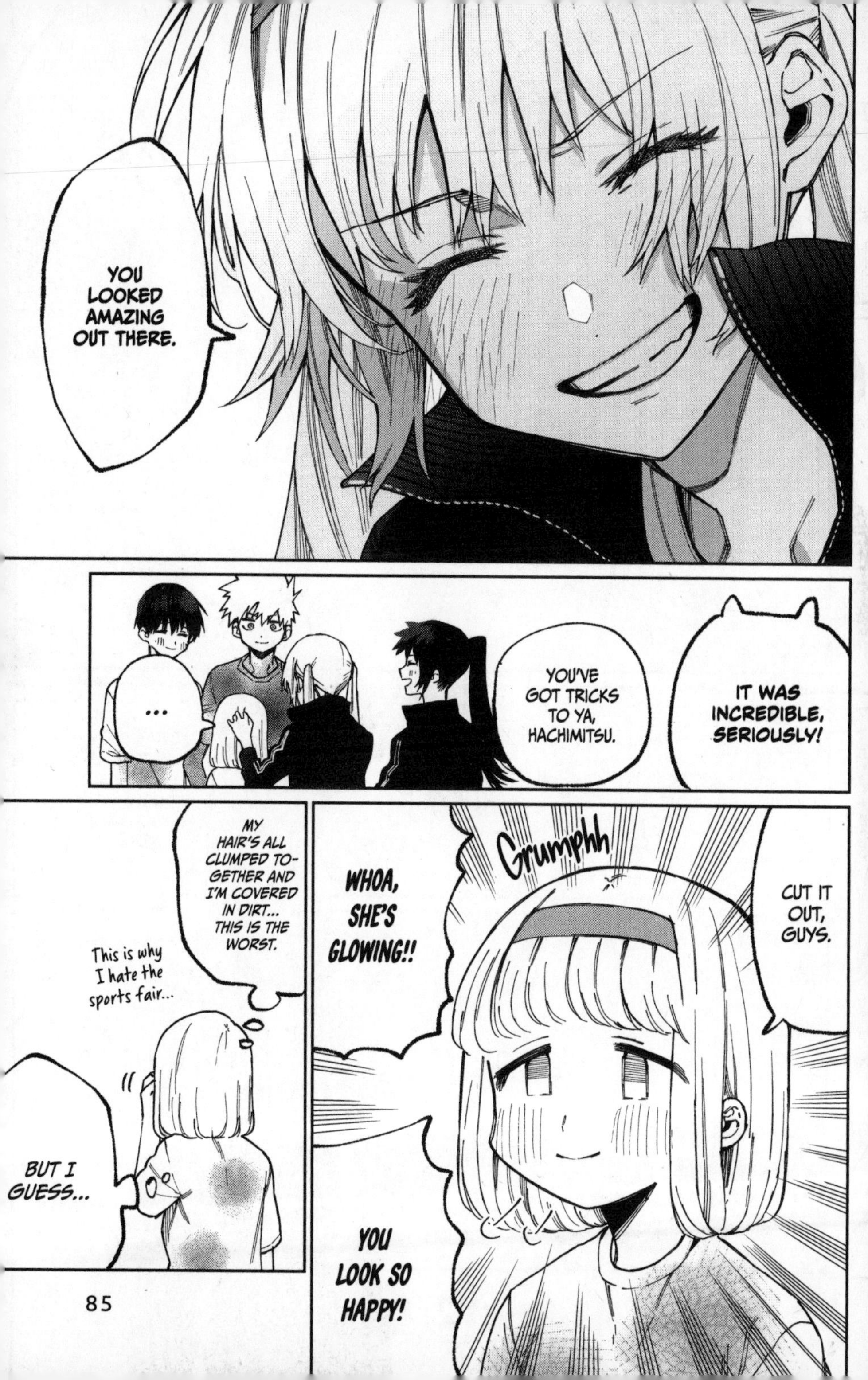
YOU LOOKED AMAZING OUT THERE.
IT WAS INCREDIBLE, SERIOUSLY!
YOU'VE GOT TRICKS TO YA, HACHIMITSU.
...
CUT IT OUT, GUYS.
Grumphh
WHOA, SHE'S GLOWING!!
YOU LOOK SO HAPPY!
MY HAIR'S ALL CLUMPED TO-GETHER AND I'M COVERED IN DIRT... THIS IS THE WORST.
This is why I hate the sports fair...
BUT I GUESS...

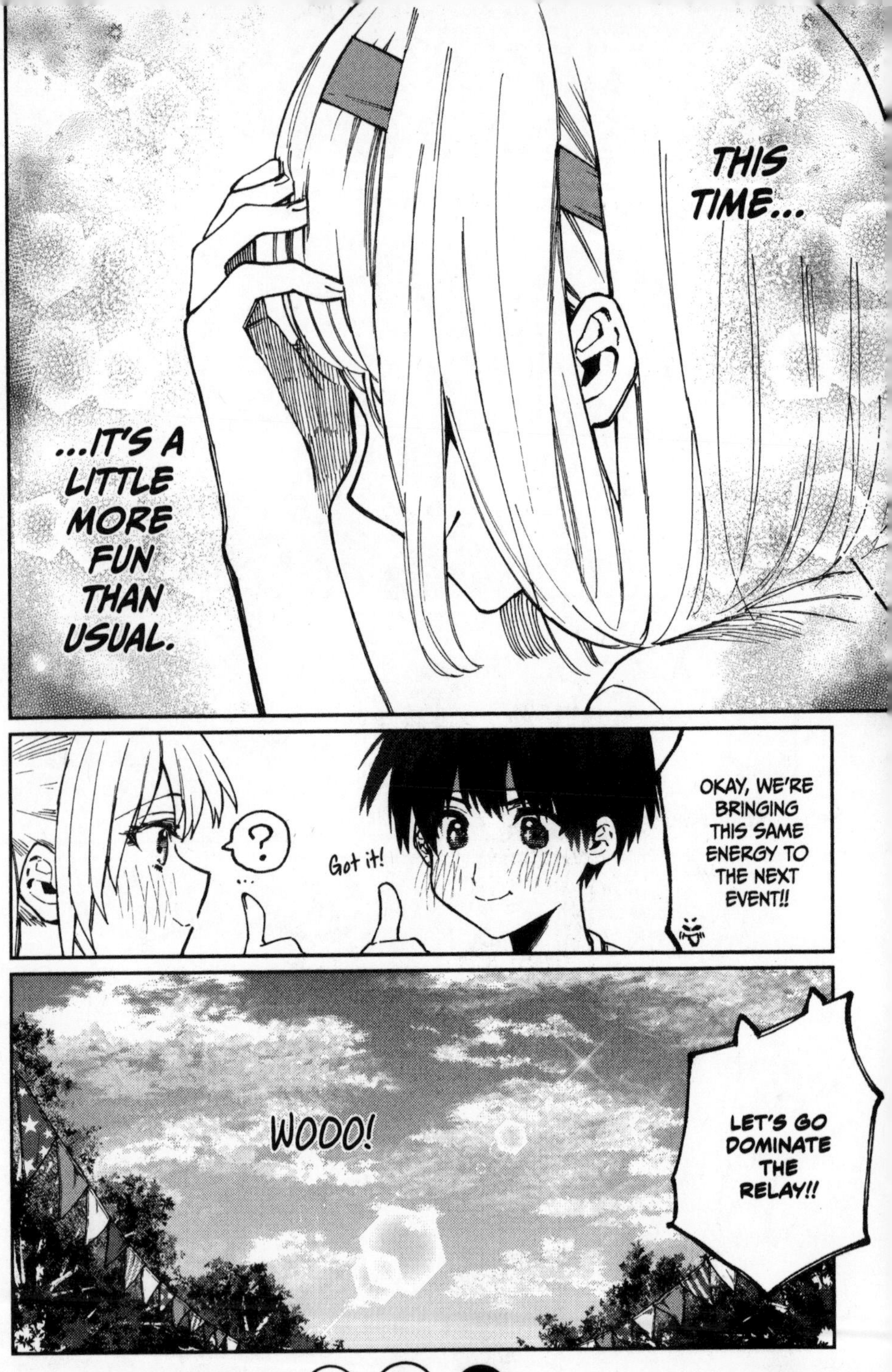
THIS TIME...
...IT'S A LITTLE MORE FUN THAN USUAL.
OKAY, WE'RE BRINGING THIS SAME ENERGY TO THE NEXT EVENT!!
Got it!
?
...
LET'S GO DOMINATE THE RELAY!!
WOOO!

Chapter 52 END

# SHIKIMORI'S
## not just a cutie

It's so cute.

She's in such a good mood.

Heh Heh Heh...

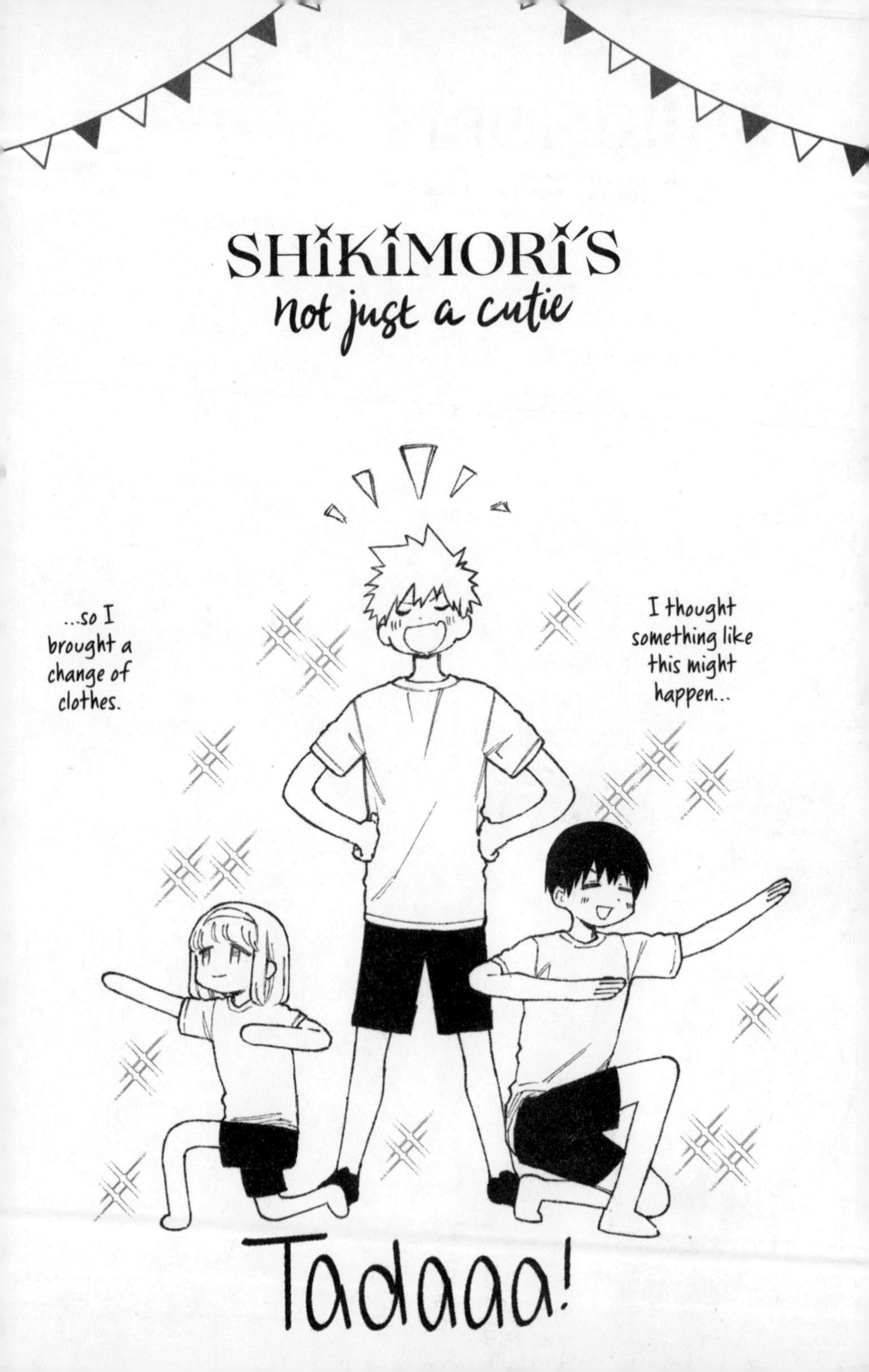
SHIKIMORI'S
not just a cutie
I thought something like this might happen...
...so I brought a change of clothes.
Tadaaa!

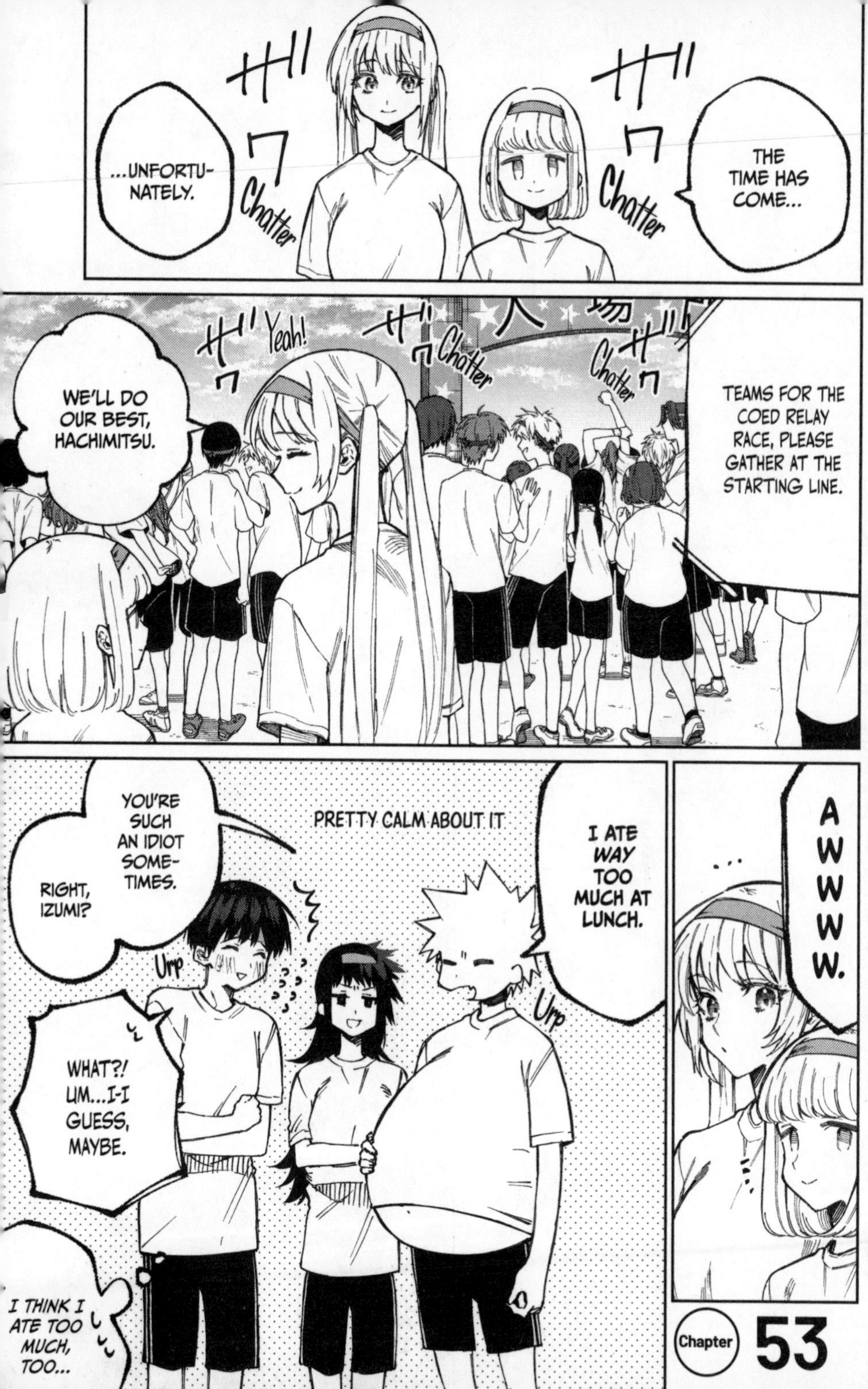
THE TIME HAS COME...
...UNFORTUNATELY.
Chatter
Chatter
TEAMS FOR THE COED RELAY RACE, PLEASE GATHER AT THE STARTING LINE.
Chatter
Chatter
Yeah!
WE'LL DO OUR BEST, HACHIMITSU.
AWWWW.
...
I ATE WAY TOO MUCH AT LUNCH.
Urp
PRETTY CALM ABOUT IT
YOU'RE SUCH AN IDIOT SOMETIMES.
RIGHT, IZUMI?
Urp
WHAT?! UM...I-I GUESS, MAYBE.
I THINK I ATE TOO MUCH, TOO...

Chapter 53

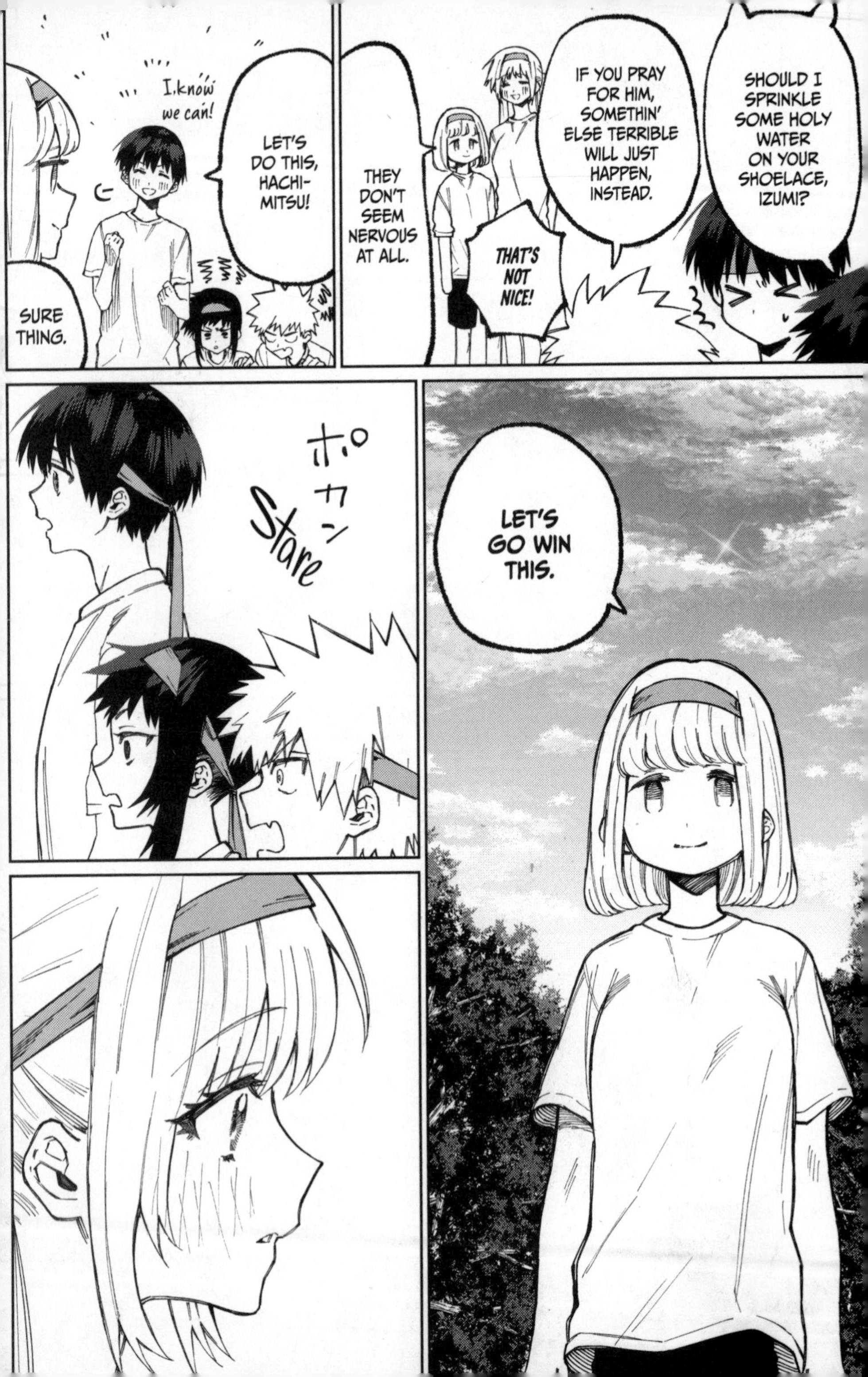
SHOULD I SPRINKLE SOME HOLY WATER ON YOUR SHOELACE, IZUMI?
IF YOU PRAY FOR HIM, SOMETHIN' ELSE TERRIBLE WILL JUST HAPPEN, INSTEAD.
THAT'S NOT NICE!
THEY DON'T SEEM NERVOUS AT ALL.
LET'S DO THIS, HACHI-MITSU!
I know we can!
SURE THING.
LET'S GO WIN THIS.
ポカン
Stare

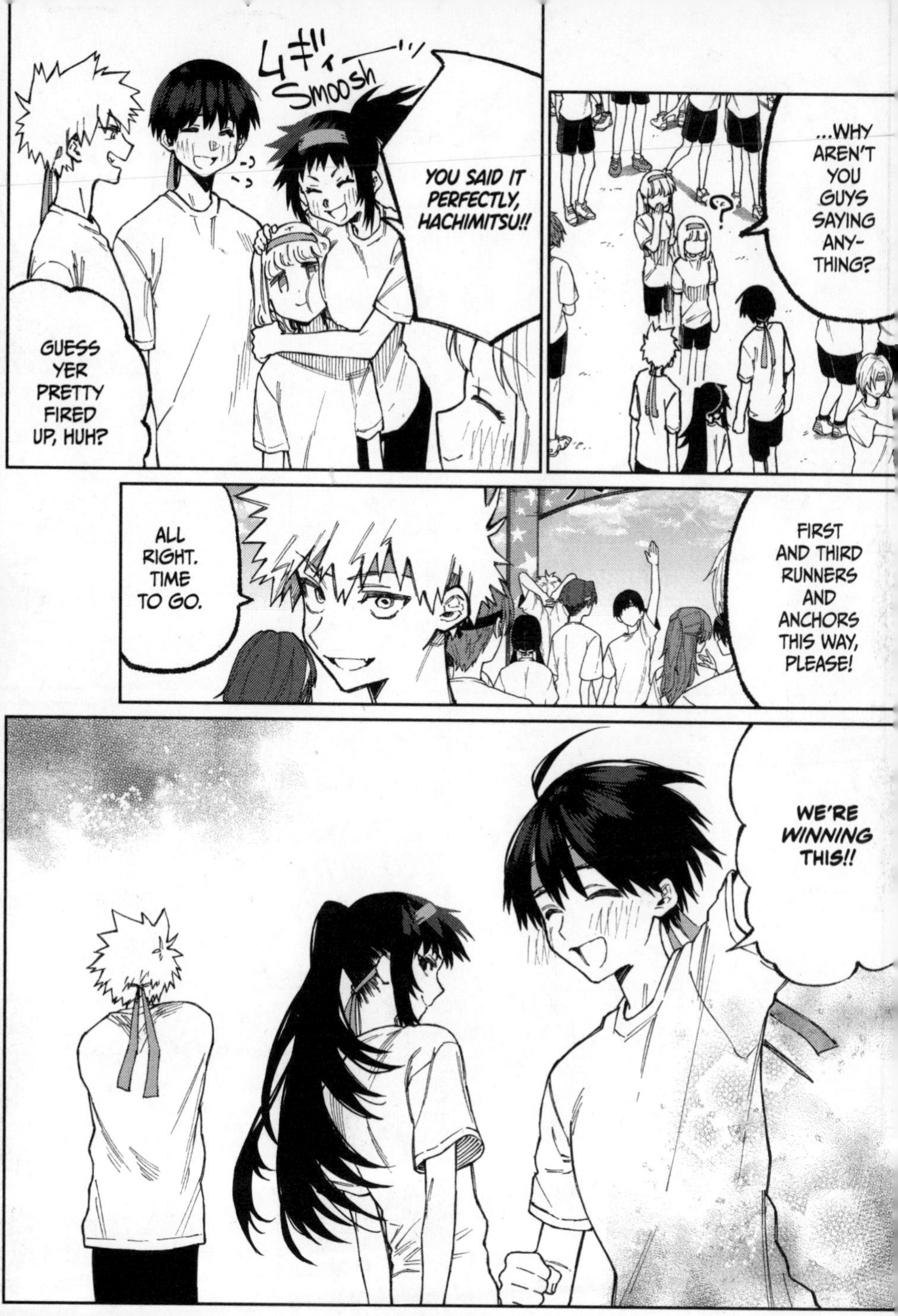
...WHY AREN'T YOU GUYS SAYING ANY-THING?
Smoosh
YOU SAID IT PERFECTLY, HACHIMITSU!!
GUESS YER PRETTY FIRED UP, HUH?
FIRST AND THIRD RUNNERS AND ANCHORS THIS WAY, PLEASE!
ALL RIGHT. TIME TO GO.
WE'RE WINNING THIS!!

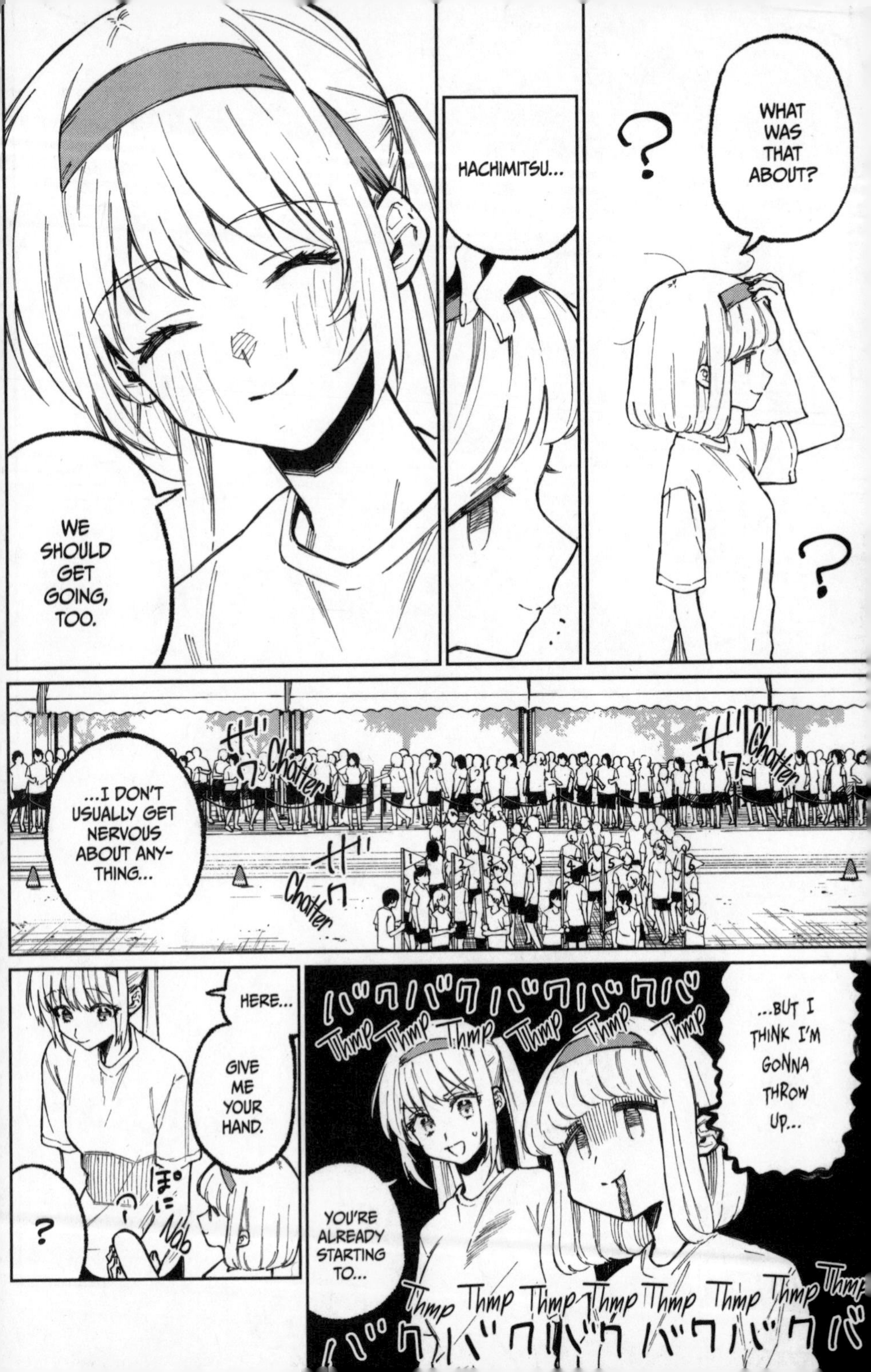
WHAT WAS THAT ABOUT?
HACHIMITSU...
WE SHOULD GET GOING, TOO.
Chatter
Chatter
...I DON'T USUALLY GET NERVOUS ABOUT ANY-THING...
Chatter
Thmp Thmp Thmp Thmp Thmp Thmp
...BUT I THINK I'M GONNA THROW UP...
YOU'RE ALREADY STARTING TO...
Thmp Thmp Thmp Thmp Thmp Thmp Thmp
HERE...
GIVE ME YOUR HAND.
Nab
?

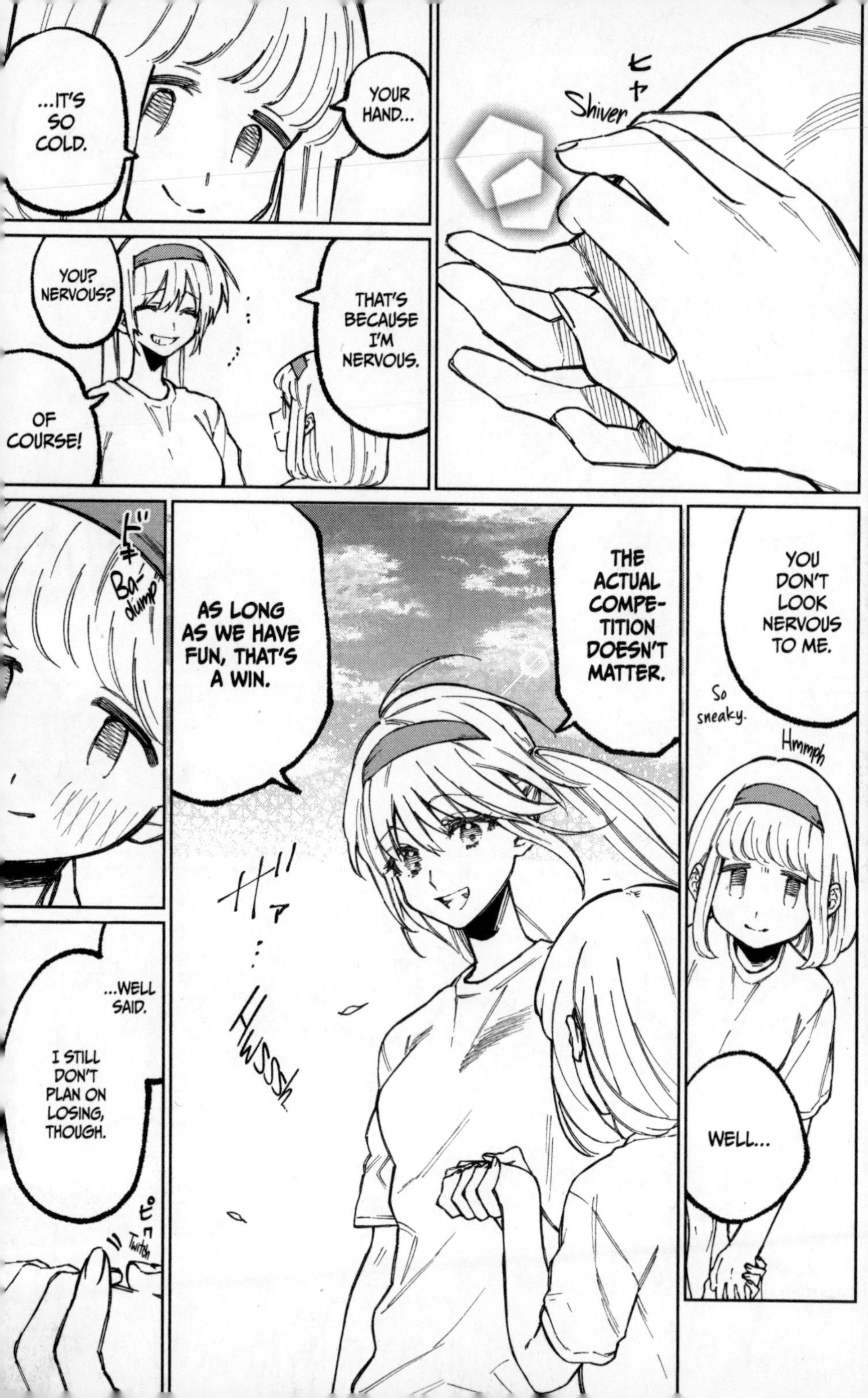
ヒヤ
Shiver
YOUR HAND...
...IT'S SO COLD.
THAT'S BECAUSE I'M NERVOUS.
YOU? NERVOUS?
OF COURSE!
YOU DON'T LOOK NERVOUS TO ME.
So sneaky.
Hmmph
WELL...
THE ACTUAL COMPETITION DOESN'T MATTER.
AS LONG AS WE HAVE FUN, THAT'S A WIN.
Hwsssh
ドキ
Ba-dump
...WELL SAID.
I STILL DON'T PLAN ON LOSING, THOUGH.
Twitch

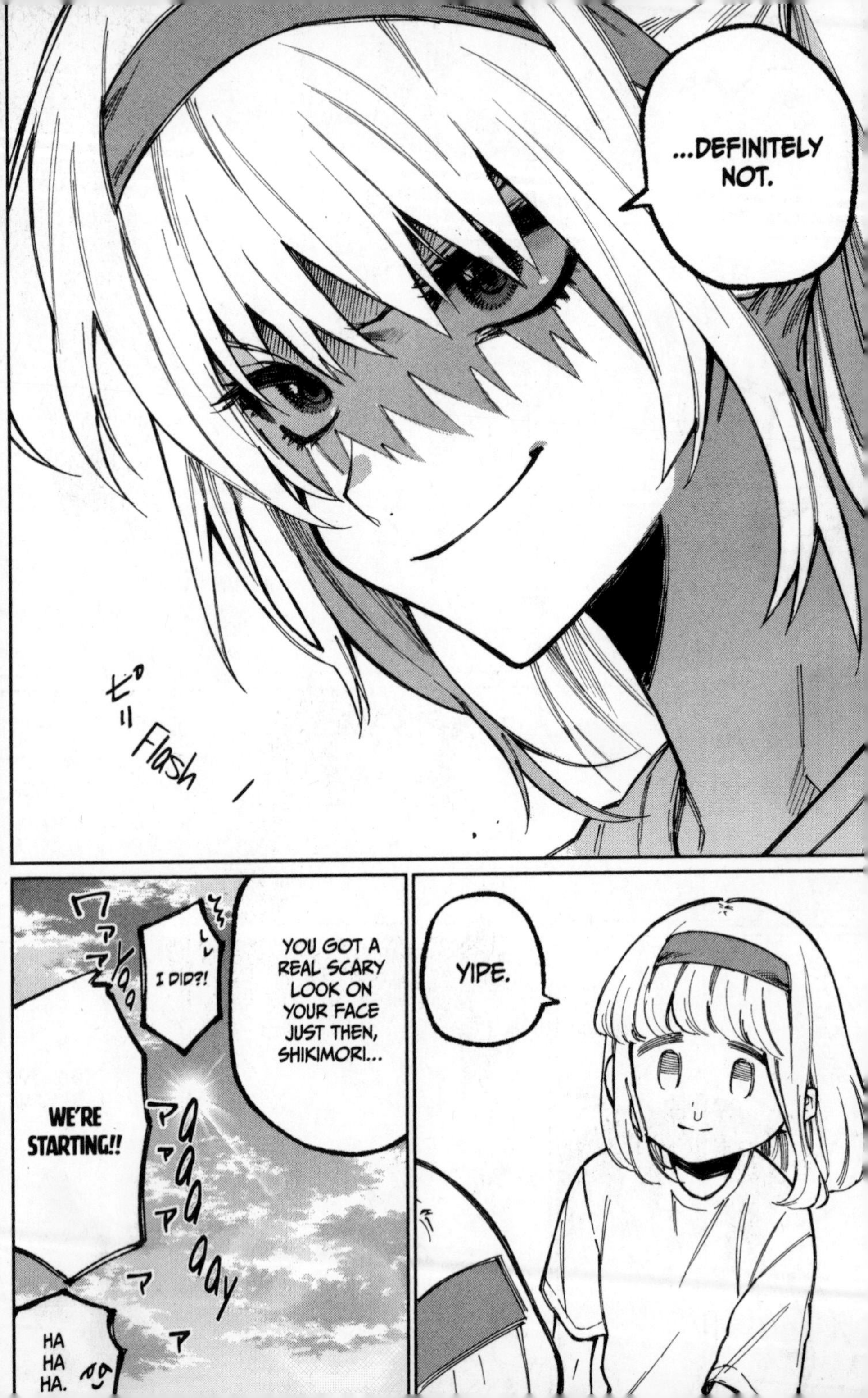
...DEFINITELY NOT.
Flash
YIPE.
YOU GOT A REAL SCARY LOOK ON YOUR FACE JUST THEN, SHIKIMORI...
I DID?!
Yaa
WE'RE STARTING!!
aaaaay
HA HA HA.

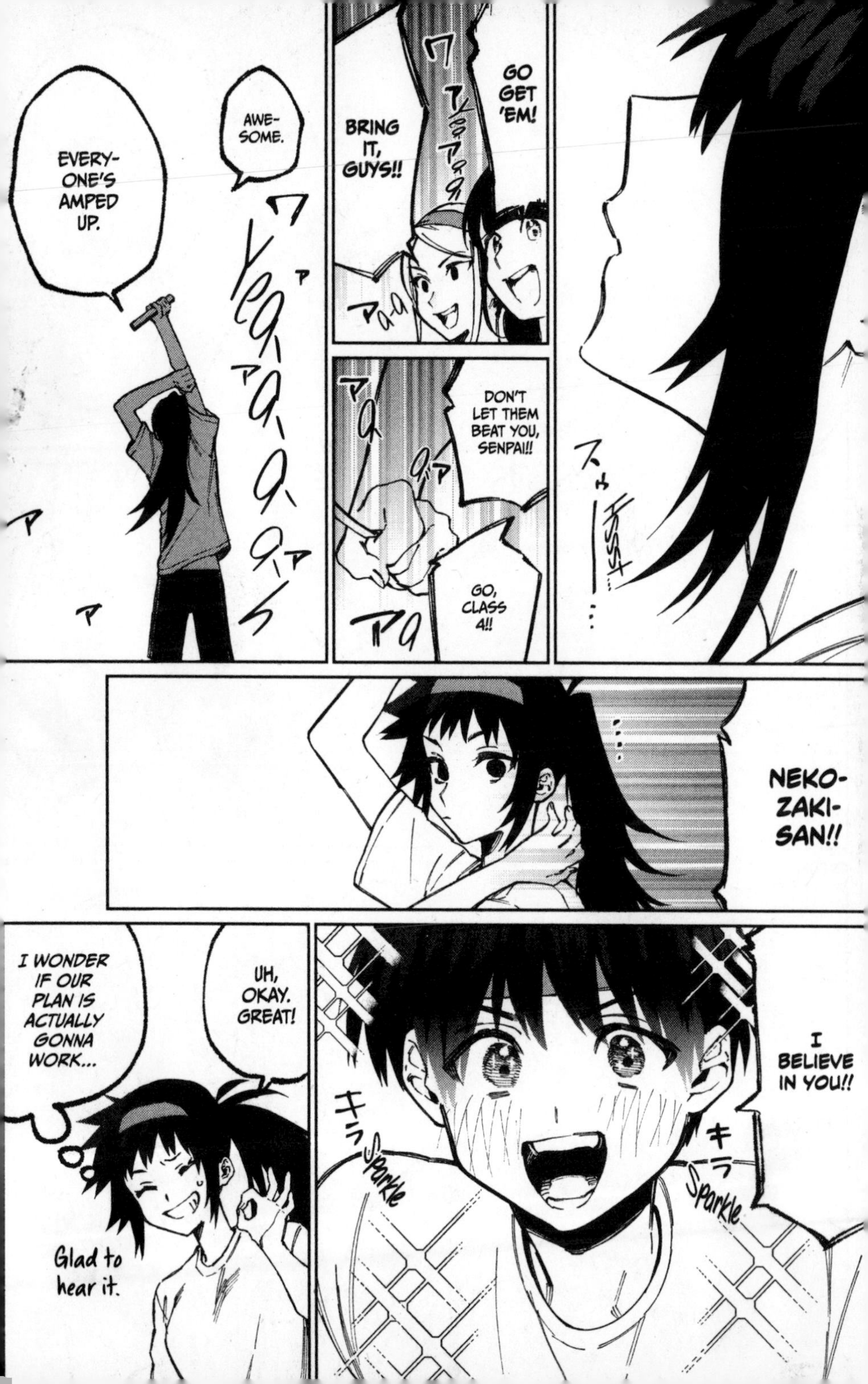
Hssst...
GO GET 'EM!
BRING IT, GUYS!!
DON'T LET THEM BEAT YOU, SENPAI!!
GO, CLASS 4!!
AWE-SOME.
EVERY-ONE'S AMPED UP.
NEKO-ZAKI-SAN!!
I BELIEVE IN YOU!!
Sparkle
Sparkle
UH, OKAY. GREAT!
I WONDER IF OUR PLAN IS ACTUALLY GONNA WORK...
Glad to hear it.

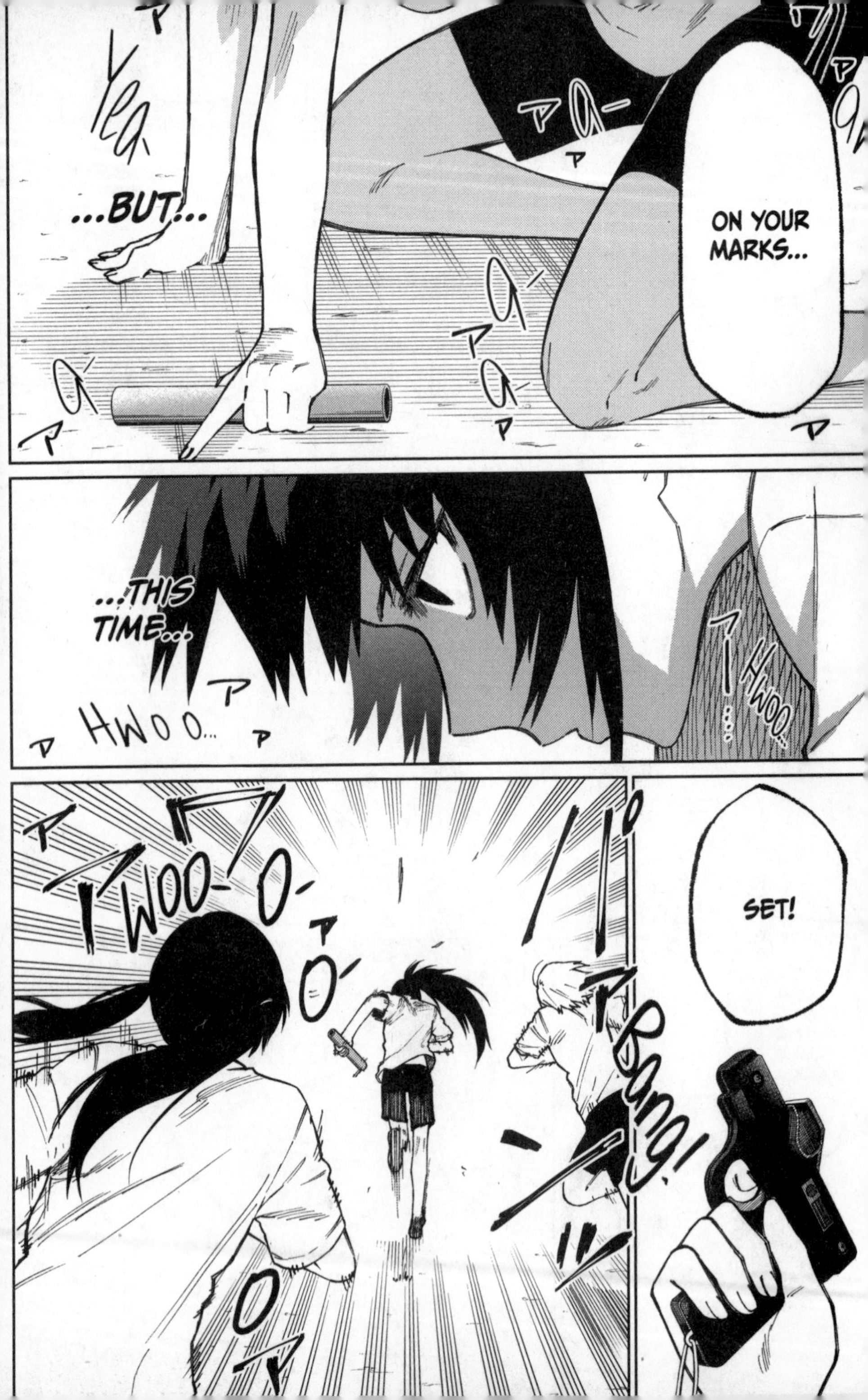
ON YOUR MARKS...
...BUT...
...THIS TIME...
HWOO...
HWOO...
SET!
BANG!
WOO-

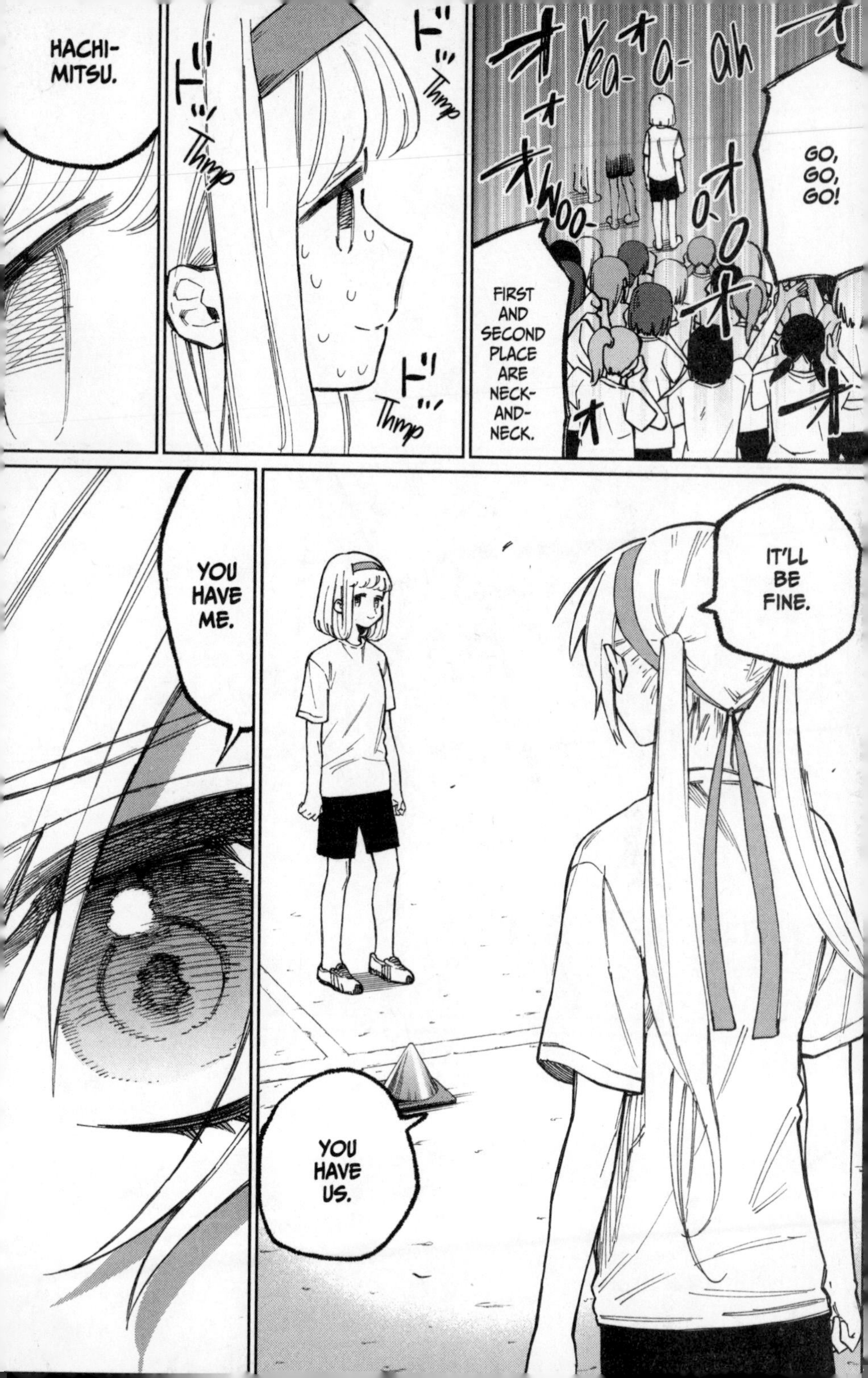
Yea-a-ah
WOO-
GO, GO, GO!
FIRST AND SECOND PLACE ARE NECK-AND-NECK.
Thmp
Thmp
Thmp
HACHI-MITSU.
IT'LL BE FINE.
YOU HAVE US.
YOU HAVE ME.

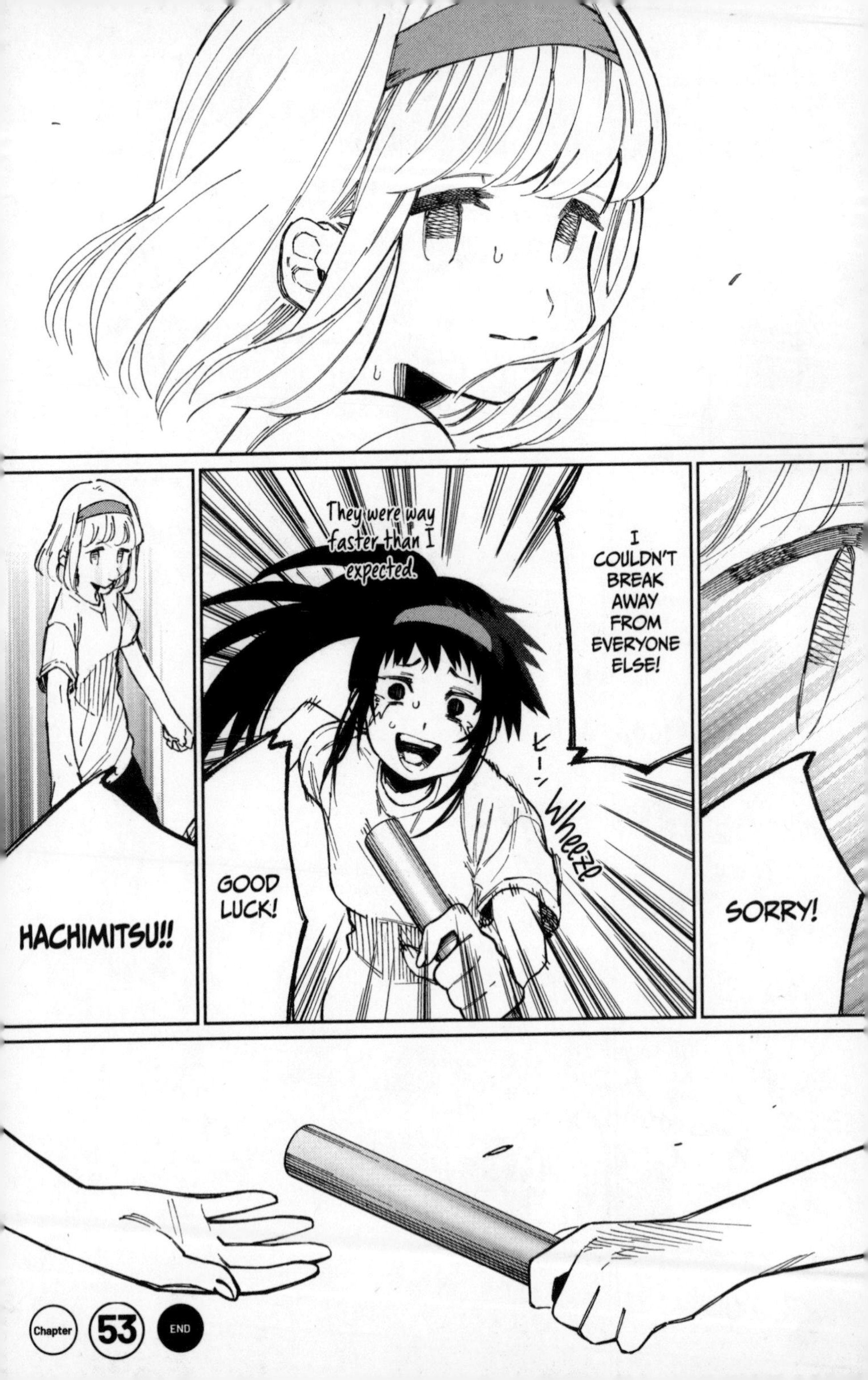
SORRY!
I COULDN'T BREAK AWAY FROM EVERYONE ELSE!
They were way faster than I expected.
Wheeze
GOOD LUCK!
HACHIMITSU!!
Chapter 53 END

# SHIKIMORI'S not just a cutie

Sigh...
She just remembered we have the relay.
She was laughing just a second ago...

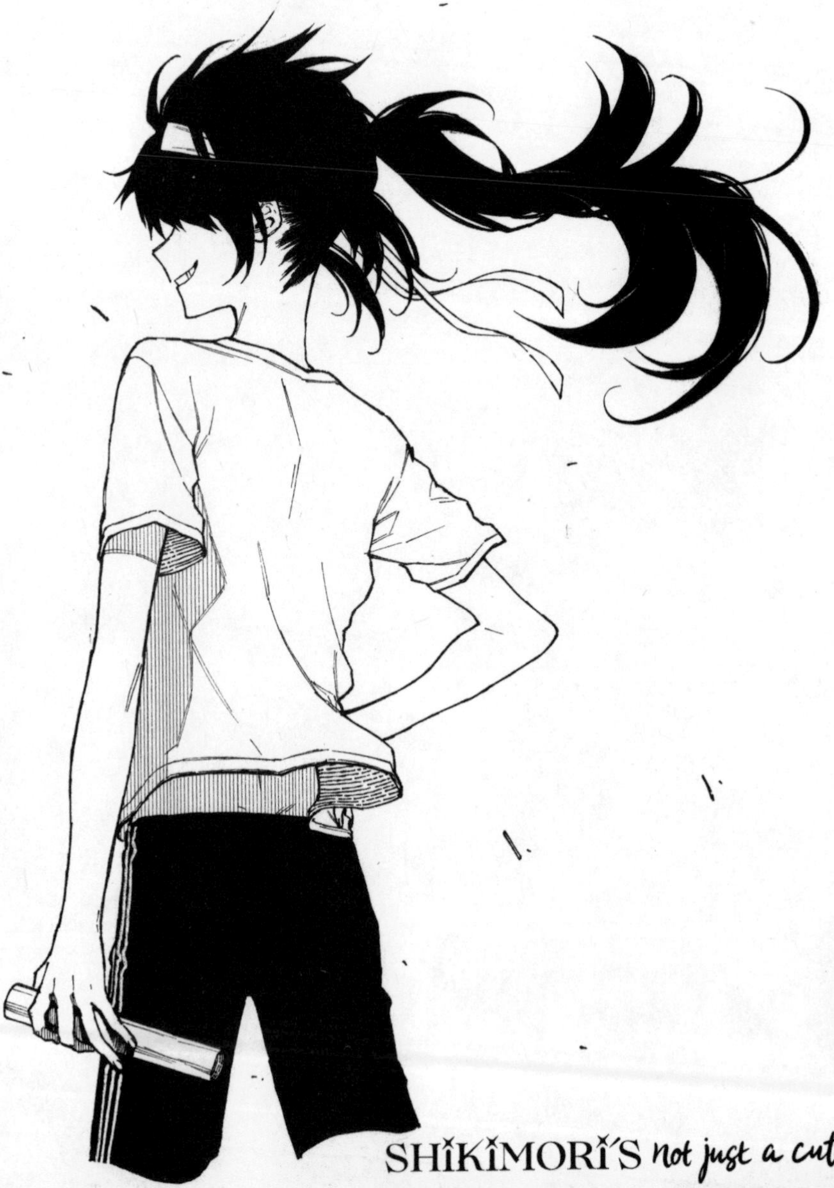

SHIKIMORI'S not just a cutie

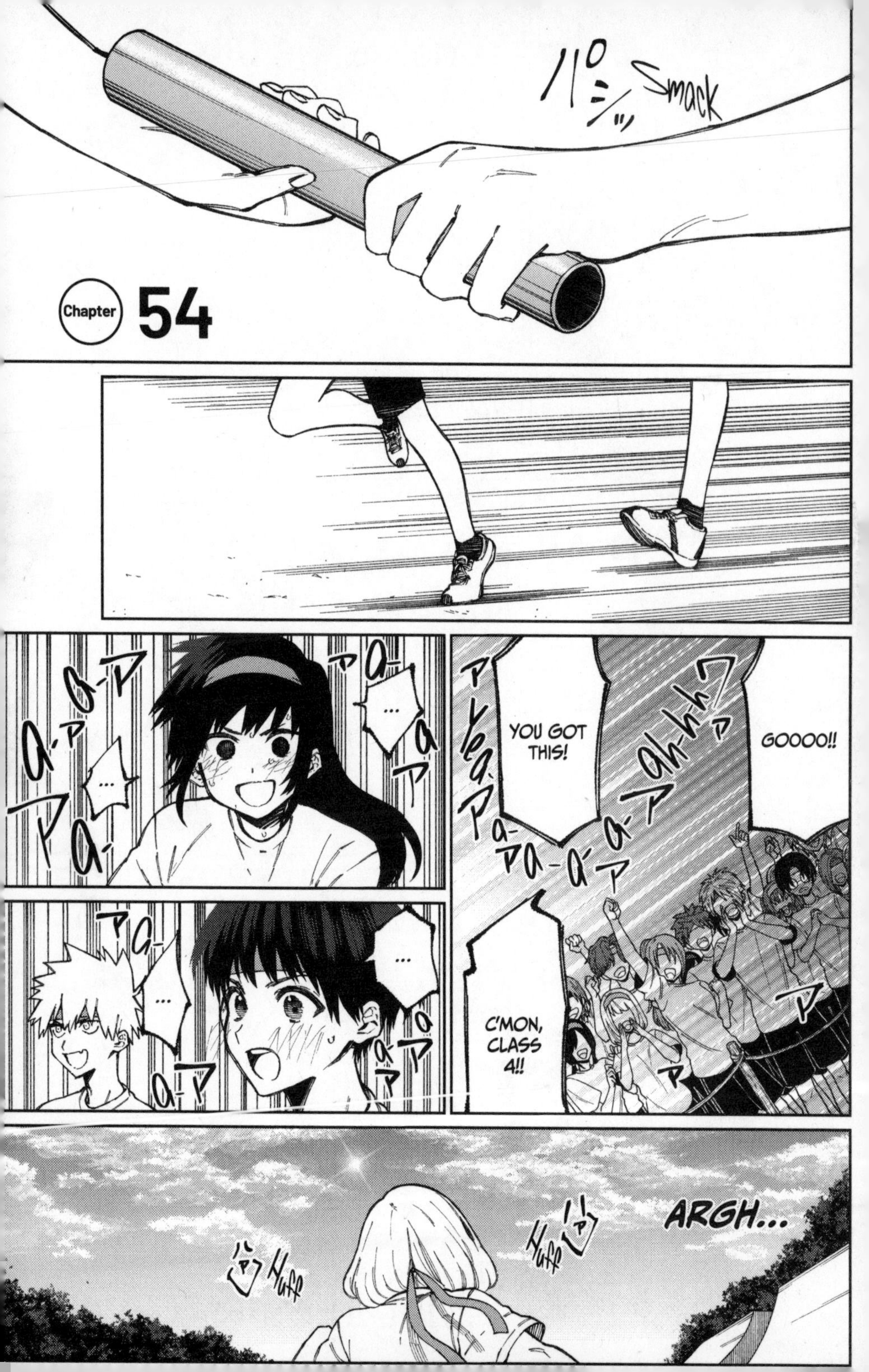
Smack
Chapter 54
GOOOO!!
YOU GOT THIS!
C'MON, CLASS 4!!
...
...
...
...
ARGH...
Huff
Huff

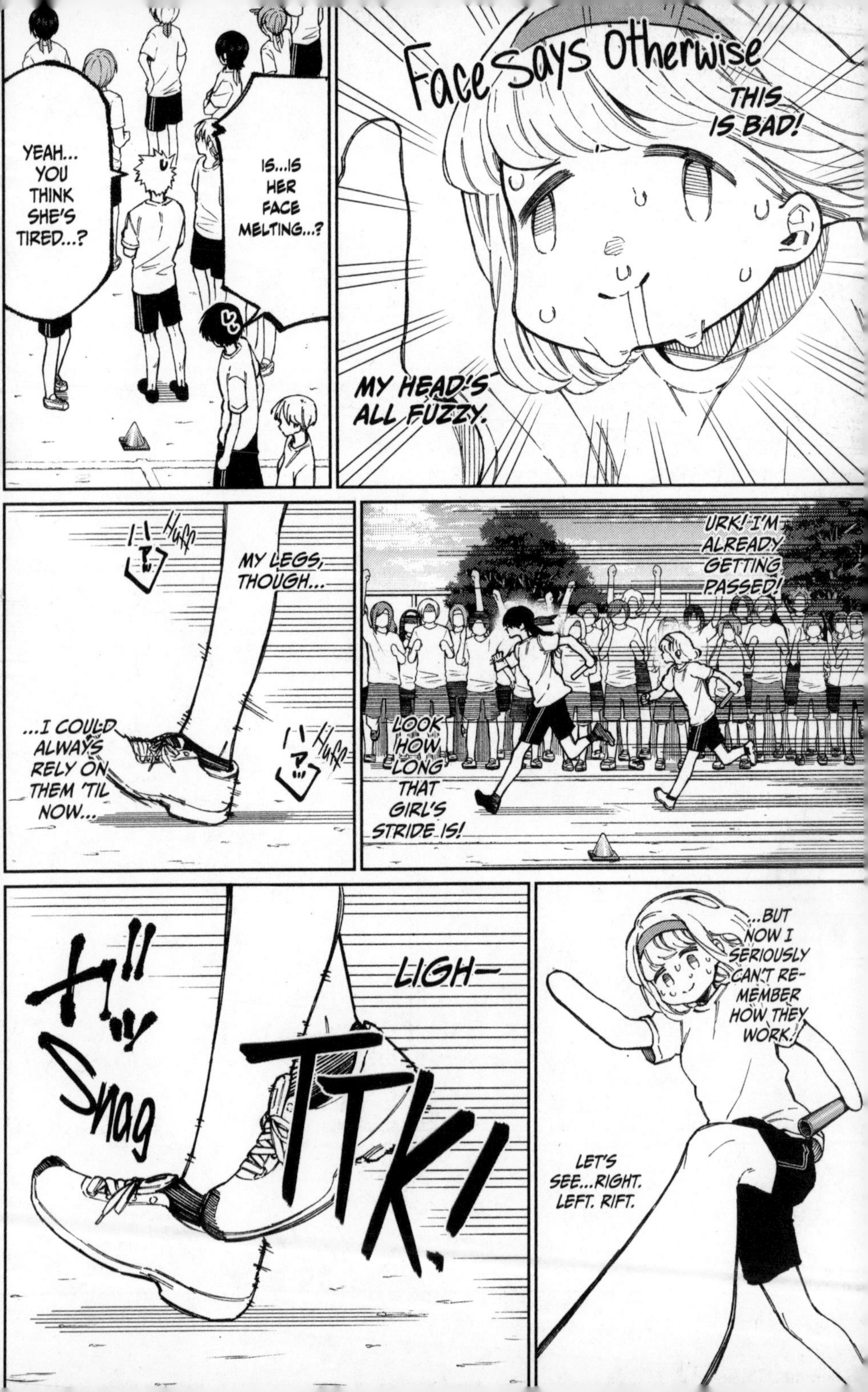
Face Says Otherwise
THIS IS BAD!
MY HEAD'S ALL FUZZY.
IS...IS HER FACE MELTING...?
YEAH... YOU THINK SHE'S TIRED...?
URK! I'M ALREADY GETTING PASSED!
LOOK HOW LONG THAT GIRL'S STRIDE IS!
Huff
MY LEGS, THOUGH...
...I COULD ALWAYS RELY ON THEM 'TIL NOW...
Huff
...BUT NOW I SERIOUSLY CAN'T RE-MEMBER HOW THEY WORK.
LET'S SEE...RIGHT. LEFT. RIFT.
LIGH—
TTK!
Snag

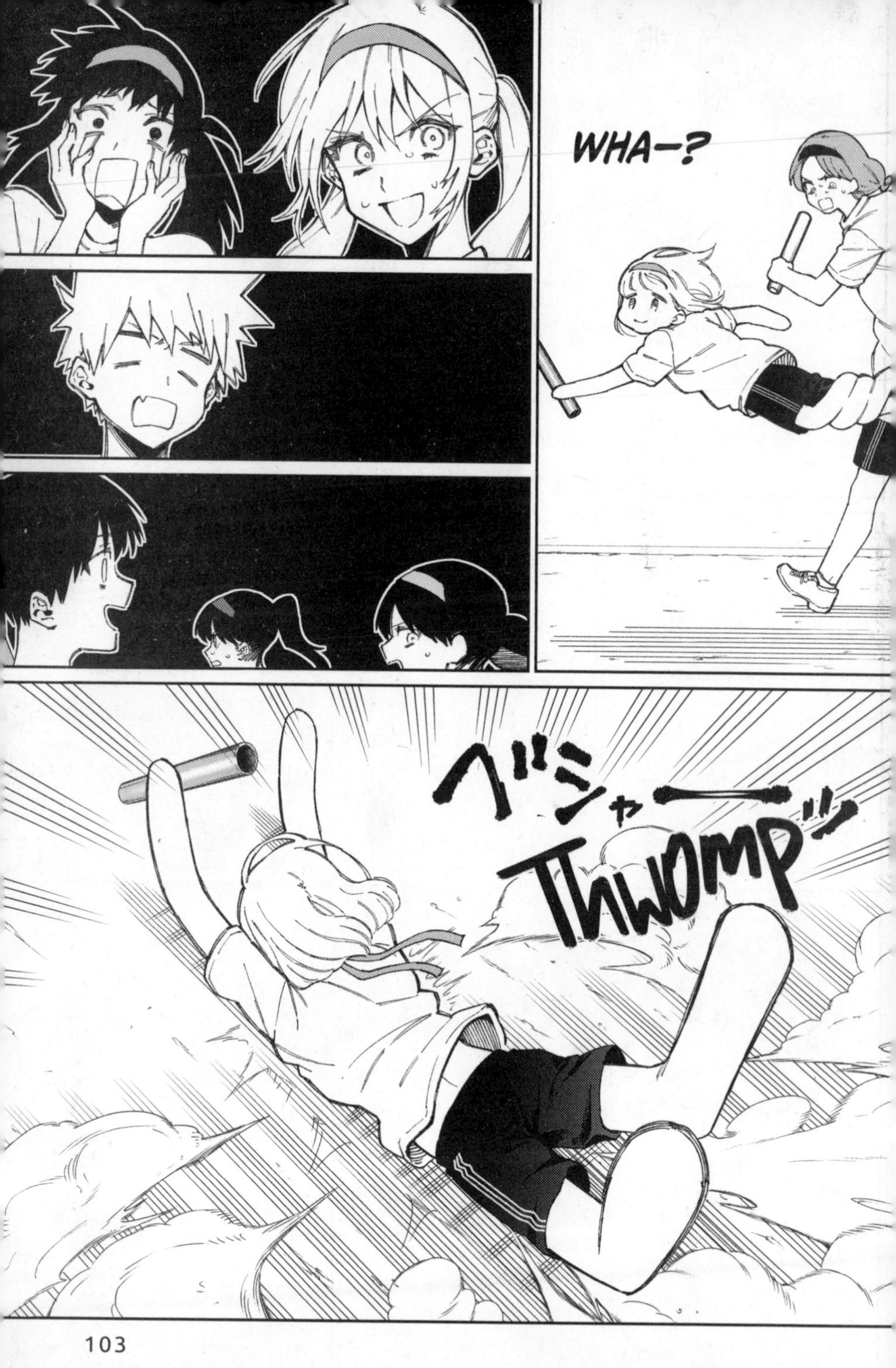
WHA—?
ベシャー
THWOMP

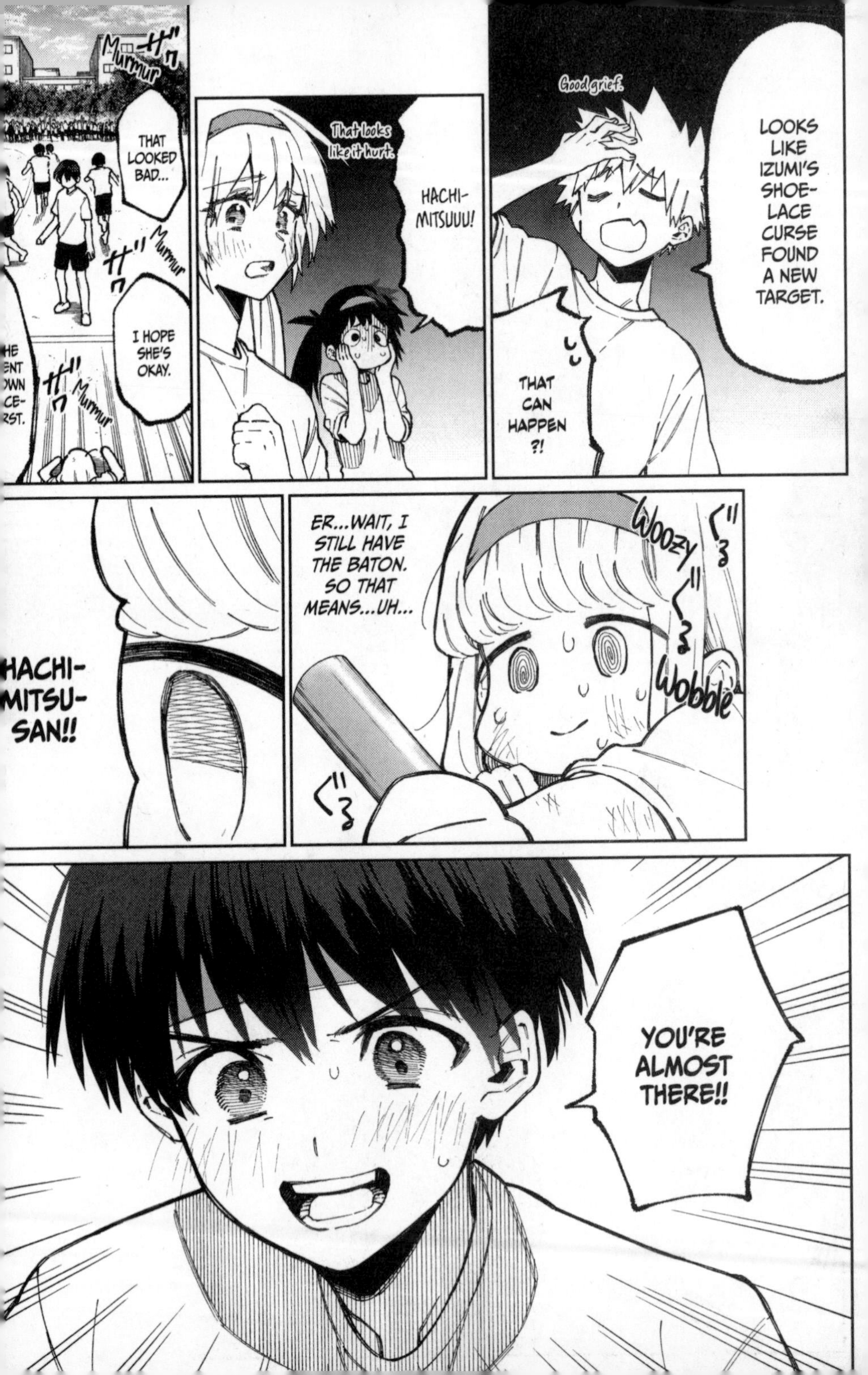
LOOKS LIKE IZUMI'S SHOE-LACE CURSE FOUND A NEW TARGET.
Good grief.
THAT CAN HAPPEN?!
HACHI-MITSUUU!
That looks like it hurt.
Murmur
THAT LOOKED BAD...
Murmur
I HOPE SHE'S OKAY.
Murmur
Woozy
Wobble
ER...WAIT, I STILL HAVE THE BATON. SO THAT MEANS...UH...
HACHI-MITSU-SAN!!
YOU'RE ALMOST THERE!!

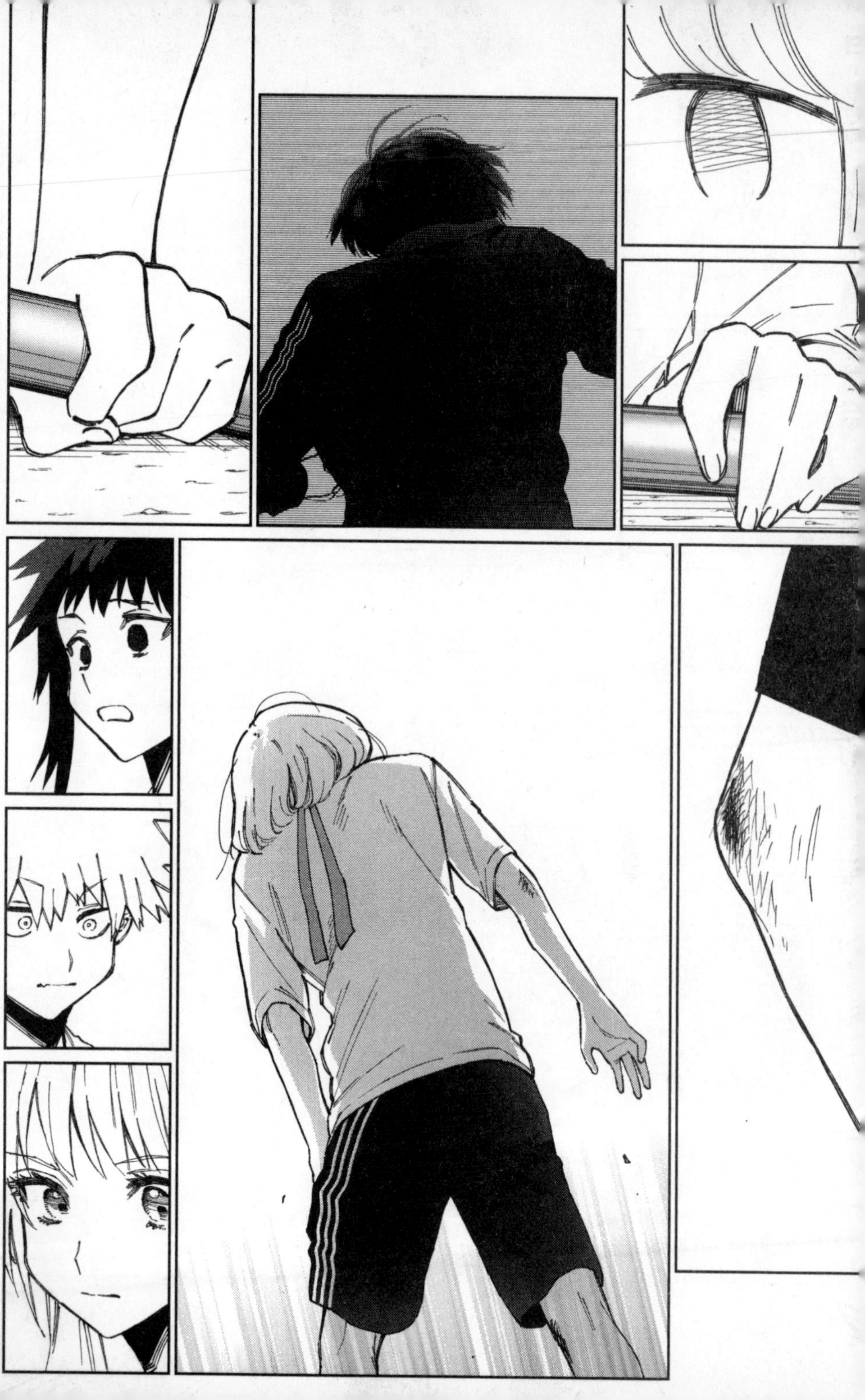

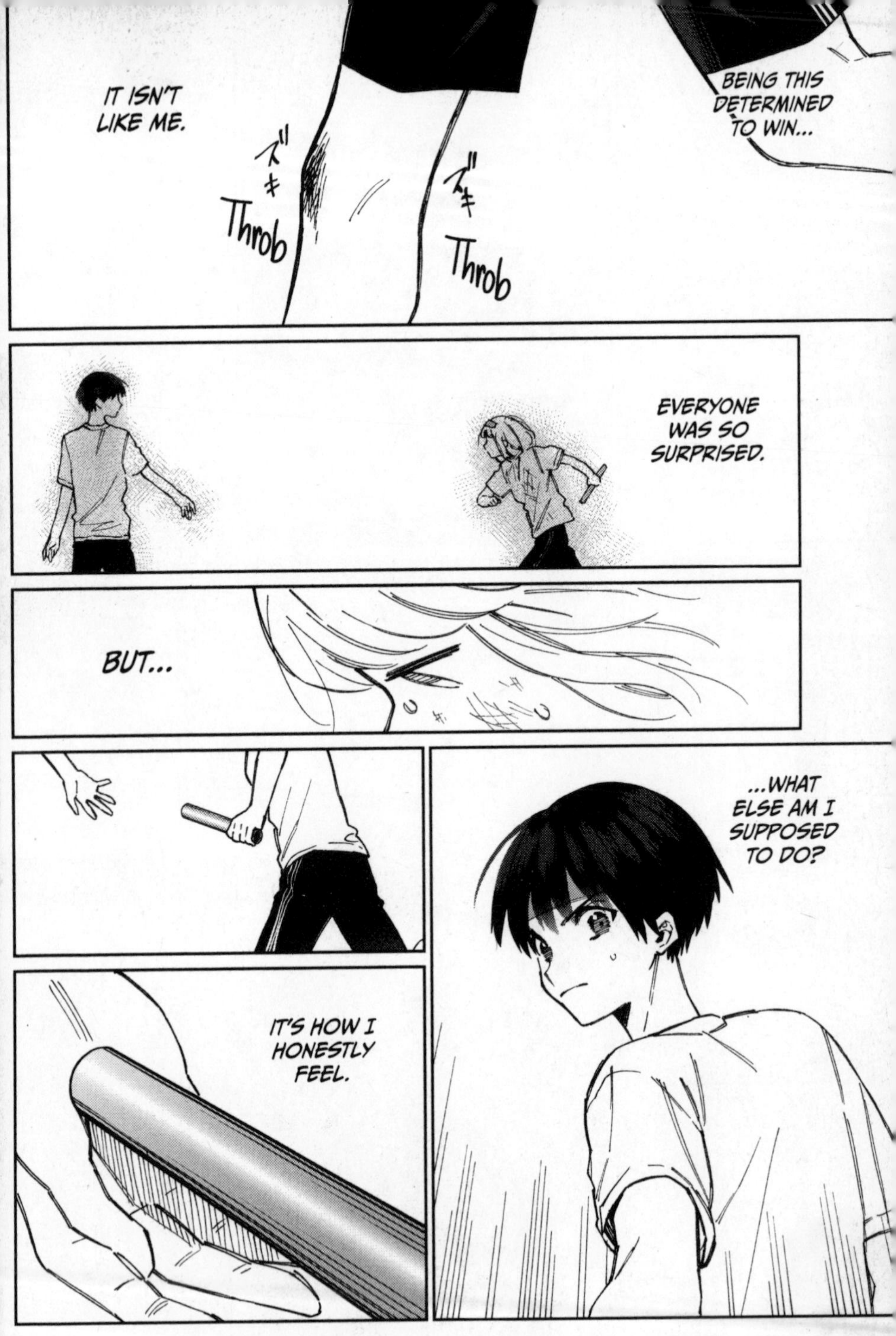
BEING THIS DETERMINED TO WIN...
IT ISN'T LIKE ME.
ズキ
Throb
ズキ
Throb
EVERYONE WAS SO SURPRISED.
BUT...
...WHAT ELSE AM I SUPPOSED TO DO?
IT'S HOW I HONESTLY FEEL.

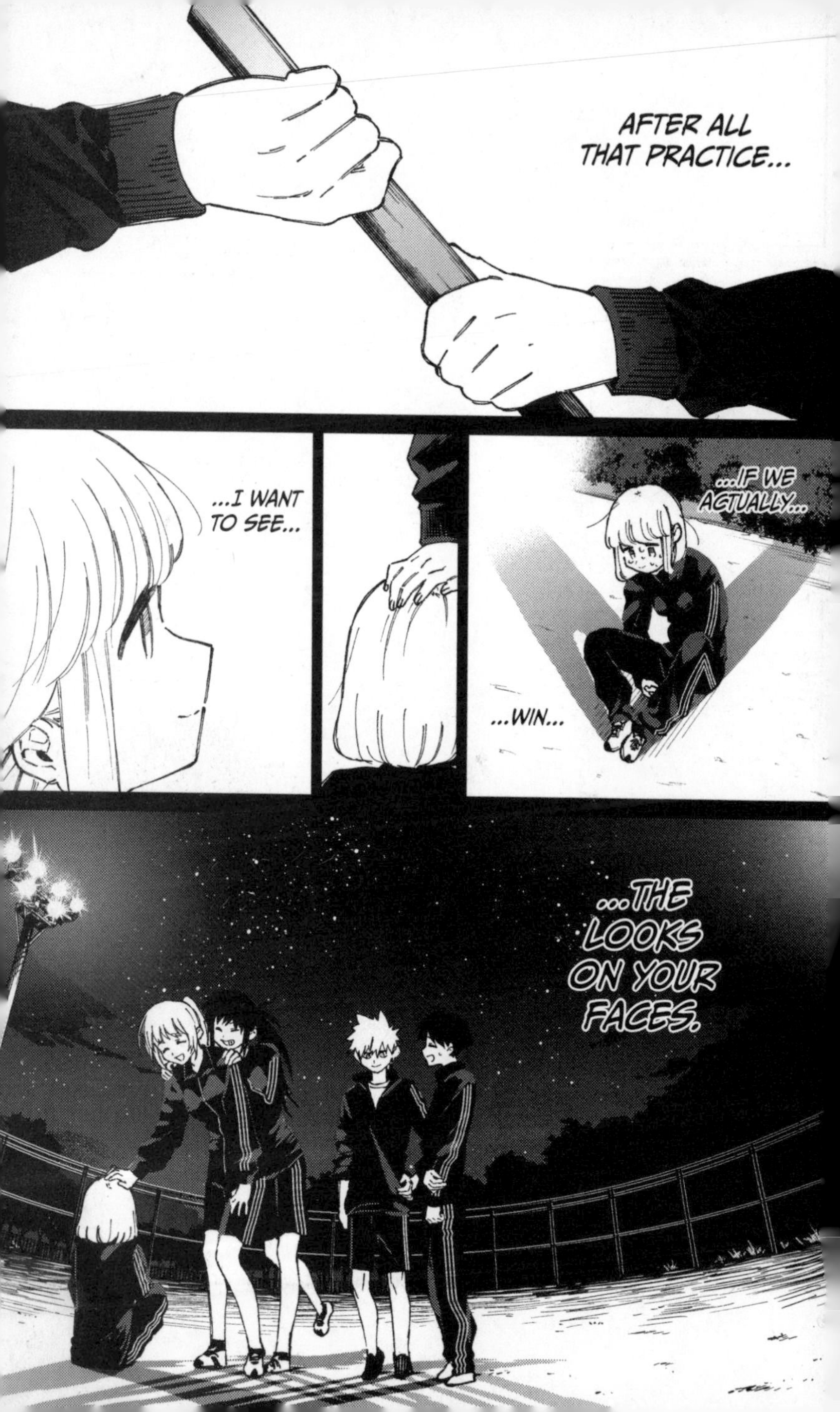
AFTER ALL THAT PRACTICE...
...IF WE ACTUALLY...
...WIN...
...I WANT TO SEE...
...THE LOOKS ON YOUR FACES.

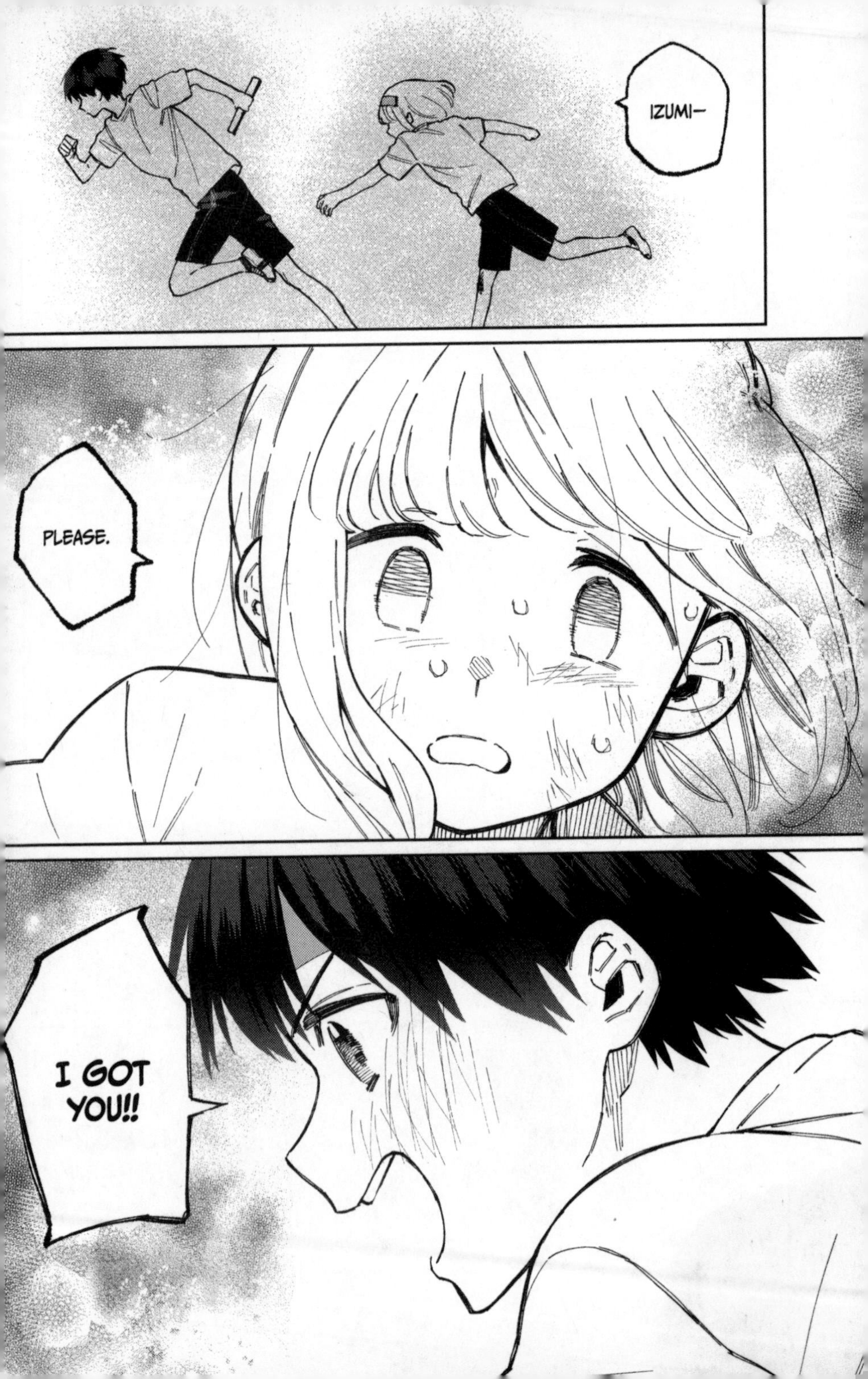
IZUMI—
PLEASE.
I GOT YOU!!

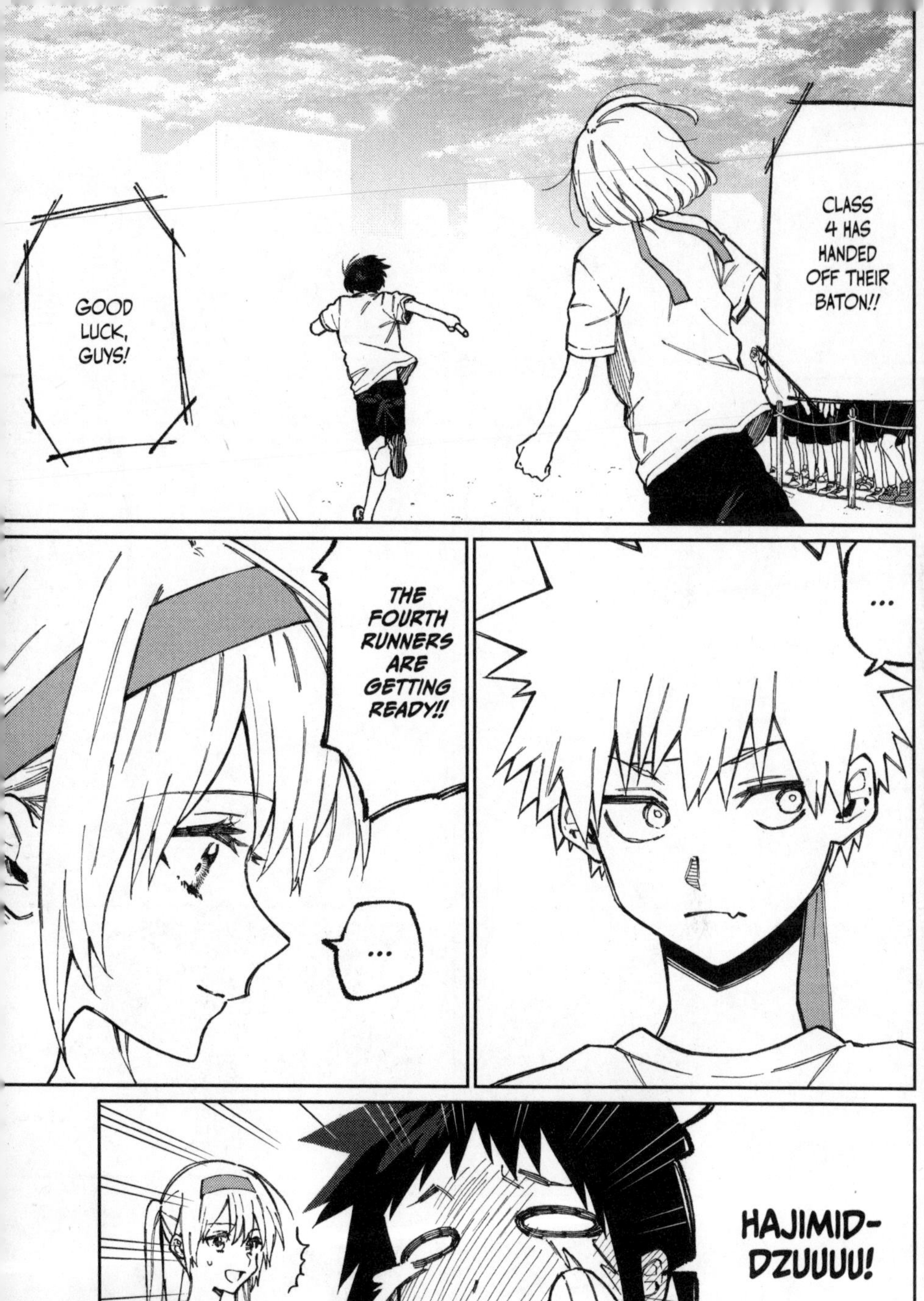
CLASS 4 HAS HANDED OFF THEIR BATON!!
GOOD LUCK, GUYS!
...
THE FOURTH RUNNERS ARE GETTING READY!!
...
HAJIMID-DZUUUU!

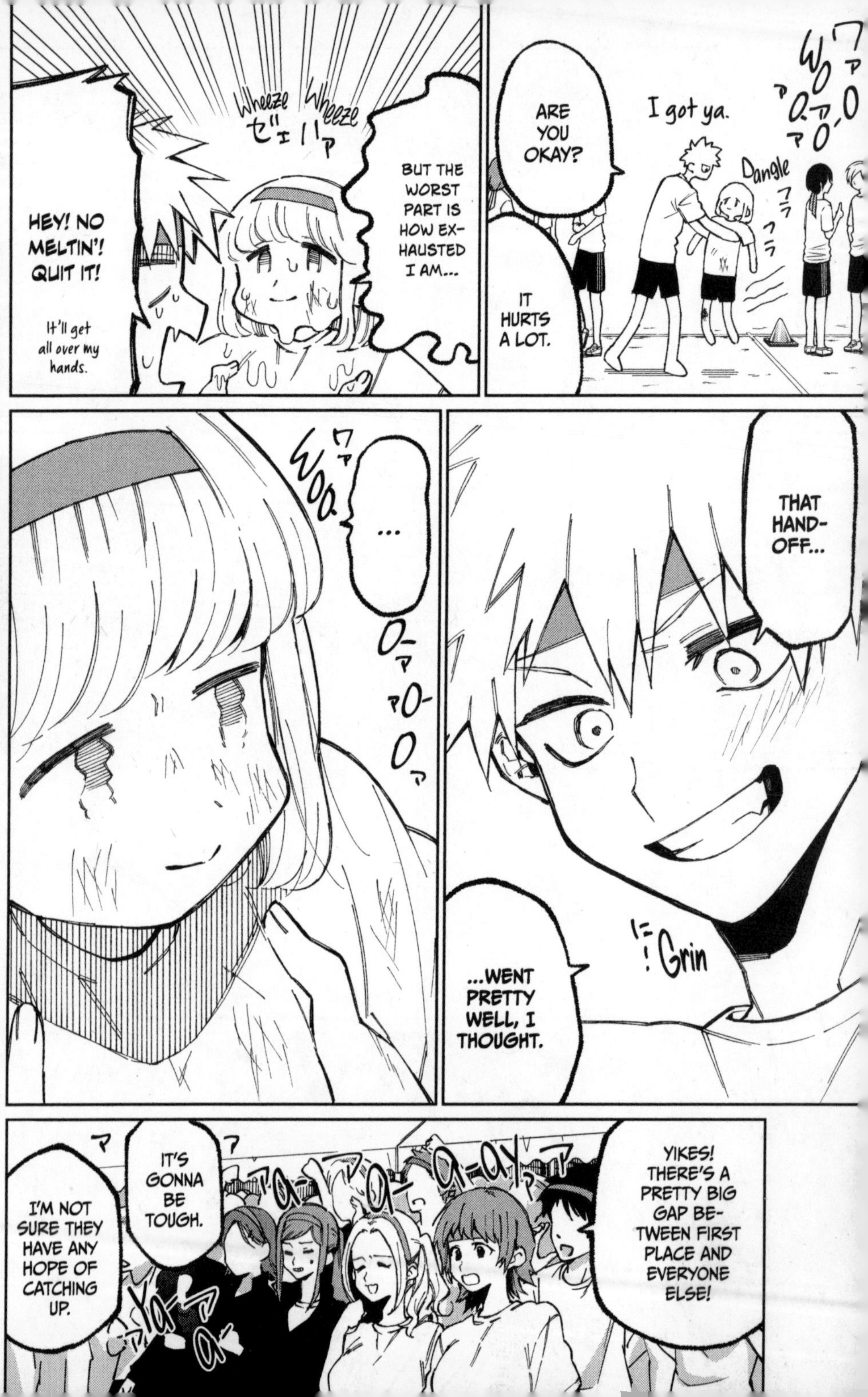
Wooo
ARE YOU OKAY?
I got ya.
Dangle
IT HURTS A LOT.
Wheeze Wheeze
BUT THE WORST PART IS HOW EX-HAUSTED I AM...
HEY! NO MELTIN'! QUIT IT!
It'll get all over my hands.
THAT HAND-OFF...
Grin
...WENT PRETTY WELL, I THOUGHT.
Wooo
...
YIKES! THERE'S A PRETTY BIG GAP BE-TWEEN FIRST PLACE AND EVERYONE ELSE!
IT'S GONNA BE TOUGH.
I'M NOT SURE THEY HAVE ANY HOPE OF CATCHING UP.

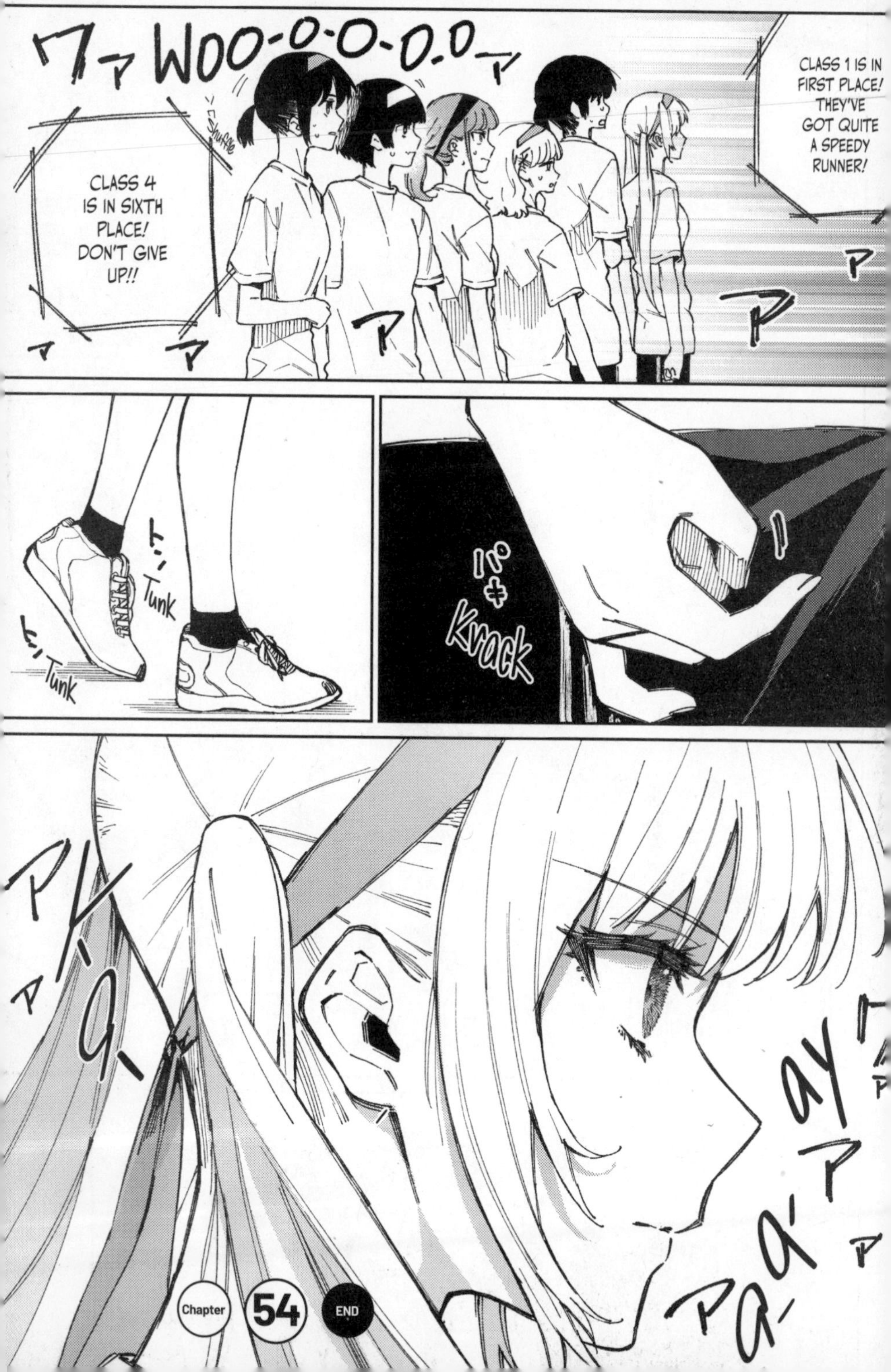
CLASS 1 IS IN FIRST PLACE! THEY'VE GOT QUITE A SPEEDY RUNNER!
WOO-O-O-O-O
CLASS 4 IS IN SIXTH PLACE! DON'T GIVE UP!!
Shuffle
Kvack
Tunk
Tunk
Chapter 54 END

**SHIKIMORI'S** *not just a cutie*

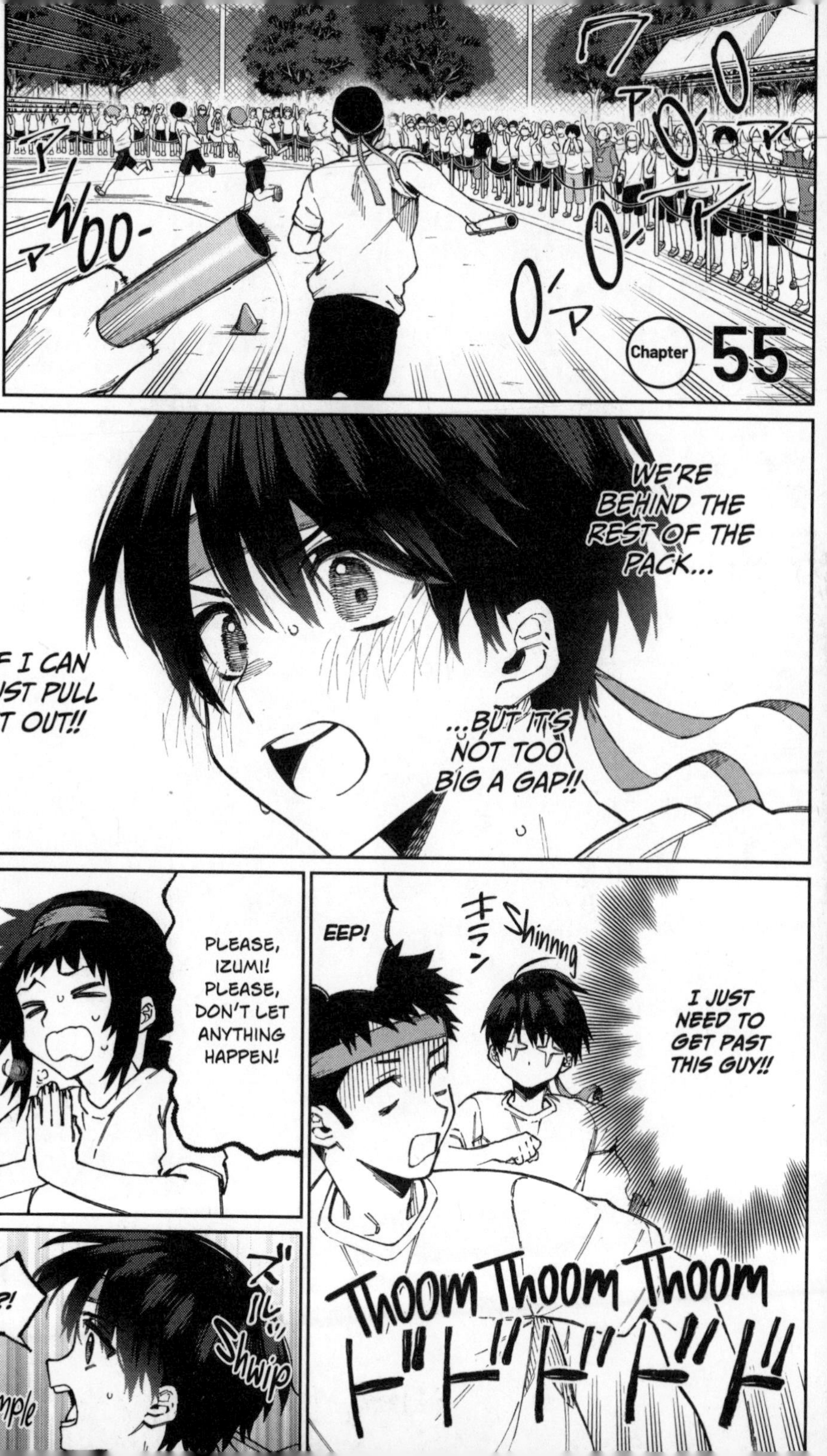

WOO-
Chapter 55
WE'RE BEHIND THE REST OF THE PACK...
...BUT IT'S NOT TOO BIG A GAP!!
IF I CAN JUST PULL IT OUT!!
EEP!
キラン Shinnng
I JUST NEED TO GET PAST THIS GUY!!
Thoom Thoom Thoom
ドドドドド
PLEASE, IZUMI! PLEASE, DON'T LET ANYTHING HAPPEN!
ハァ Pant
ハァ Pant
?!
ズルッ Shwip
グシャッ Crumple

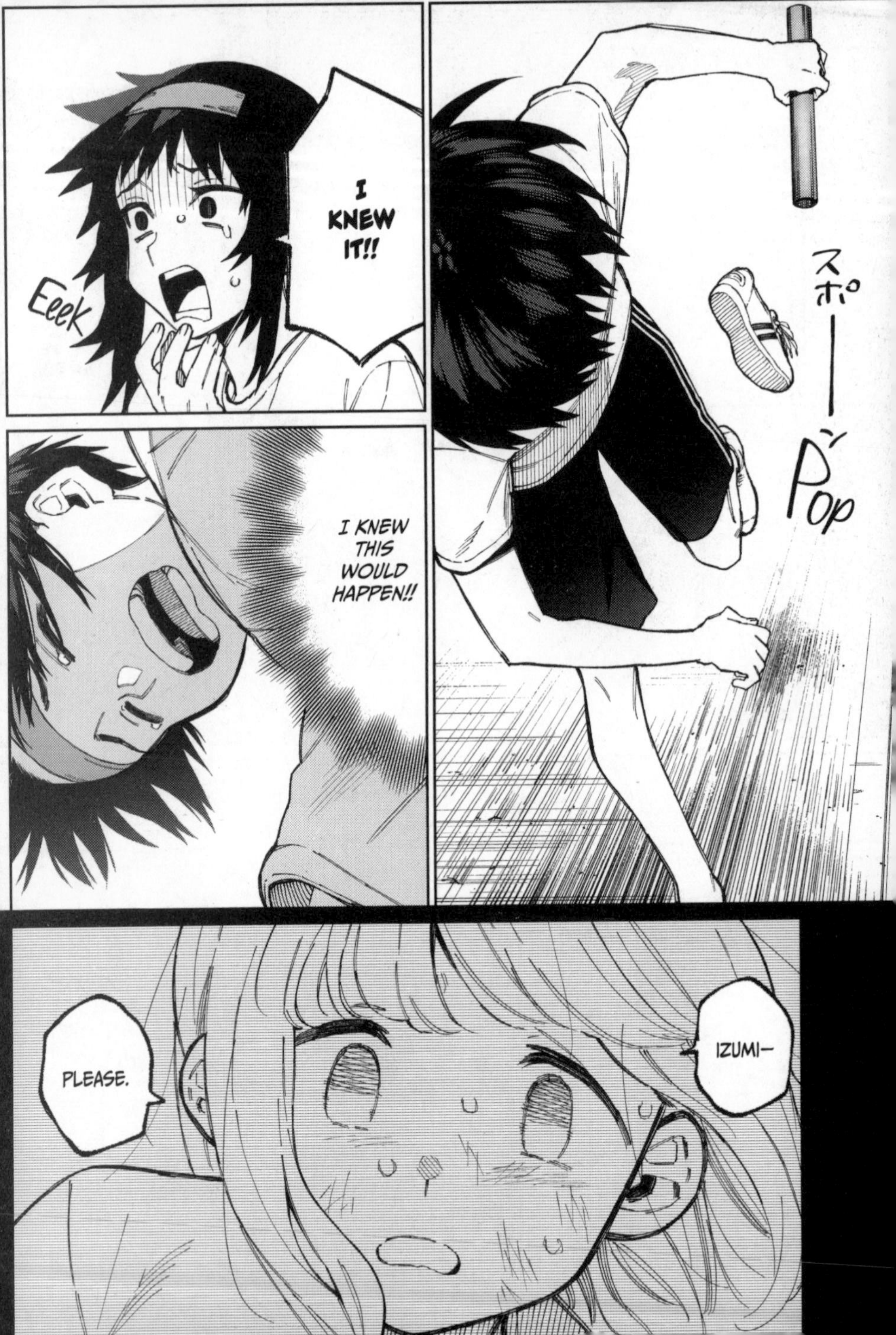
スポーン
Pop
I KNEW IT!!
Eeek
I KNEW THIS WOULD HAPPEN!!
IZUMI—
PLEASE.

I CAN'T
LET THIS
STOP ME.

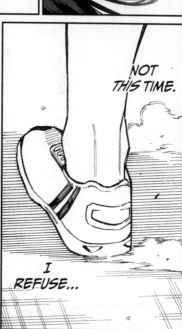

...TO LET
MY TERRIBLE
LUCK
DEFEAT US!

NOT
THIS TIME.

I
REFUSE...

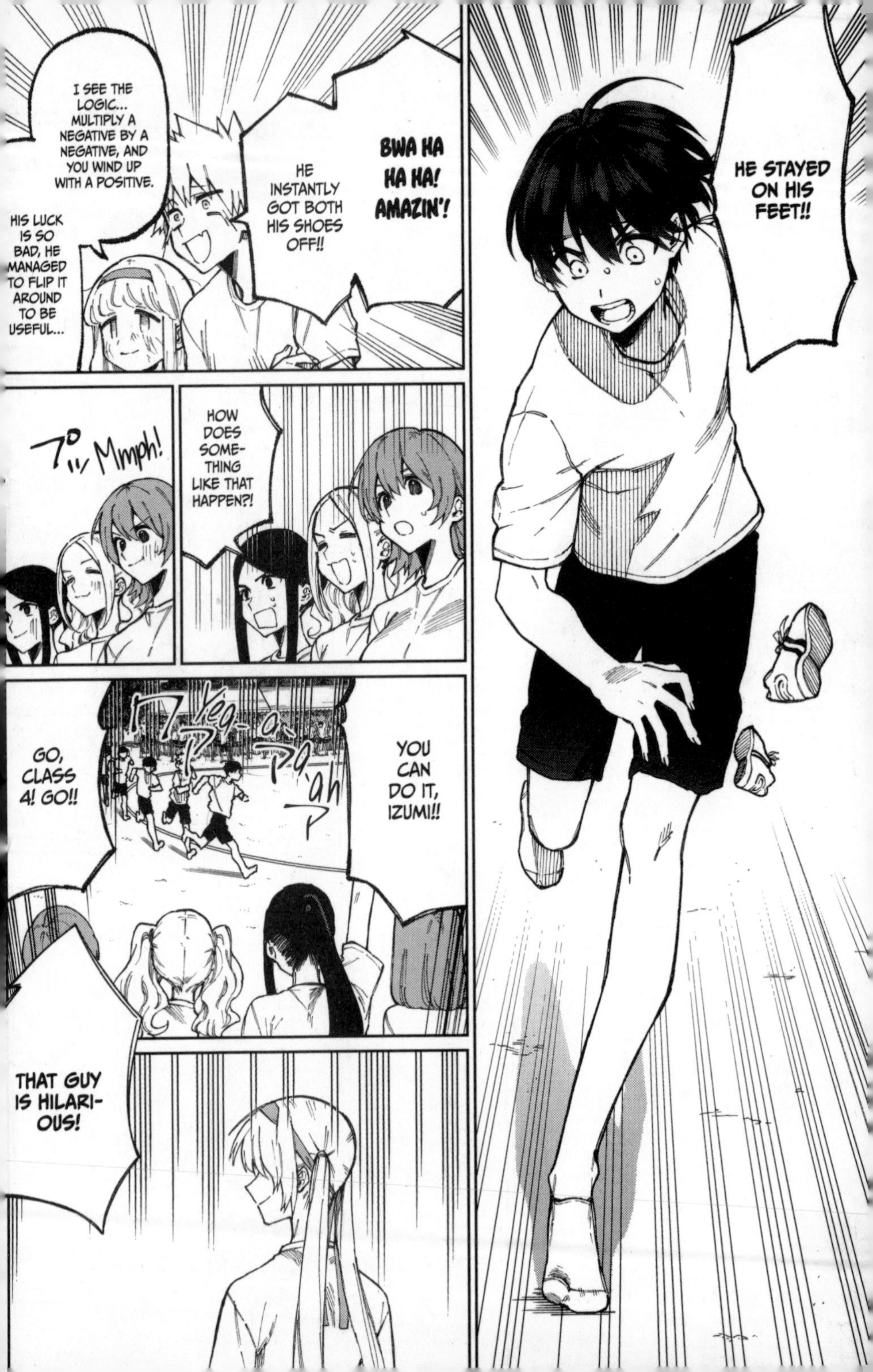
HE STAYED ON HIS FEET!!
BWA HA HA HA! AMAZIN'!
HE INSTANTLY GOT BOTH HIS SHOES OFF!!
I SEE THE LOGIC... MULTIPLY A NEGATIVE BY A NEGATIVE, AND YOU WIND UP WITH A POSITIVE.
HIS LUCK IS SO BAD, HE MANAGED TO FLIP IT AROUND TO BE USEFUL...
HOW DOES SOME-THING LIKE THAT HAPPEN?!
プッ Mmph!
YOU CAN DO IT, IZUMI!!
Yea-a-aah
GO, CLASS 4! GO!!
THAT GUY IS HILARI-OUS!

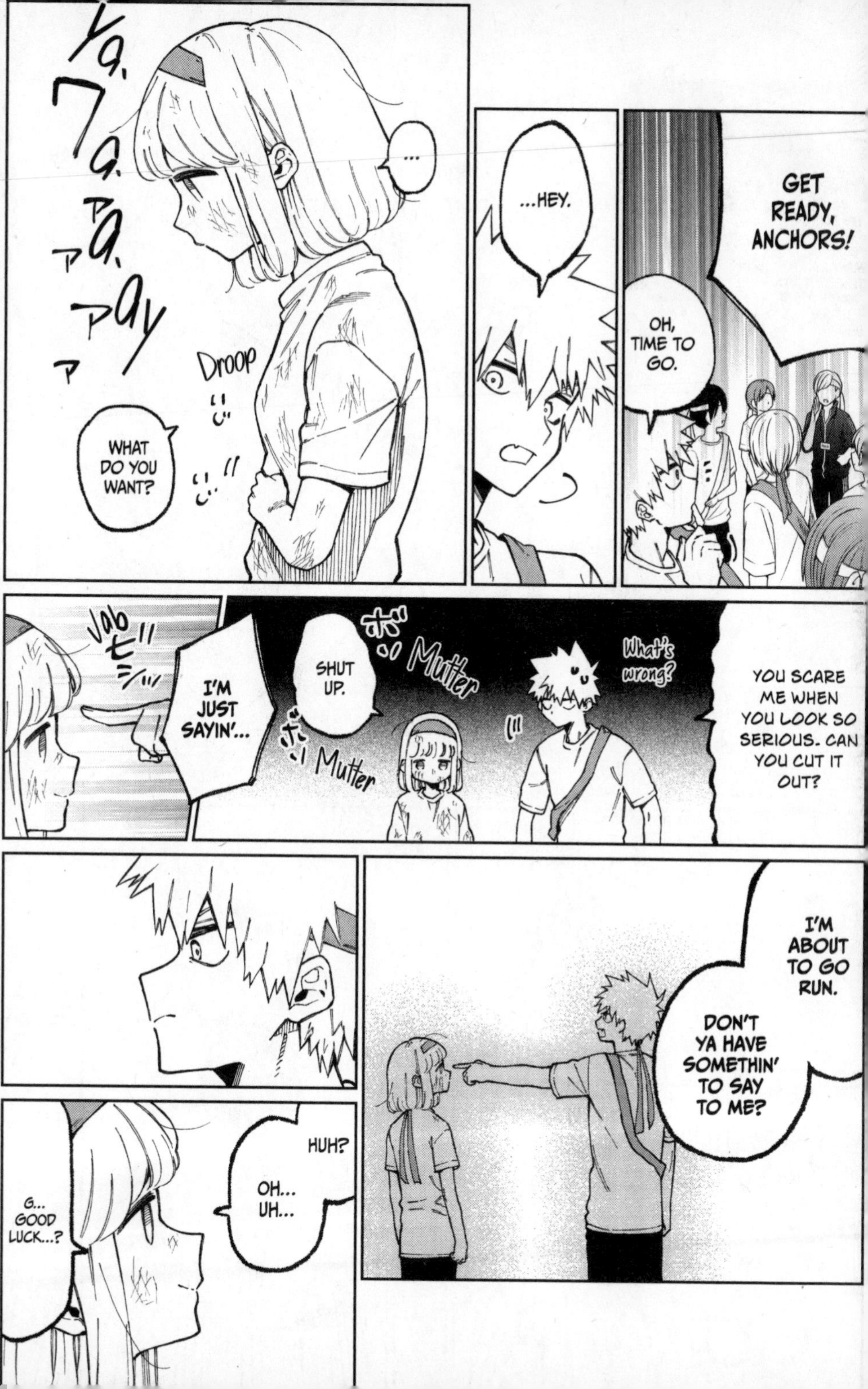
GET READY, ANCHORS!
OH, TIME TO GO.
...HEY.
...
Droop
WHAT DO YOU WANT?
YOU SCARE ME WHEN YOU LOOK SO SERIOUS. CAN YOU CUT IT OUT?
What's wrong?
SHUT UP.
Mutter
Mutter
Jab
I'M JUST SAYIN'...
I'M ABOUT TO GO RUN.
DON'T YA HAVE SOMETHIN' TO SAY TO ME?
HUH?
OH... UH...
G... GOOD LUCK...?

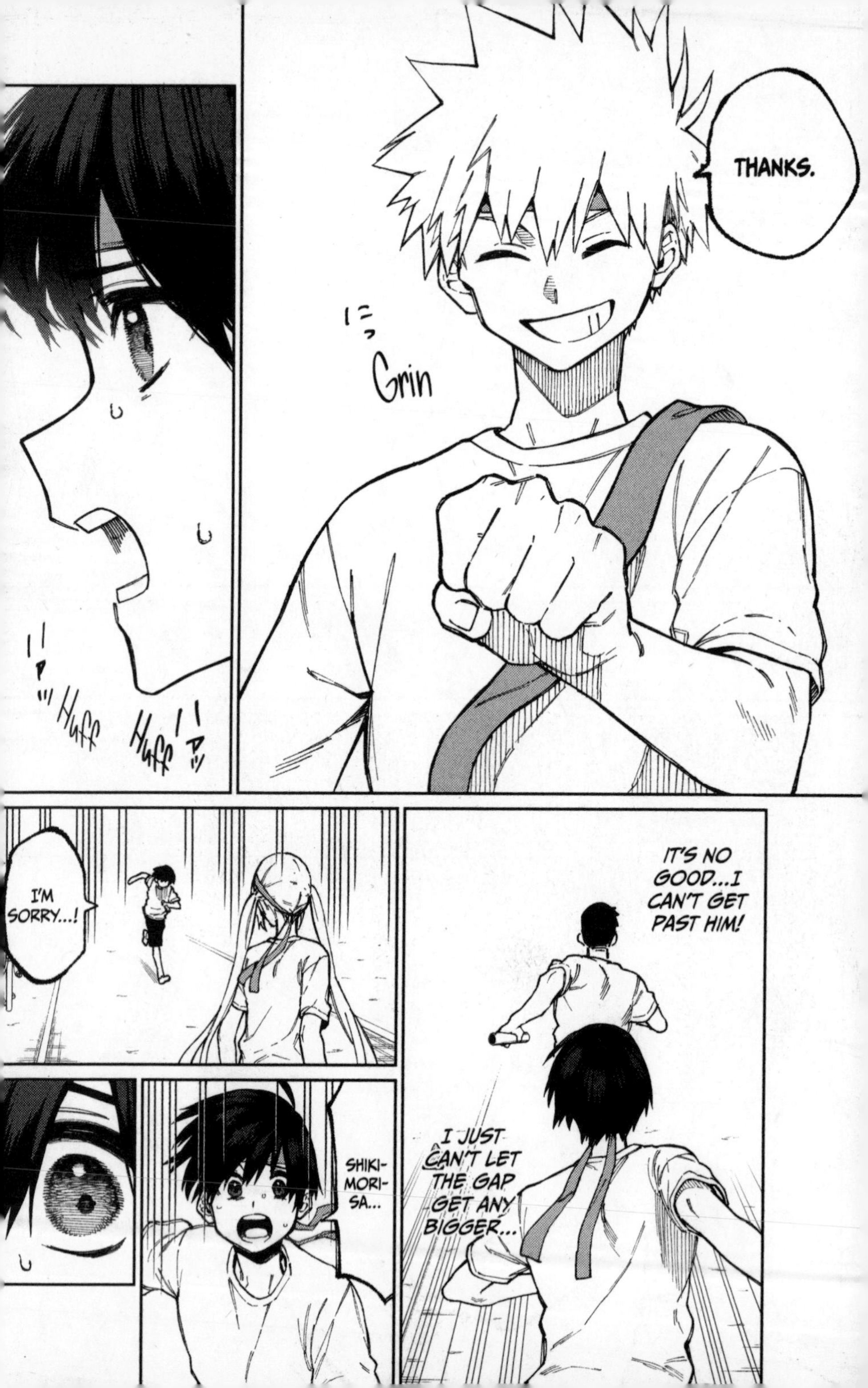
THANKS.
Grin
Huff Huff
IT'S NO GOOD...I CAN'T GET PAST HIM!
I JUST CAN'T LET THE GAP GET ANY BIGGER...
I'M SORRY...!
SHIKIMORI-SA...

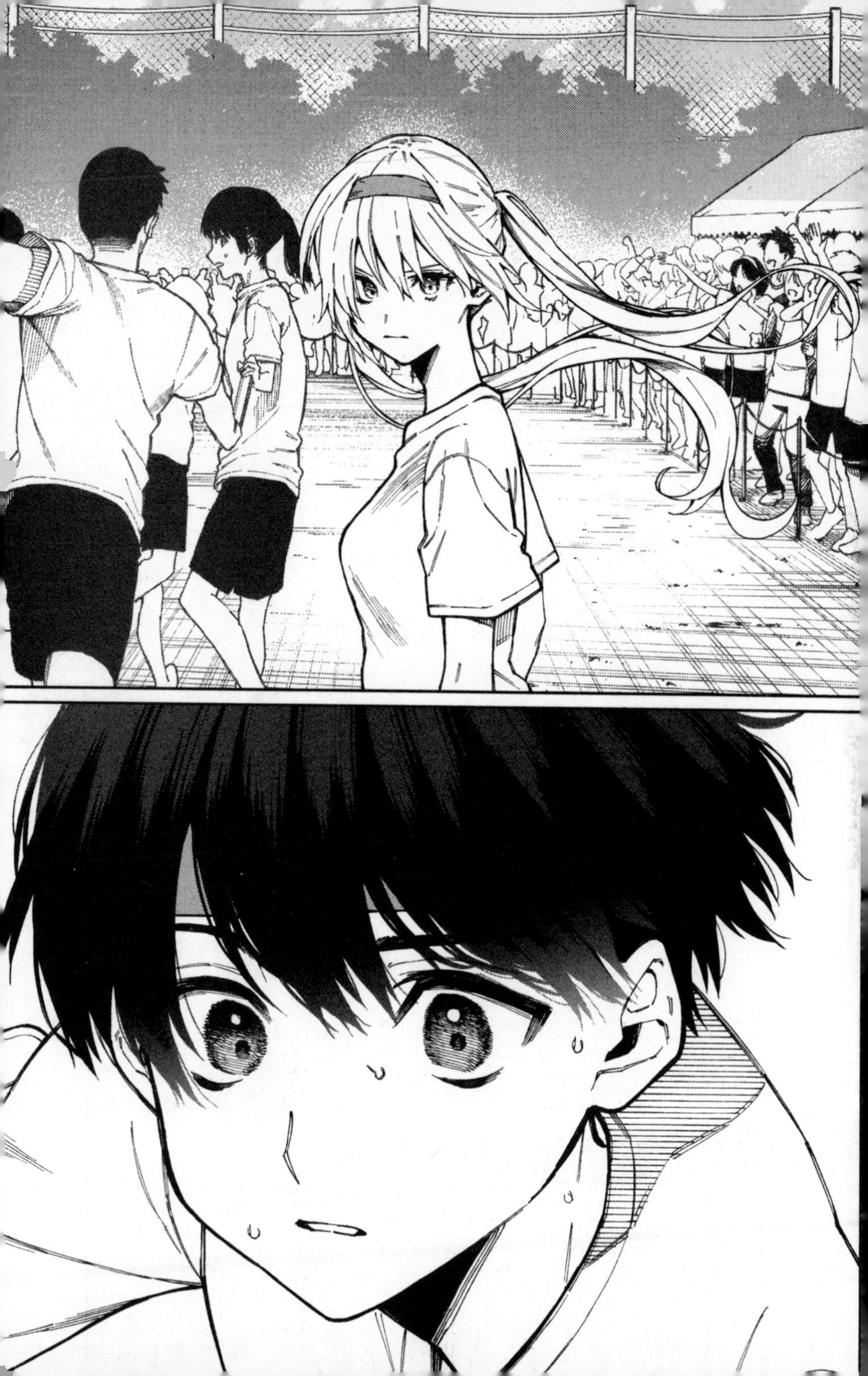

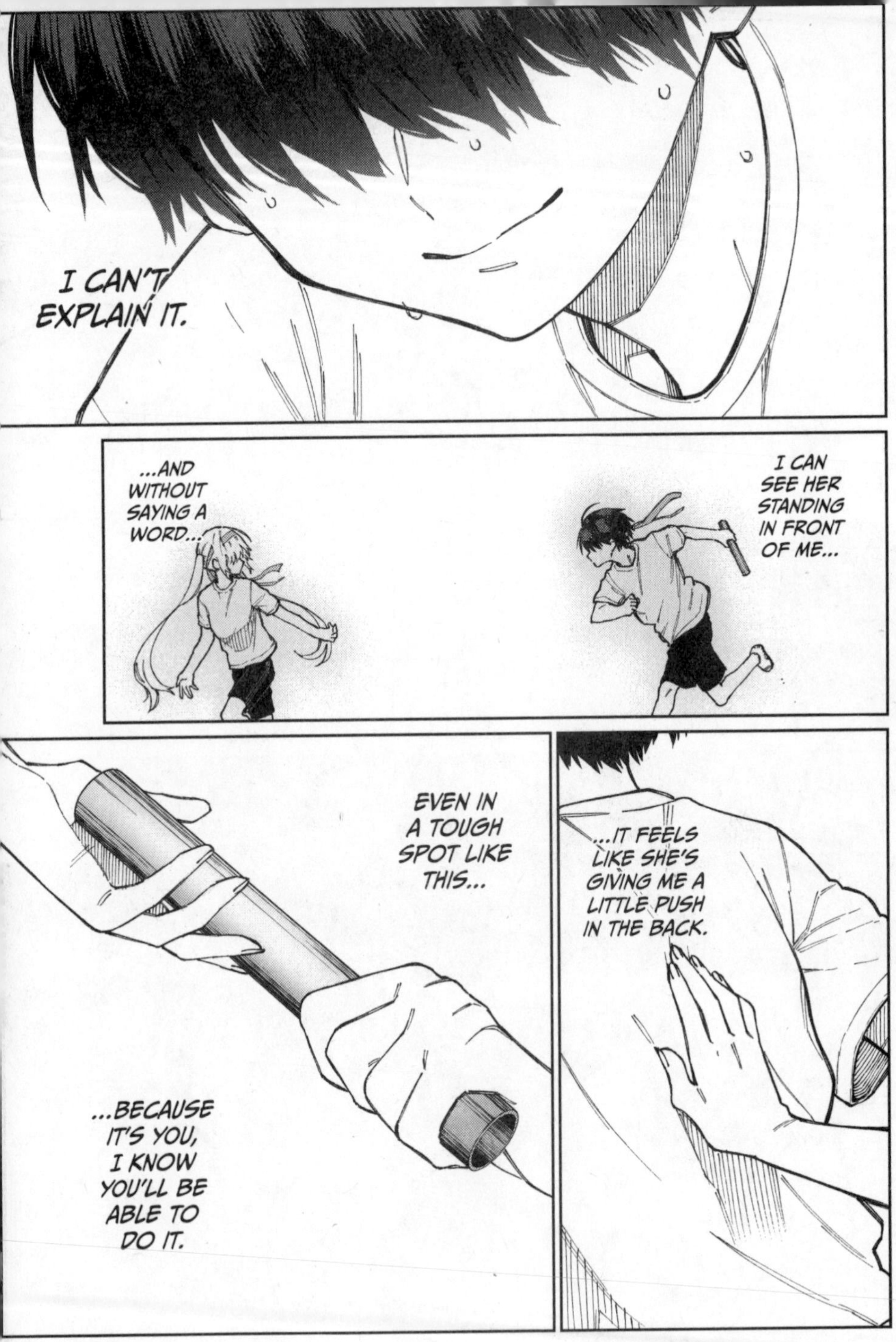
I CAN'T EXPLAIN IT.
I CAN SEE HER STANDING IN FRONT OF ME...
...AND WITHOUT SAYING A WORD...
...IT FEELS LIKE SHE'S GIVING ME A LITTLE PUSH IN THE BACK.
EVEN IN A TOUGH SPOT LIKE THIS...
...BECAUSE IT'S YOU, I KNOW YOU'LL BE ABLE TO DO IT.

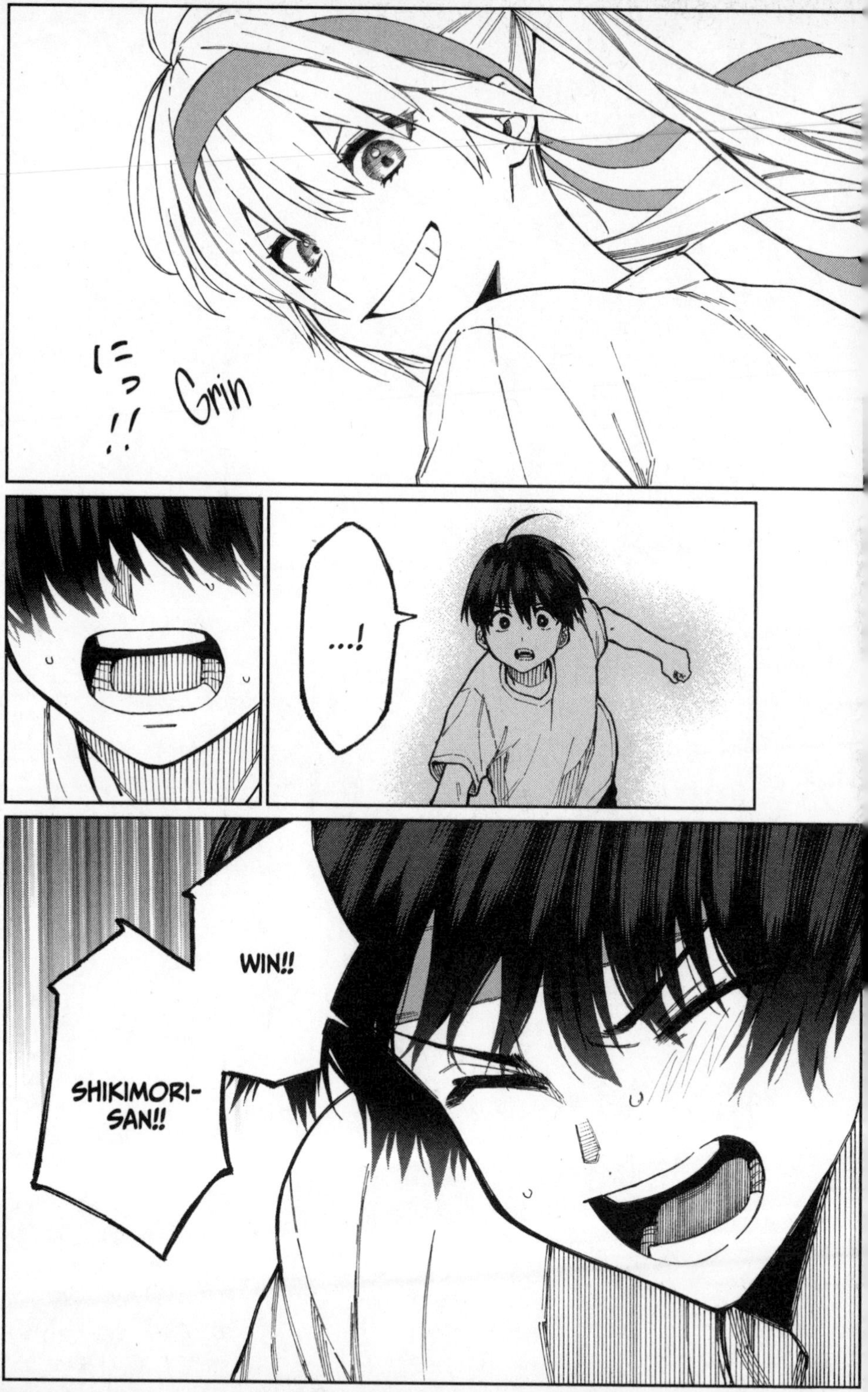
にっ!!
Grin
...!
WIN!!
SHIKIMORI-SAN!!

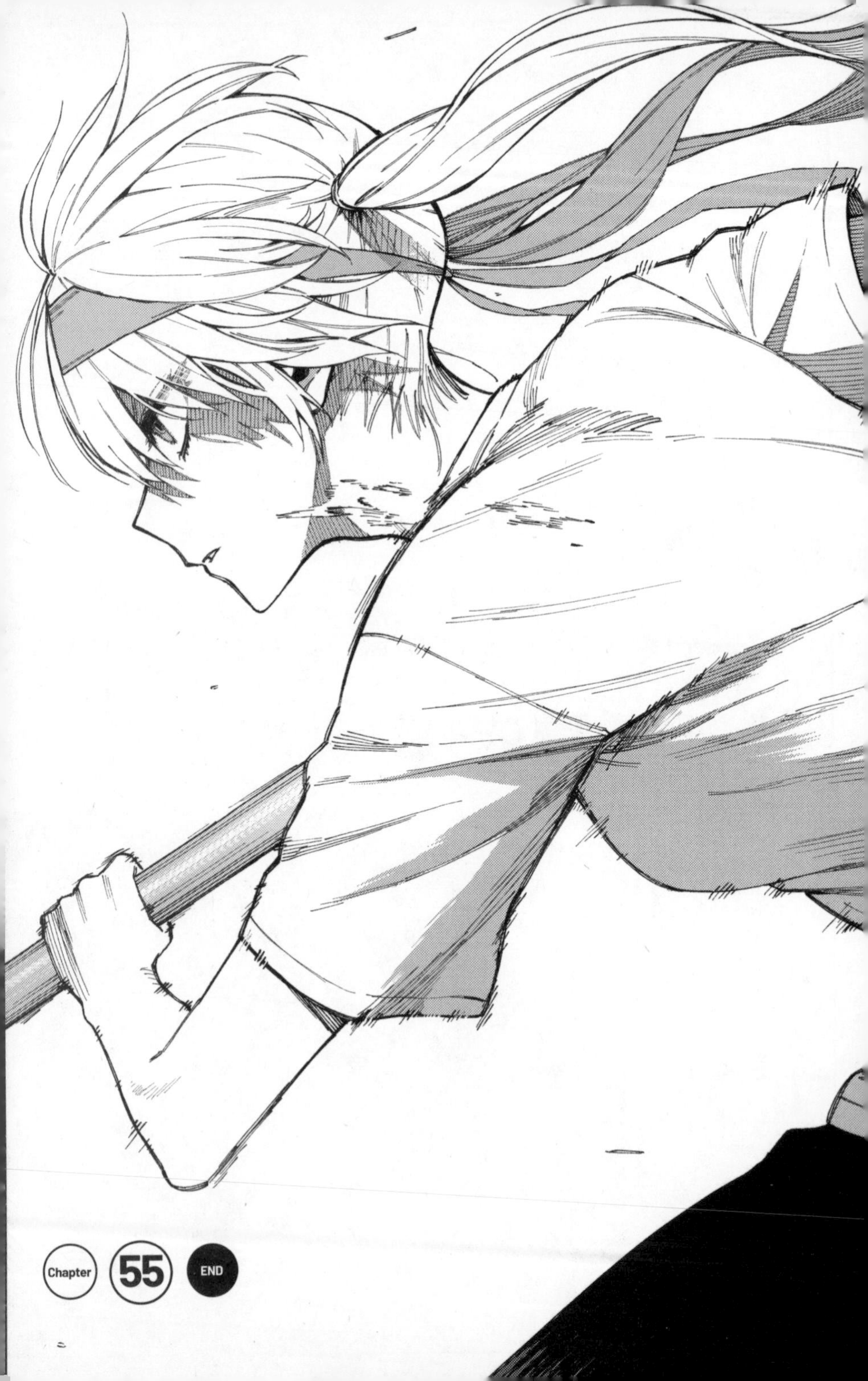

Chapter 55 END

# CONTINUED IN VOLUME 6!!!!!!

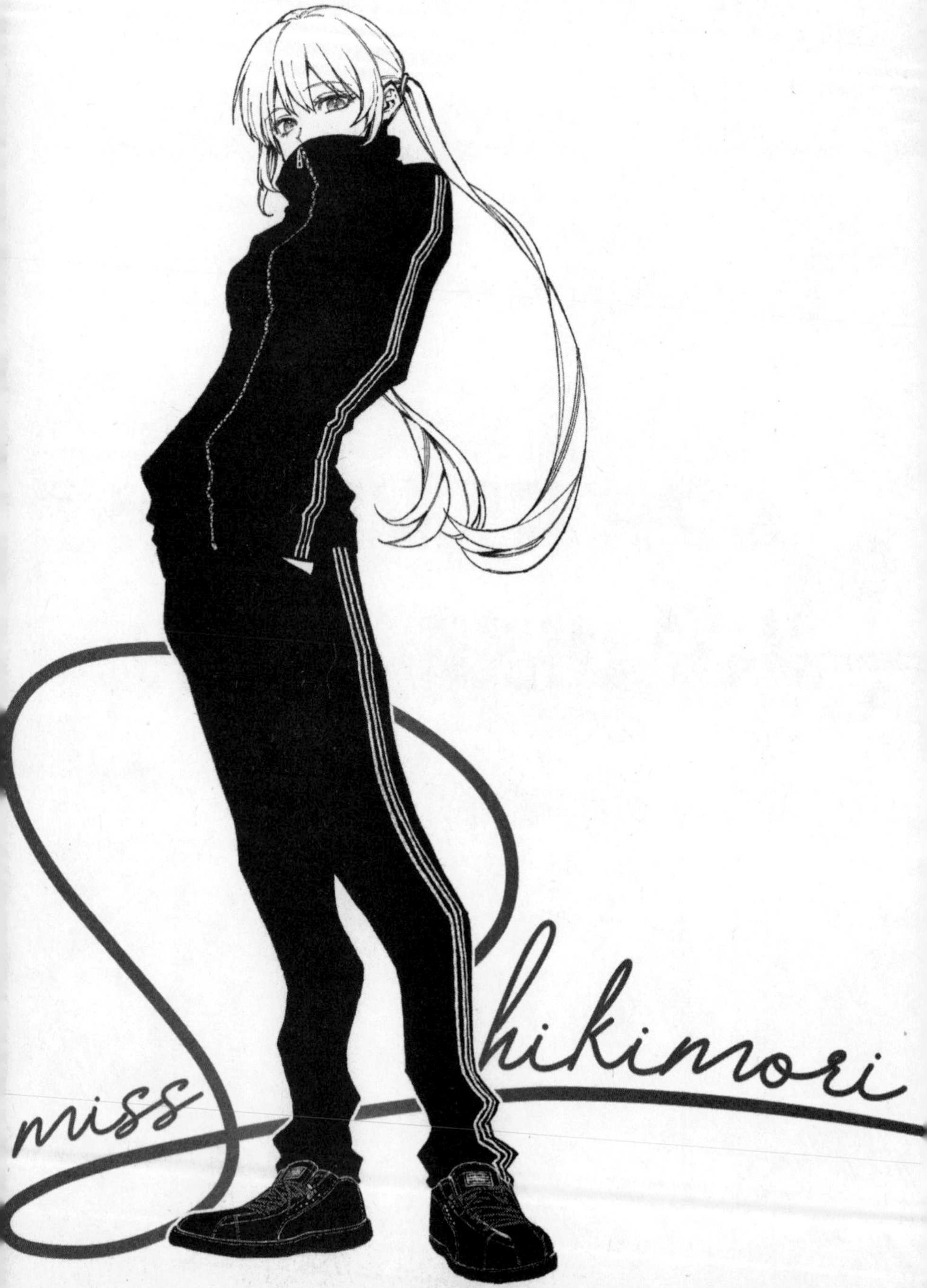
miss Shikimori

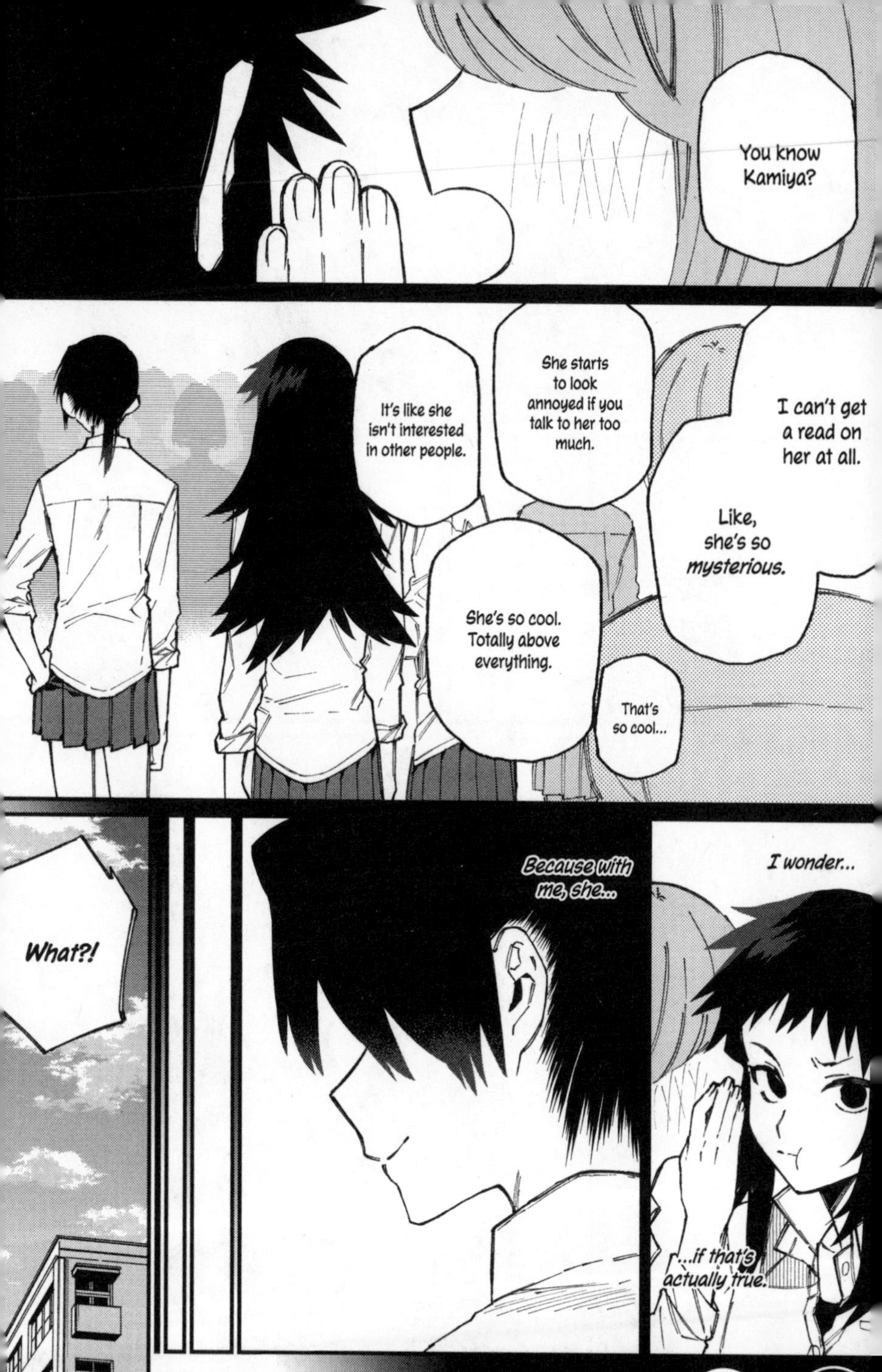
You know Kamiya?
I can't get a read on her at all.
Like, she's so *mysterious.*
She starts to look annoyed if you talk to her too much.
It's like she isn't interested in other people.
She's so cool. Totally above everything.
That's so cool...
I wonder...
...if that's actually true.
Because with me, she...
What?!

Tankobon

Bonus Story

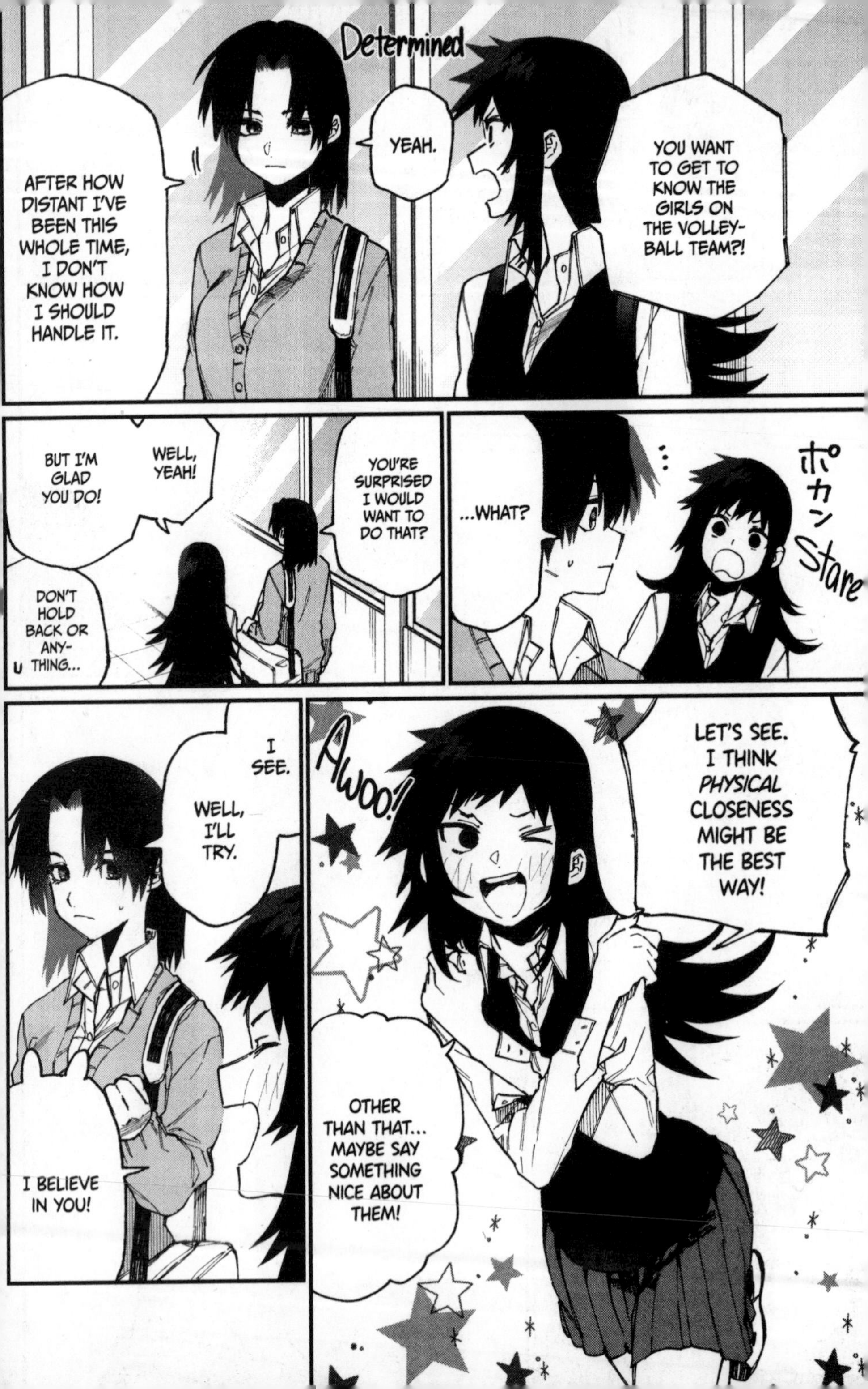
Determined
YOU WANT TO GET TO KNOW THE GIRLS ON THE VOLLEY-BALL TEAM?!
YEAH.
AFTER HOW DISTANT I'VE BEEN THIS WHOLE TIME, I DON'T KNOW HOW I SHOULD HANDLE IT.
ポカン
Stare
...WHAT?
YOU'RE SURPRISED I WOULD WANT TO DO THAT?
WELL, YEAH!
BUT I'M GLAD YOU DO!
DON'T HOLD BACK OR ANY-THING...
Awoo!!
LET'S SEE. I THINK *PHYSICAL* CLOSENESS MIGHT BE THE BEST WAY!
OTHER THAN THAT... MAYBE SAY SOMETHING NICE ABOUT THEM!
I SEE.
WELL, I'LL TRY.
I BELIEVE IN YOU!

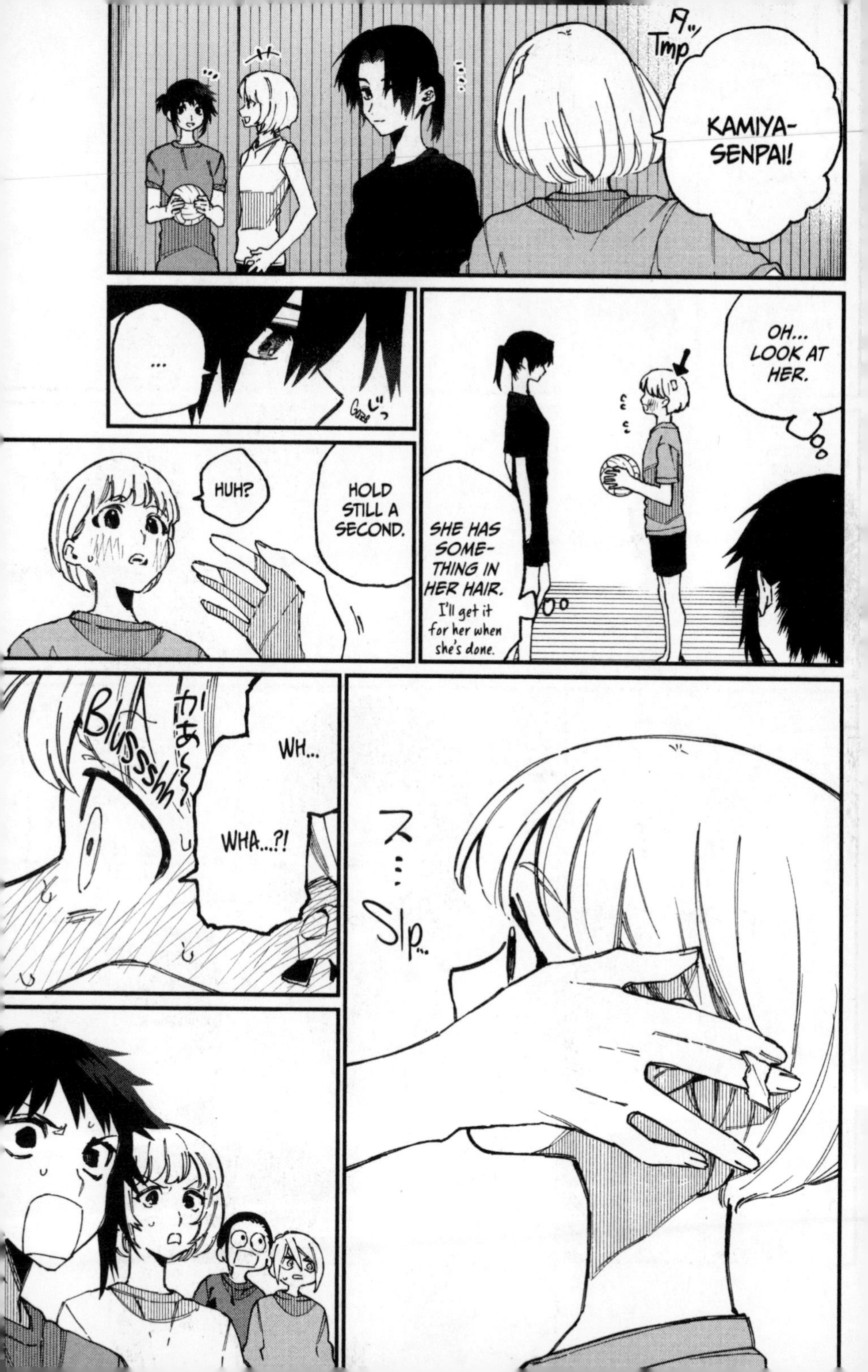
タッ
Tmp
KAMIYA-SENPAI!
OH... LOOK AT HER.
SHE HAS SOME-THING IN HER HAIR.
I'll get it for her when she's done.
...
じっ
Gaze
HOLD STILL A SECOND.
HUH?
ス…
Slp...
Blussshh
WH...
WHA...?!

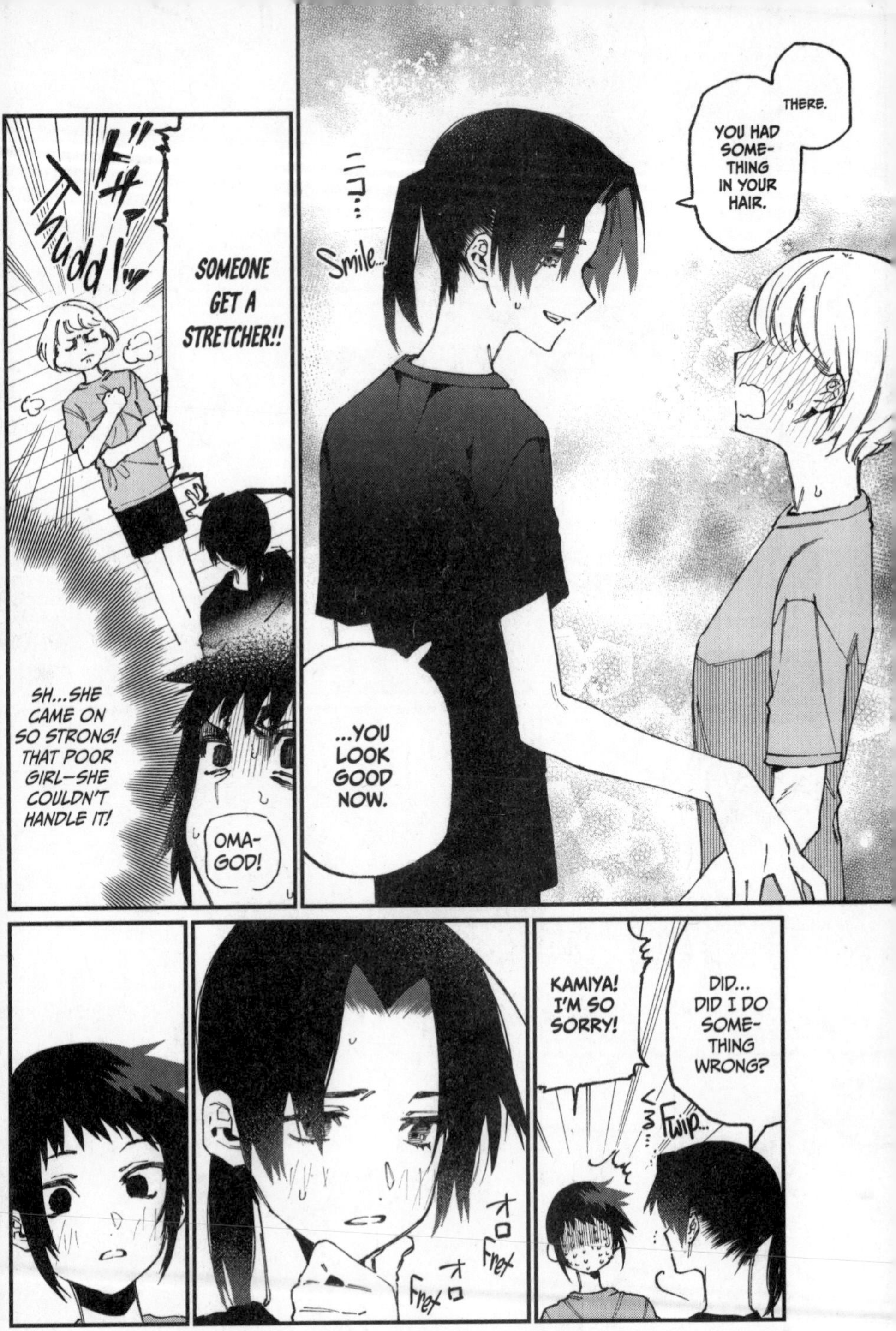
THERE.
YOU HAD SOME-THING IN YOUR HAIR.
ニコ…
Smile...
...YOU LOOK GOOD NOW.
ドサァ
Thudd!!
SOMEONE GET A STRETCHER!!
SH...SHE CAME ON SO STRONG! THAT POOR GIRL—SHE COULDN'T HANDLE IT!
OMA-GOD!
DID... DID I DO SOME-THING WRONG?
KAMIYA! I'M SO SORRY!
くる…
Fwip...
オロ
Fret
オロ
Fret

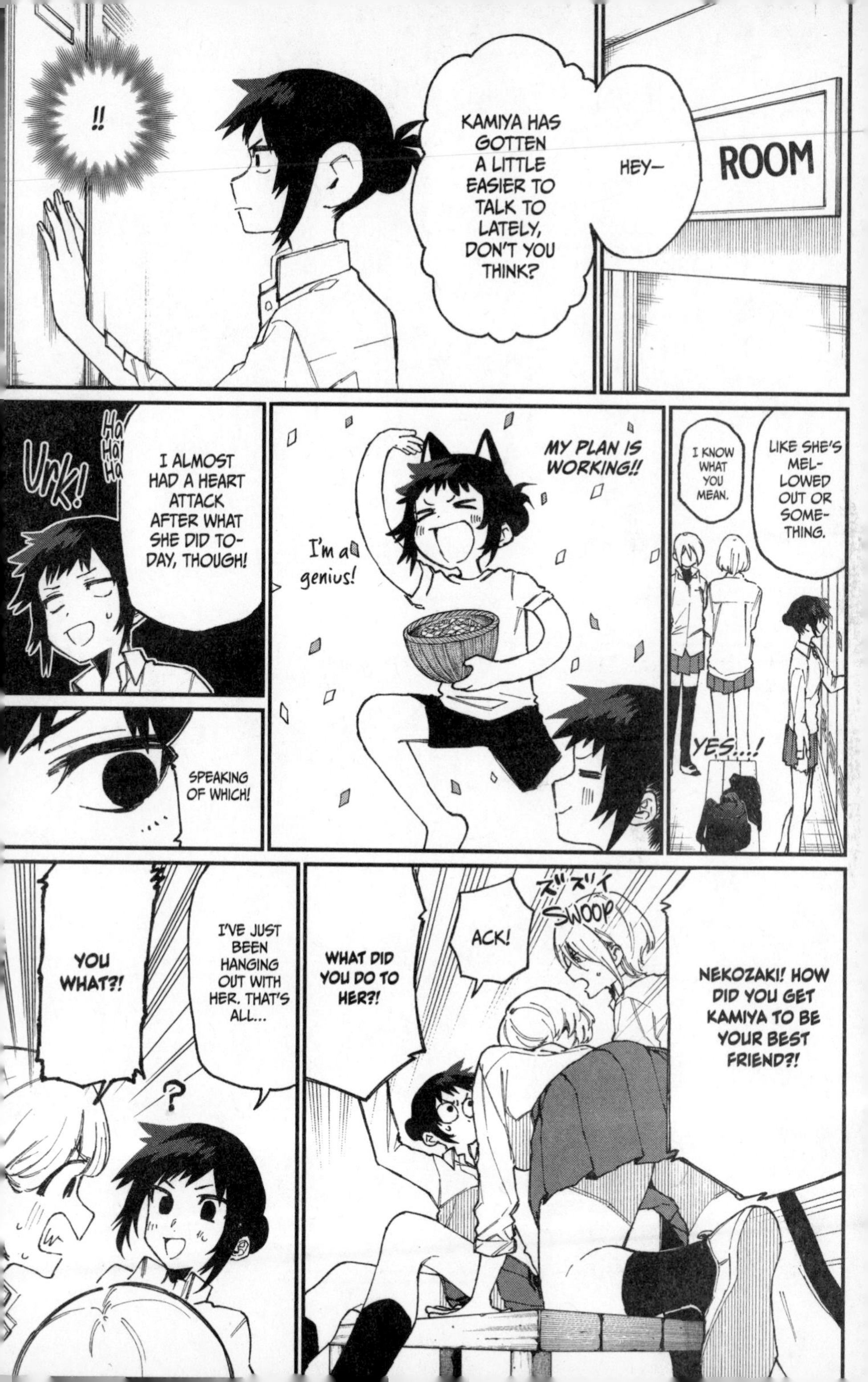

ROOM
HEY—
KAMIYA HAS GOTTEN A LITTLE EASIER TO TALK TO LATELY, DON'T YOU THINK?
!!
LIKE SHE'S MEL-LOWED OUT OR SOME-THING.
I KNOW WHAT YOU MEAN.
YES...!
MY PLAN IS WORKING!!
I'm a genius!
Ha Ha Ha
I ALMOST HAD A HEART ATTACK AFTER WHAT SHE DID TO-DAY, THOUGH!
Urk!
SPEAKING OF WHICH!
...
NEKOZAKI! HOW DID YOU GET KAMIYA TO BE YOUR BEST FRIEND?!
ズズイ
SWOOP
ACK!
WHAT DID YOU DO TO HER?!
I'VE JUST BEEN HANGING OUT WITH HER. THAT'S ALL...
YOU WHAT?!
?

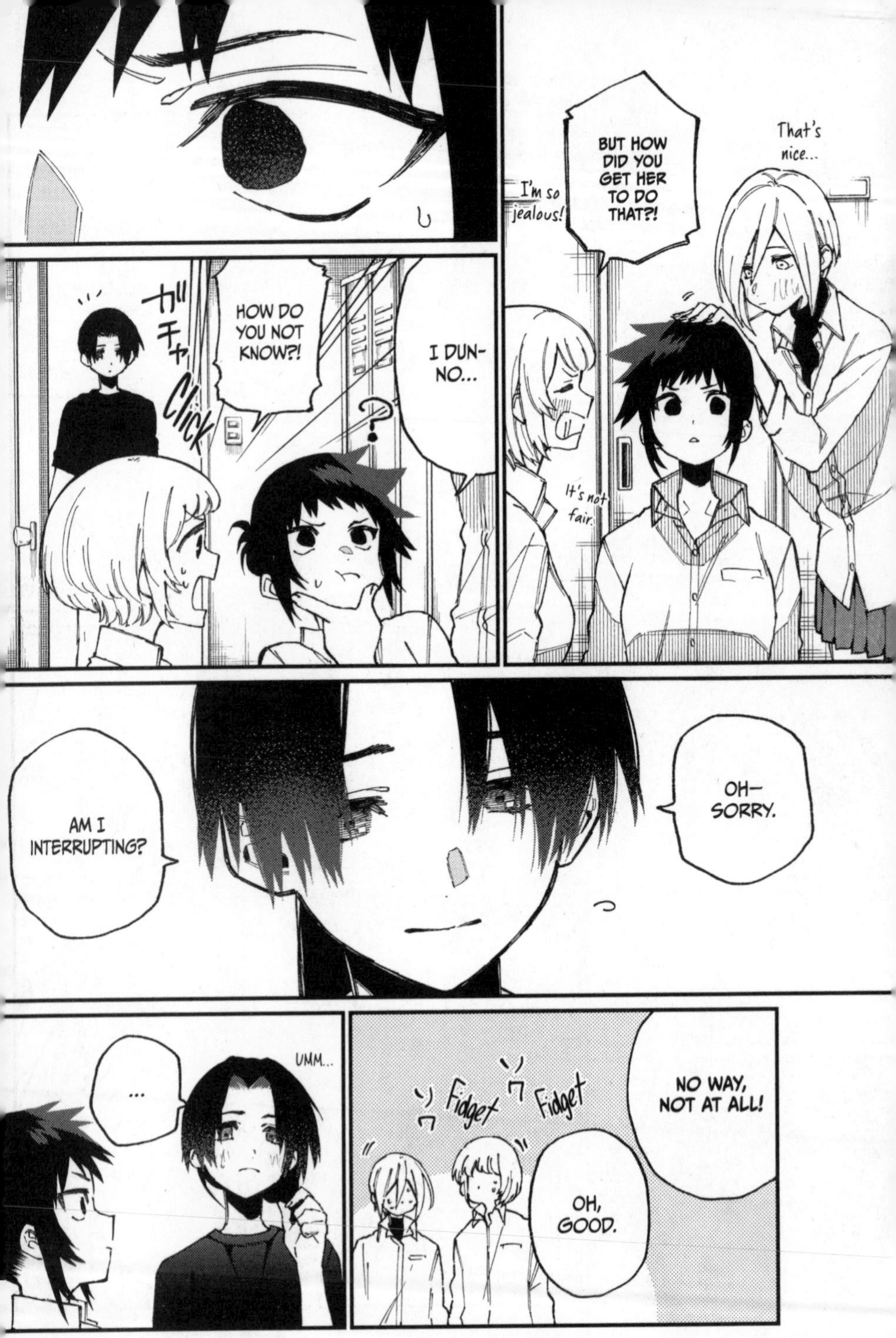
That's nice...
BUT HOW DID YOU GET HER TO DO THAT?!
I'm so jealous!
It's not fair.
I DUN-NO...
HOW DO YOU NOT KNOW?!
ガチャ
Click
OH—SORRY.
AM I INTERRUPTING?
NO WAY, NOT AT ALL!
OH, GOOD.
ソワ Fidget
ソワ Fidget
UMM...
...

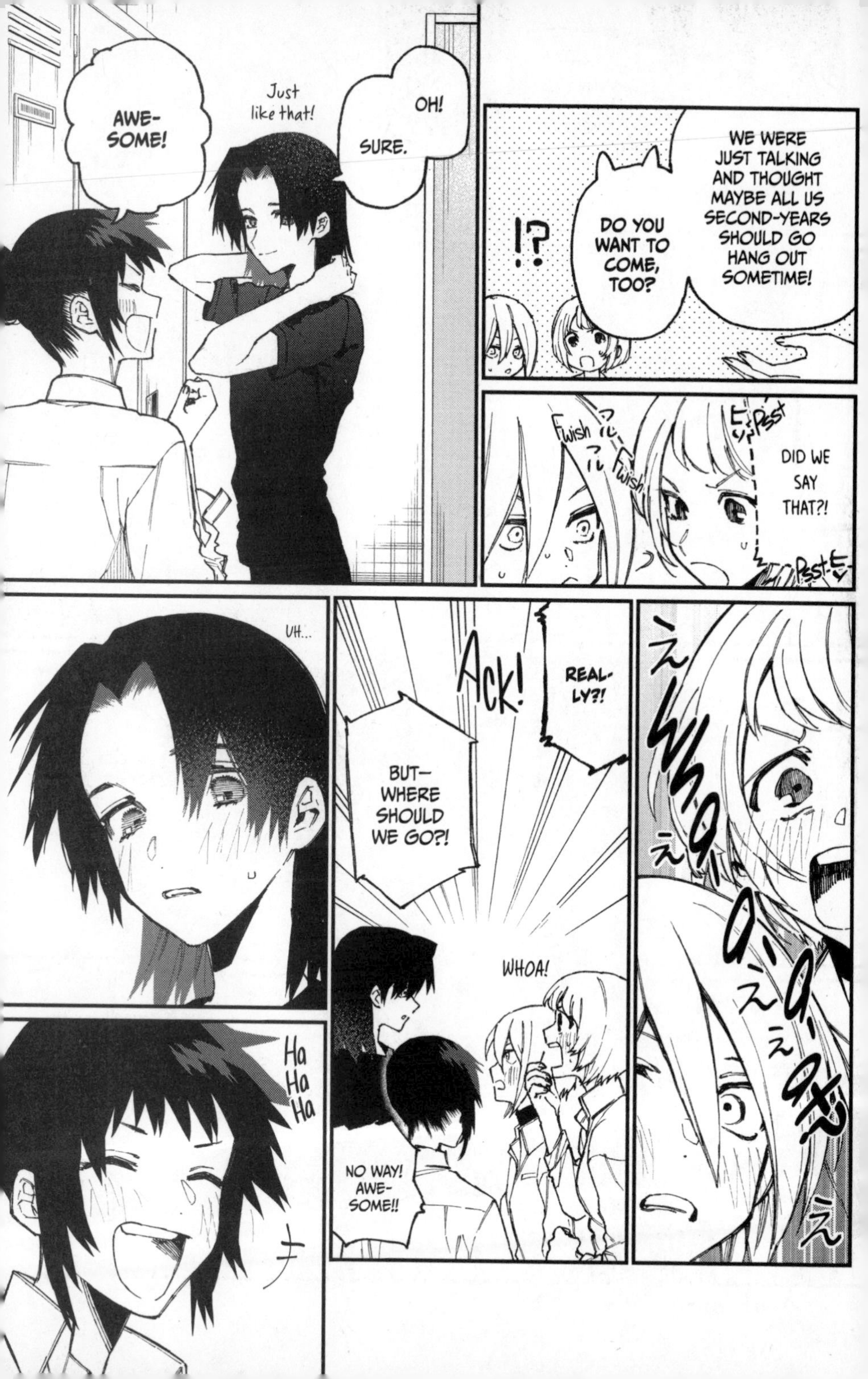
WE WERE JUST TALKING AND THOUGHT MAYBE ALL US SECOND-YEARS SHOULD GO HANG OUT SOMETIME!
DO YOU WANT TO COME, TOO?
!?
Fwish
Fwish
Psst
DID WE SAY THAT?!
Psst
OH!
SURE.
Just like that!
AWE-SOME!
Ack!
REAL-LY?!
BUT— WHERE SHOULD WE GO?!
WHOA!
NO WAY! AWE-SOME!!
UH...
Ha Ha Ha

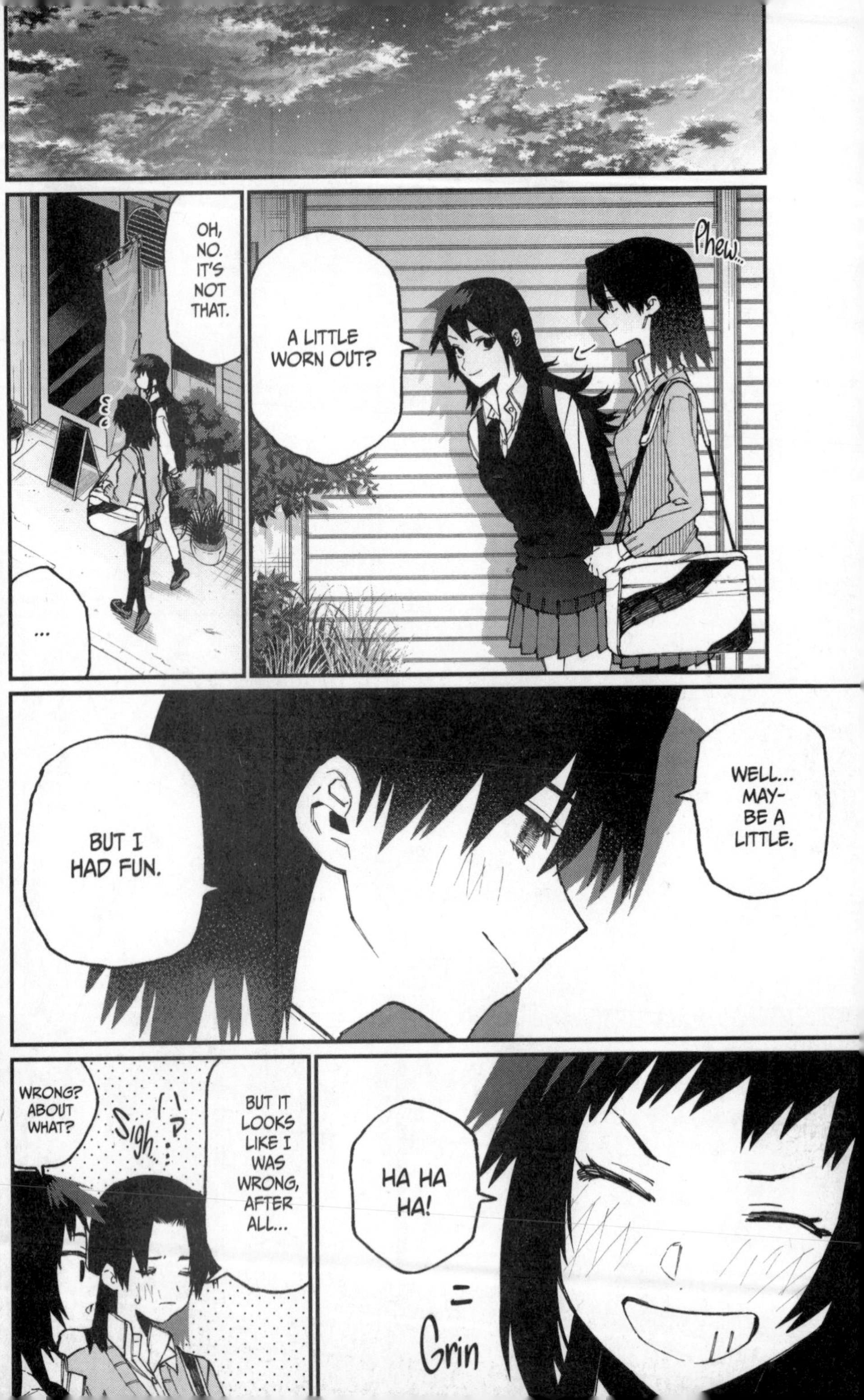
Phew...
A LITTLE WORN OUT?
OH, NO. IT'S NOT THAT.
...
WELL... MAY-BE A LITTLE.
BUT I HAD FUN.
HA HA HA!
Grin
BUT IT LOOKS LIKE I WAS WRONG, AFTER ALL...
Sigh...
WRONG? ABOUT WHAT?

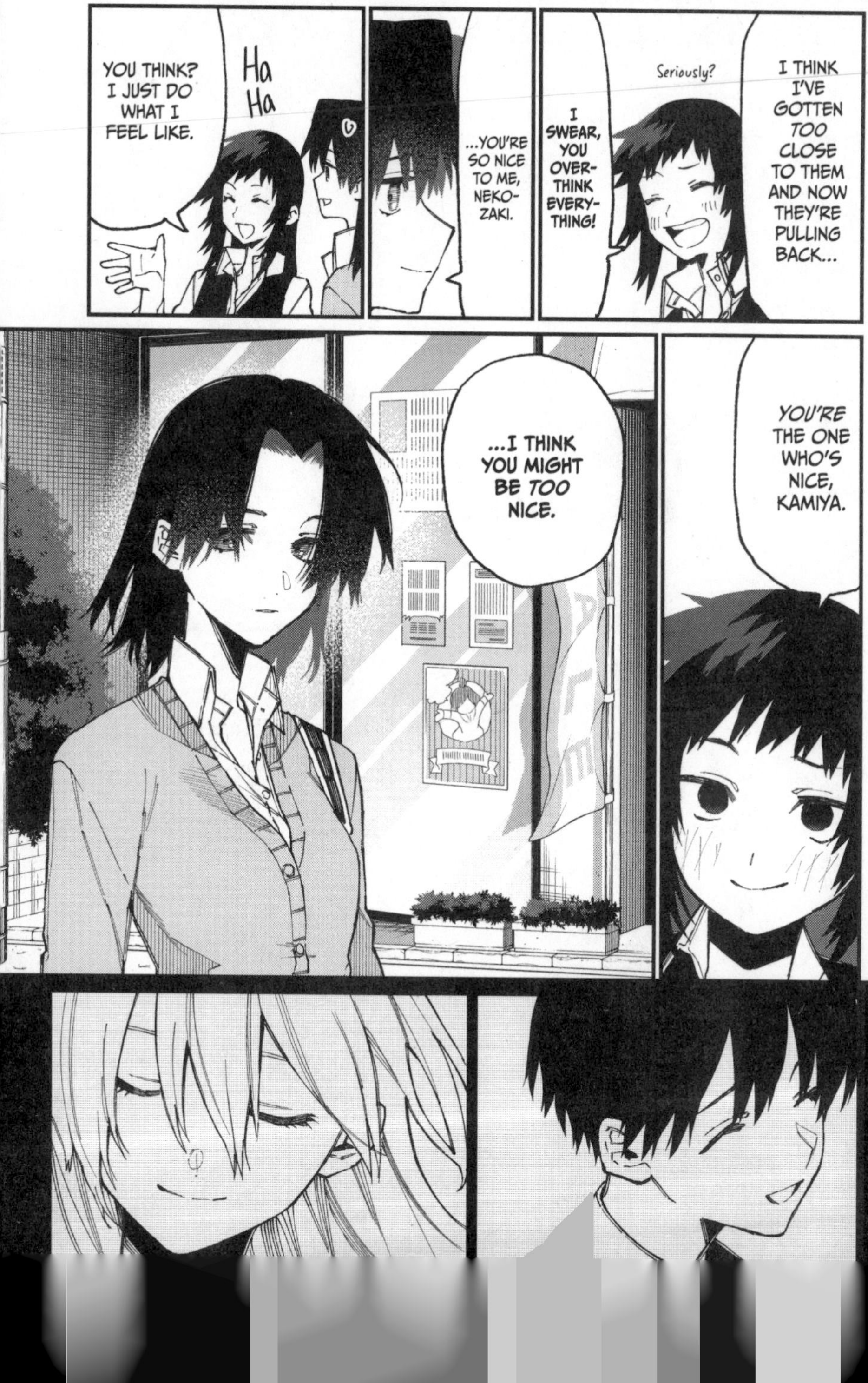
I THINK I'VE GOTTEN *TOO* CLOSE TO THEM AND NOW THEY'RE PULLING BACK...
Seriously?
I SWEAR, YOU OVER-THINK EVERY-THING!
...YOU'RE SO NICE TO ME, NEKO-ZAKI.
Ha Ha
YOU THINK? I JUST DO WHAT I FEEL LIKE.
*YOU'RE* THE ONE WHO'S NICE, KAMIYA.
...I THINK YOU MIGHT BE *TOO* NICE.

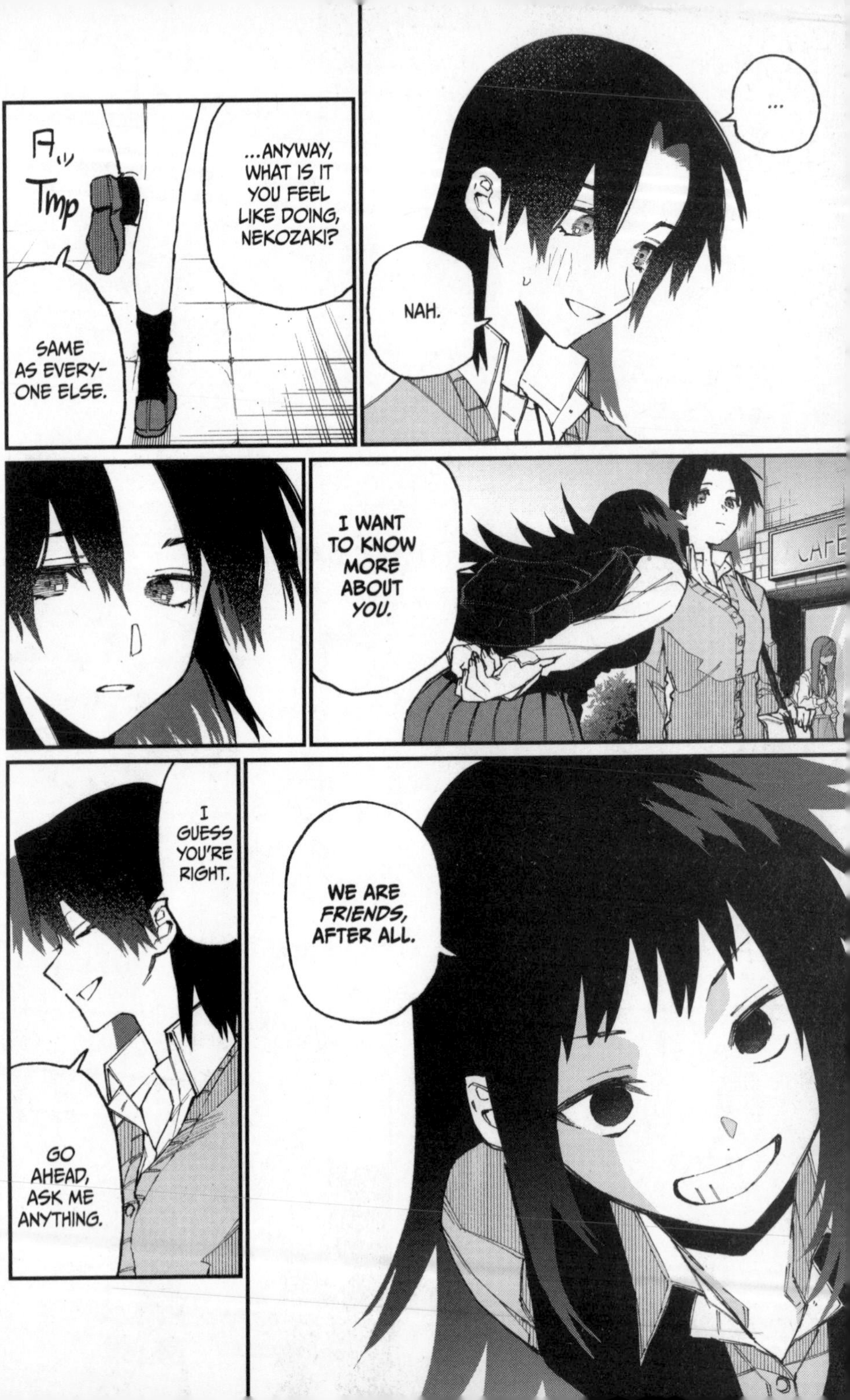
...
NAH.
...ANYWAY, WHAT IS IT YOU FEEL LIKE DOING, NEKOZAKI?
Tmp
SAME AS EVERY-ONE ELSE.
I WANT TO KNOW MORE ABOUT *YOU.*
CAFE
WE ARE *FRIENDS,* AFTER ALL.
I GUESS YOU'RE RIGHT.
GO AHEAD, ASK ME ANYTHING.

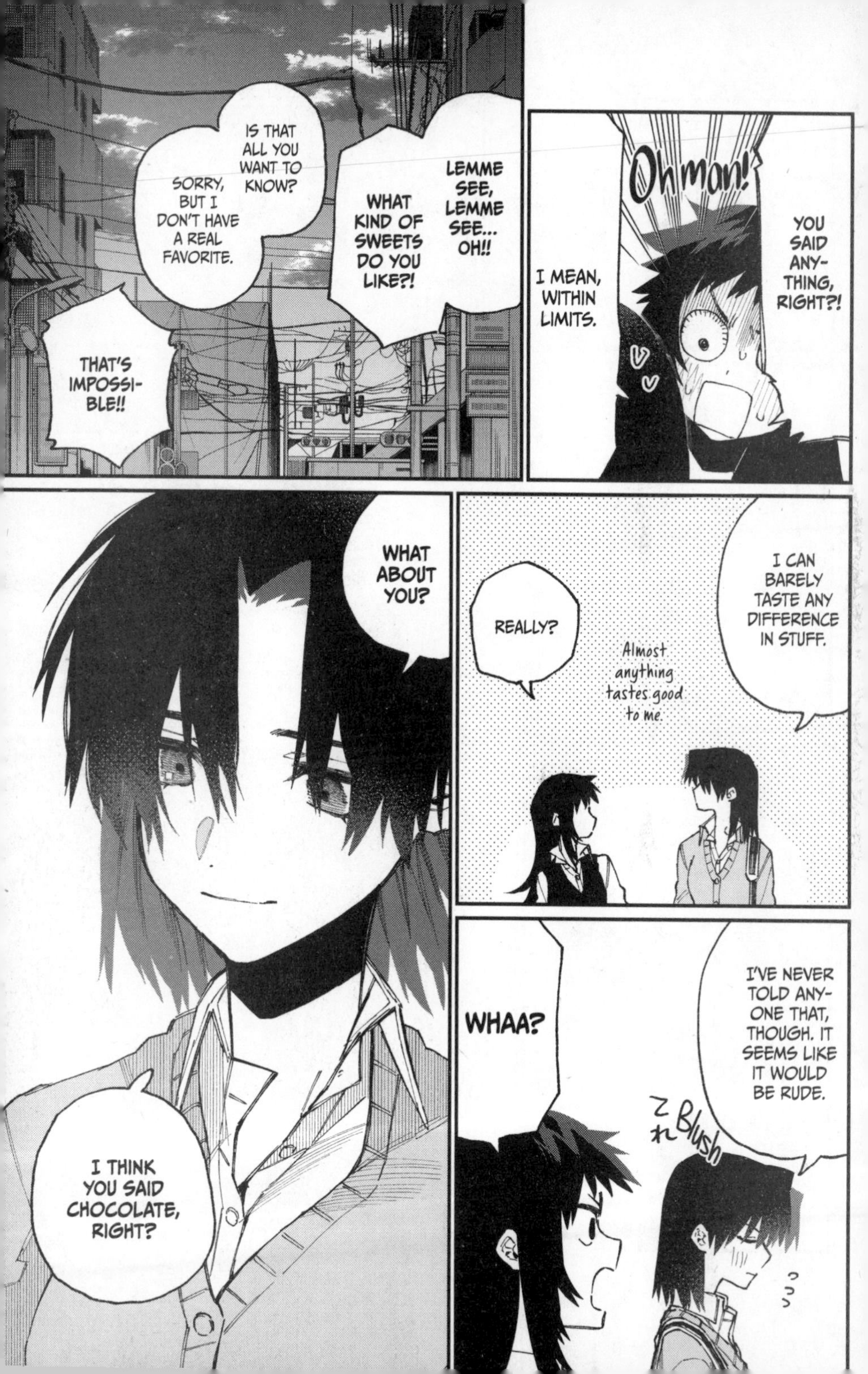
Oh man!
YOU SAID ANY-THING, RIGHT?!
I MEAN, WITHIN LIMITS.
LEMME SEE, LEMME SEE... OH!! WHAT KIND OF SWEETS DO YOU LIKE?!
IS THAT ALL YOU WANT TO KNOW? SORRY, BUT I DON'T HAVE A REAL FAVORITE.
THAT'S IMPOSSI-BLE!!
I CAN BARELY TASTE ANY DIFFERENCE IN STUFF.
Almost anything tastes good to me.
REALLY?
I'VE NEVER TOLD ANY-ONE THAT, THOUGH. IT SEEMS LIKE IT WOULD BE RUDE.
Blush
WHAA?
WHAT ABOUT YOU?
I THINK YOU SAID CHOCOLATE, RIGHT?

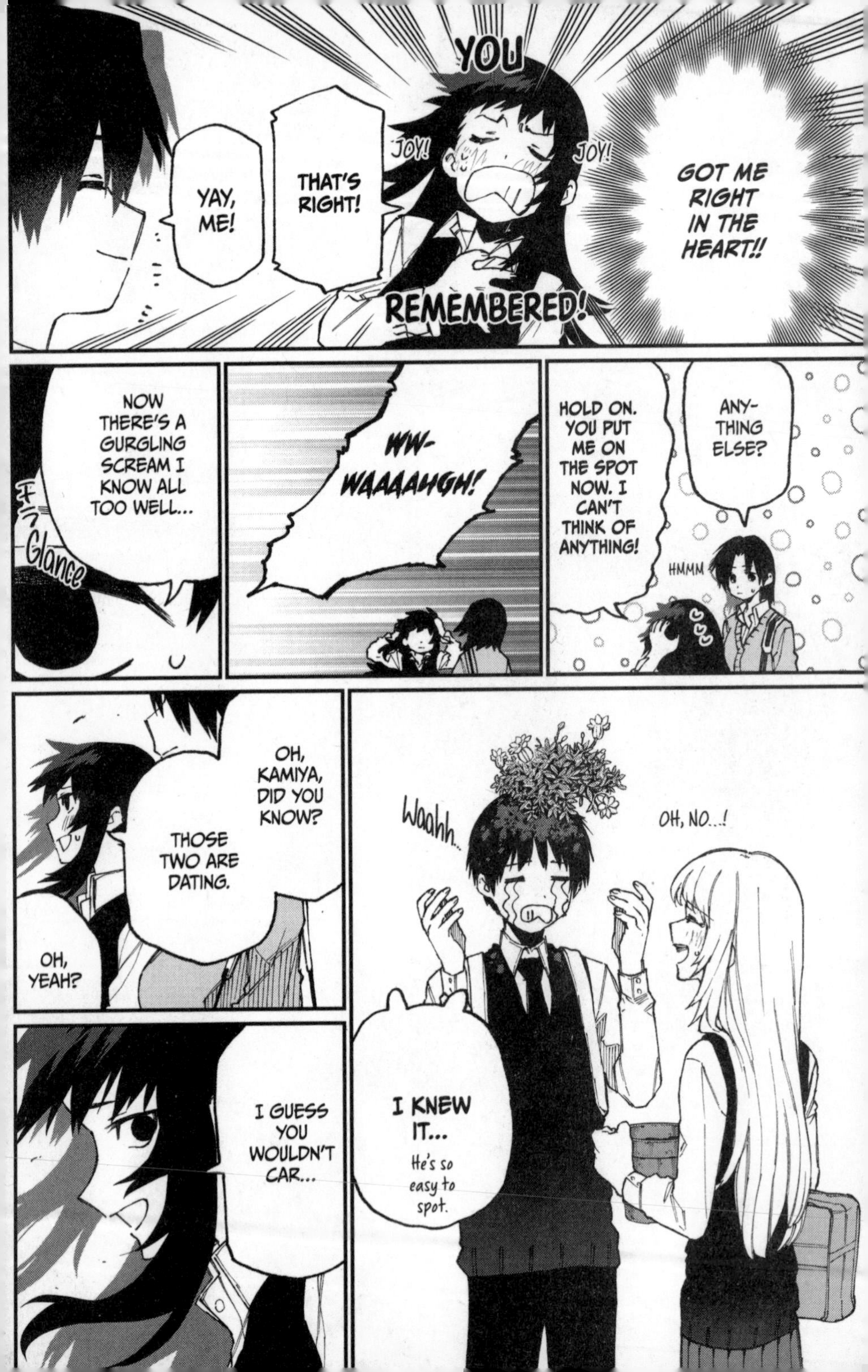
GOT ME RIGHT IN THE HEART!!
YOU
JOY!
JOY!
THAT'S RIGHT!
YAY, ME!
REMEMBERED!
ANY-THING ELSE?
HOLD ON. YOU PUT ME ON THE SPOT NOW. I CAN'T THINK OF ANYTHING!
HMMM
WW-WAAAAHGH!
NOW THERE'S A GURGLING SCREAM I KNOW ALL TOO WELL...
チラ
Glance
OH, NO...!
Waahh...
I KNEW IT...
He's so easy to spot.
OH, KAMIYA, DID YOU KNOW?
THOSE TWO ARE DATING.
OH, YEAH?
I GUESS YOU WOULDN'T CAR...

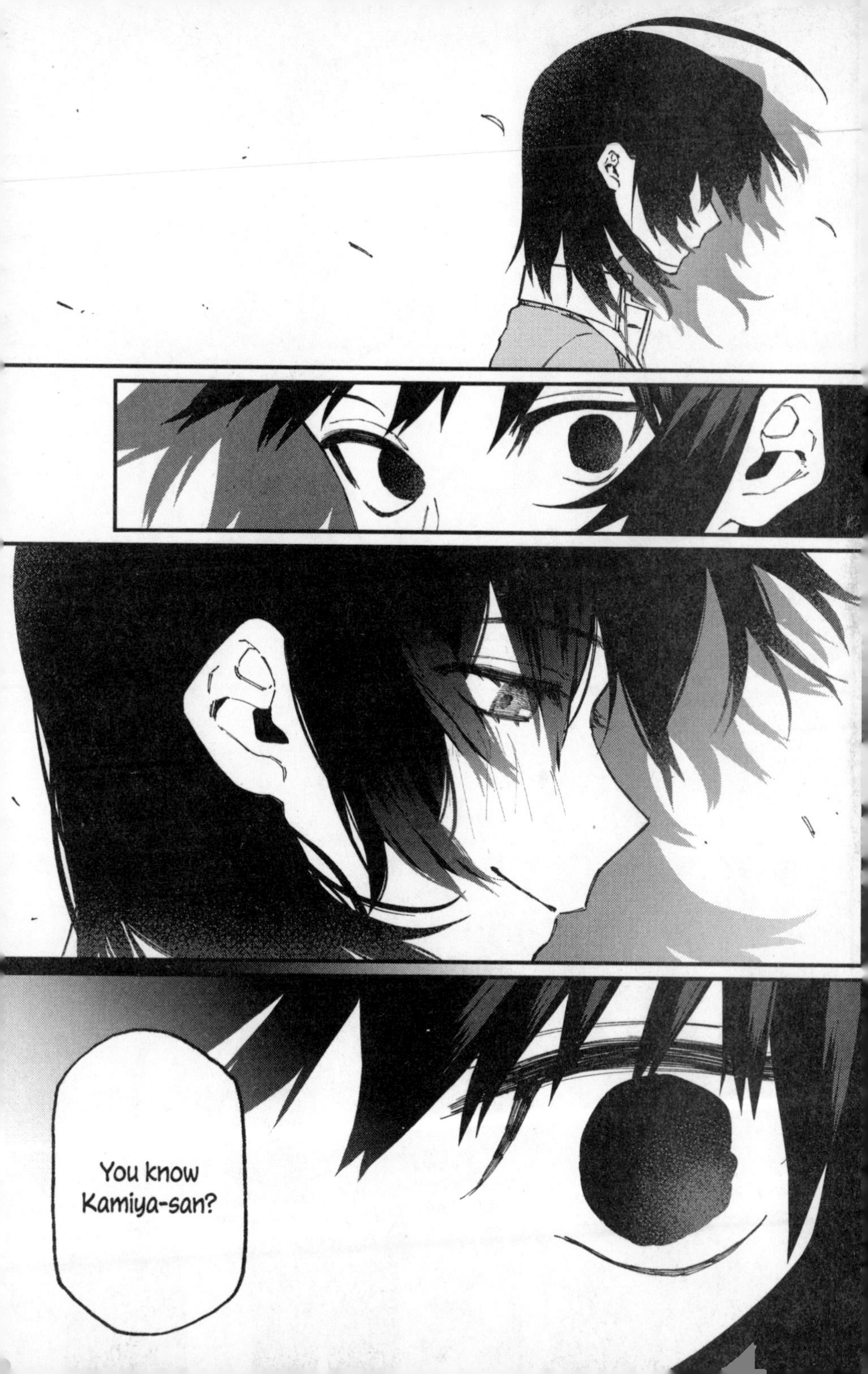
You know Kamiya-san?

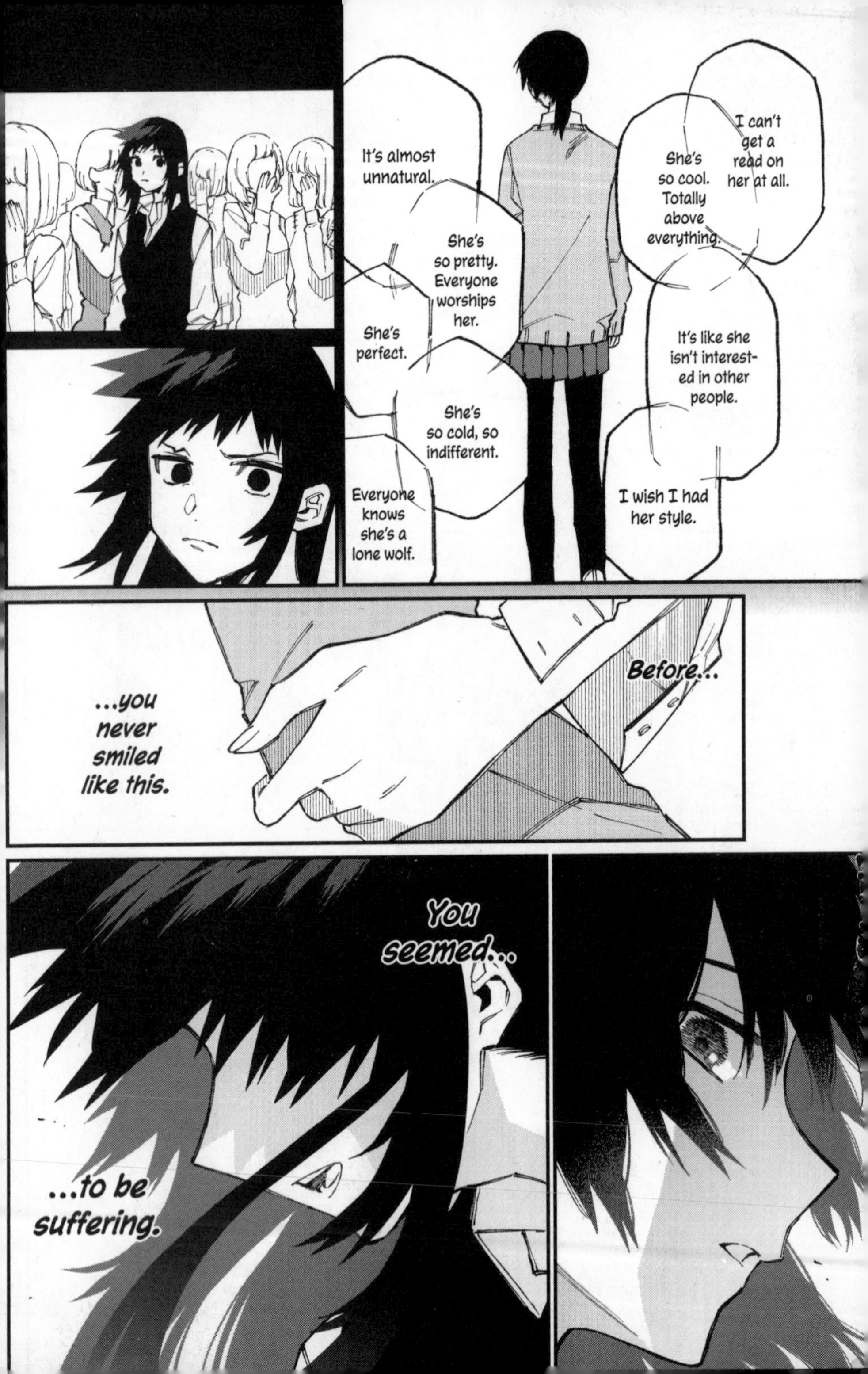
I can't get a read on her at all.
She's so cool. Totally above everything.
It's like she isn't interested in other people.
I wish I had her style.
It's almost unnatural.
She's so pretty. Everyone worships her.
She's perfect.
She's so cold, so indifferent.
Everyone knows she's a lone wolf.
Before...
...you never smiled like this.
You seemed...
...to be suffering.

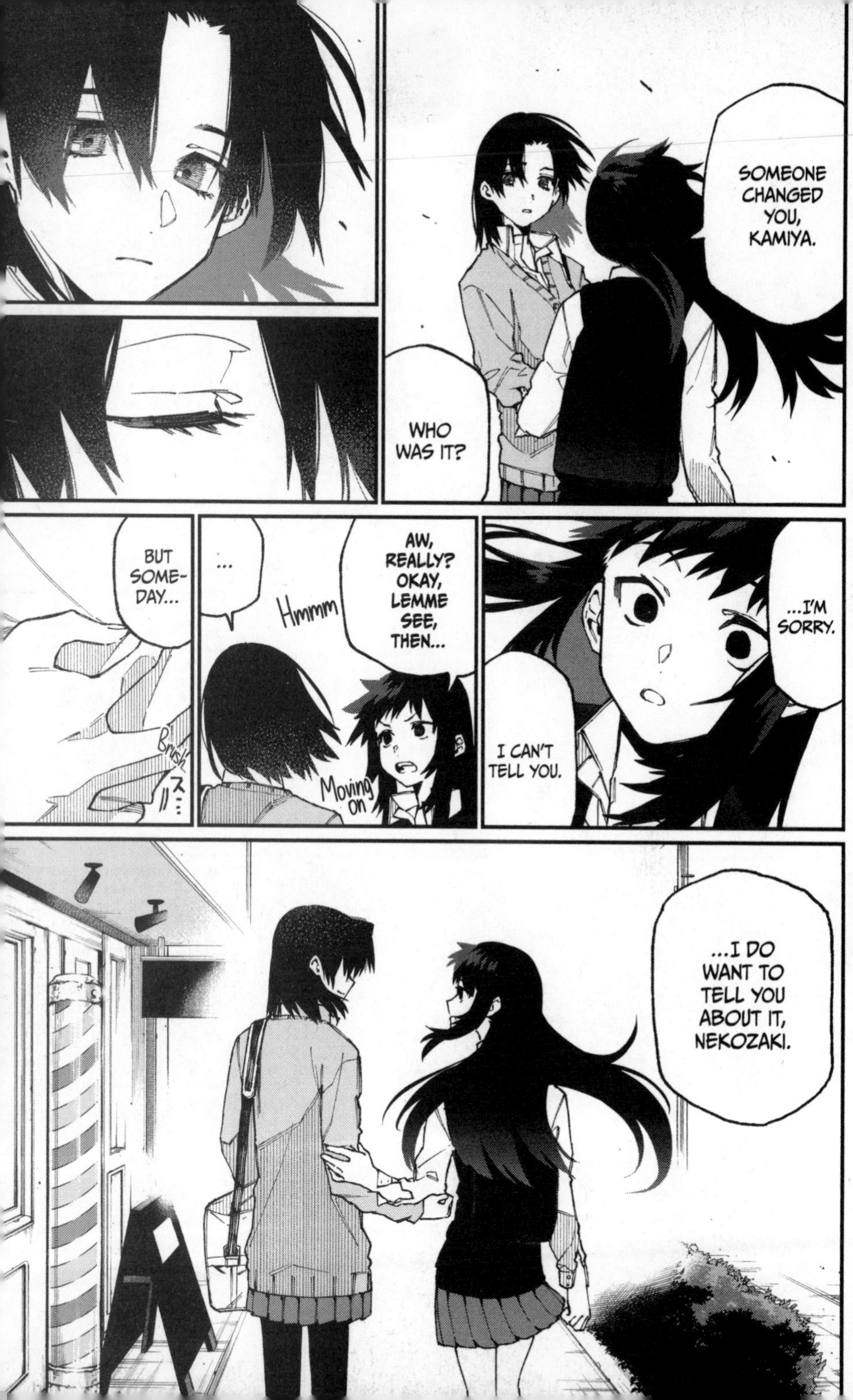
SOMEONE CHANGED YOU, KAMIYA.
WHO WAS IT?
...I'M SORRY.
I CAN'T TELL YOU.
AW, REALLY? OKAY, LEMME SEE, THEN...
Hmmm
...
Moving on
BUT SOME-DAY...
Brush
スー…
...I DO WANT TO TELL YOU ABOUT IT, NEKOZAKI.

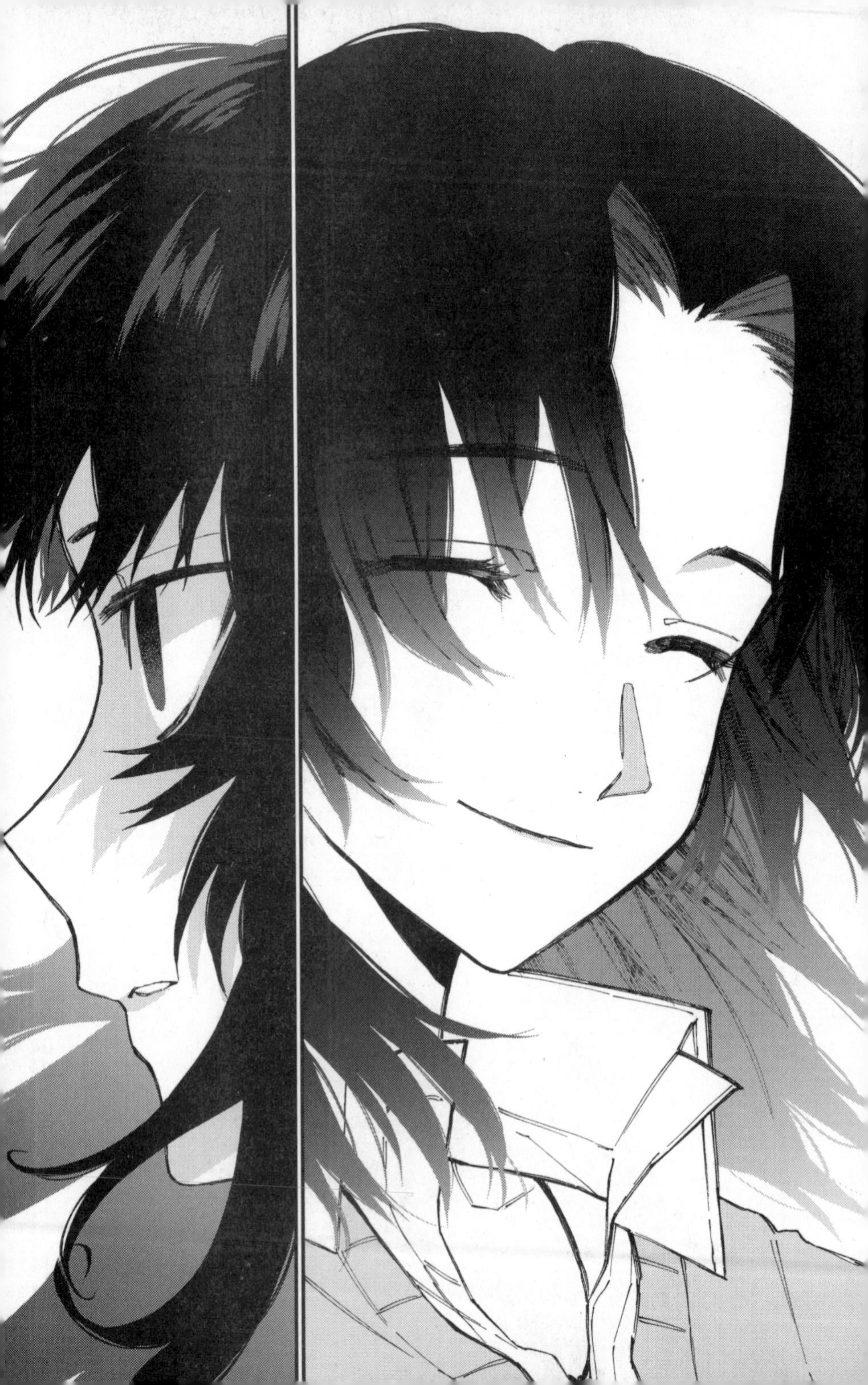

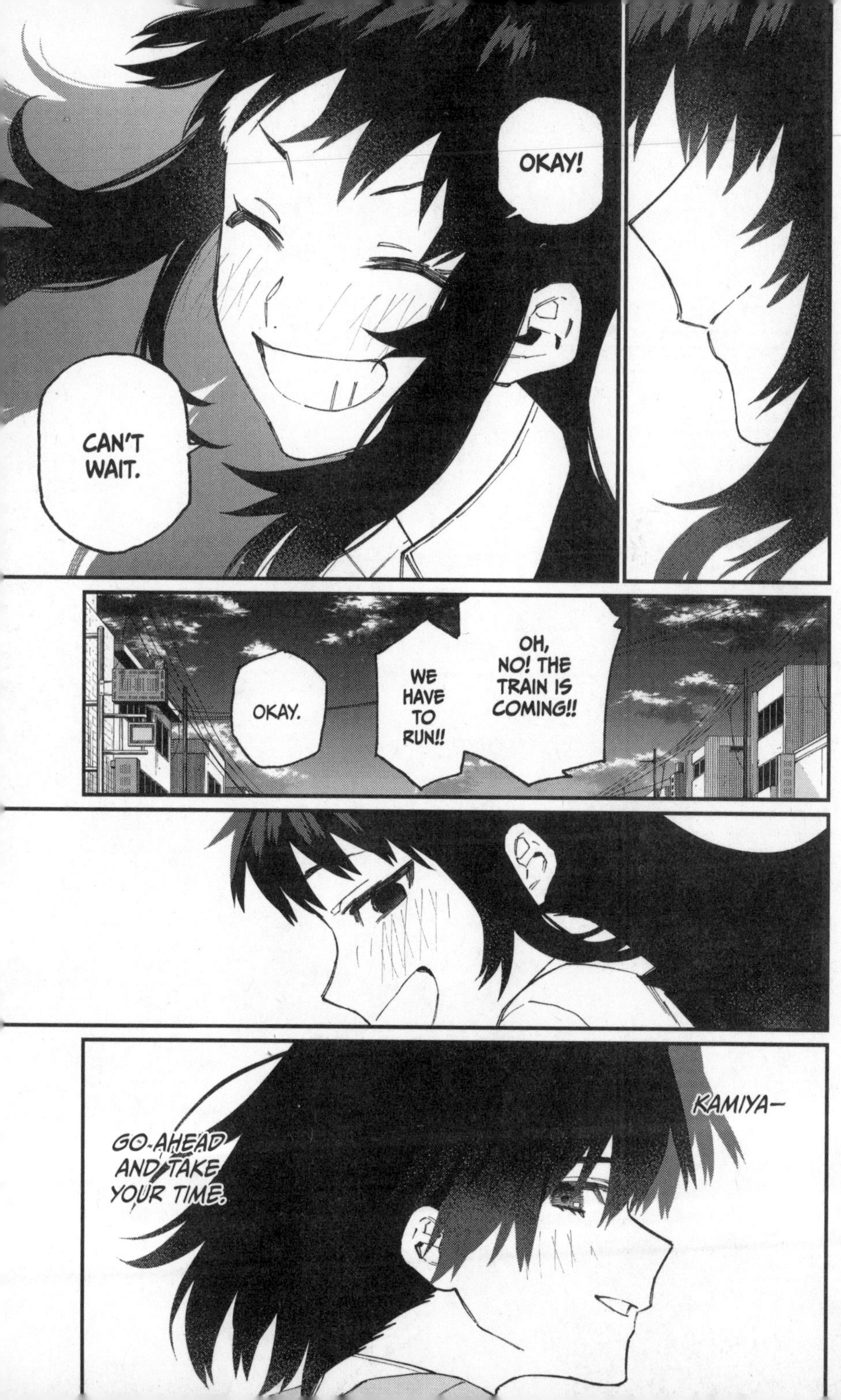
OKAY!
CAN'T WAIT.
OH, NO! THE TRAIN IS COMING!!
WE HAVE TO RUN!!
OKAY.
KAMIYA—
GO AHEAD AND TAKE YOUR TIME.

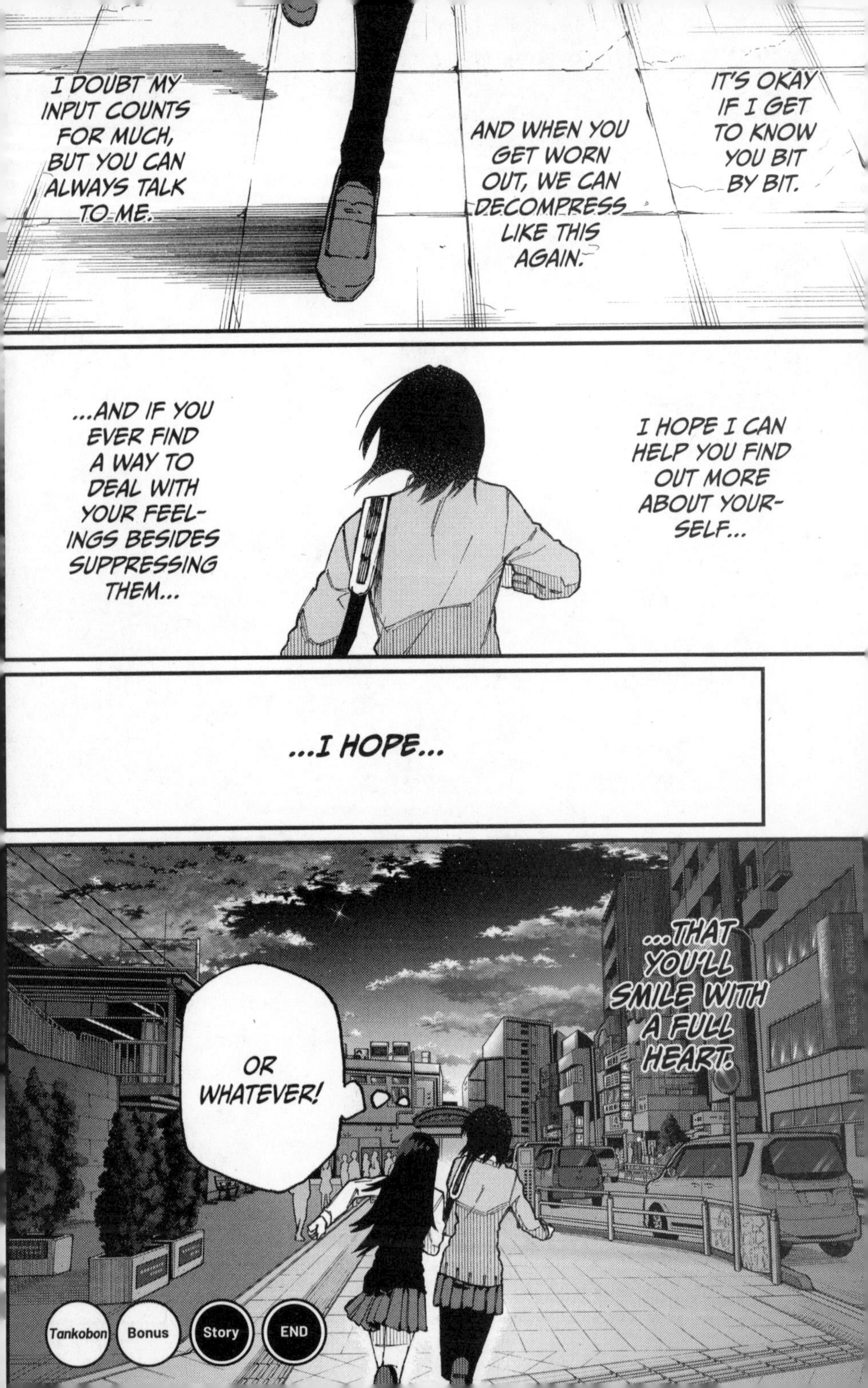
IT'S OKAY IF I GET TO KNOW YOU BIT BY BIT.
AND WHEN YOU GET WORN OUT, WE CAN DECOMPRESS LIKE THIS AGAIN.
I DOUBT MY INPUT COUNTS FOR MUCH, BUT YOU CAN ALWAYS TALK TO ME.
I HOPE I CAN HELP YOU FIND OUT MORE ABOUT YOUR-SELF...
...AND IF YOU EVER FIND A WAY TO DEAL WITH YOUR FEEL-INGS BESIDES SUPPRESSING THEM...
...I HOPE...
...THAT YOU'LL SMILE WITH A FULL HEART.
OR WHATEVER!
Tankobon
Bonus
Story
END

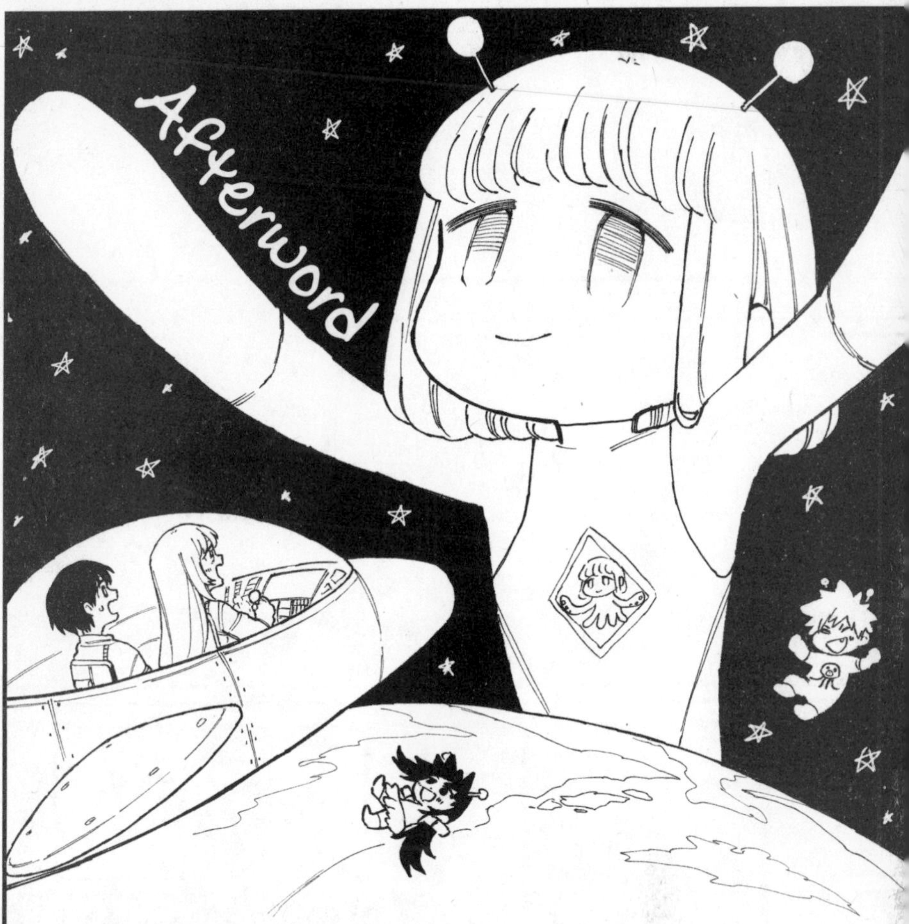
Afterword

Thank you all so much for picking up volume 5.
The other day I moved my studio and the person who came to pick up my junk asked me, "Hey, are you a manga-ka?" and I just blurted out, "Bwhaa?!"
We're still all sleeping huddled together on the sofa in the new studio and we haven't figured out how to open the mailbox.
But I'm going to do my best and try to approach people more, darn it!

Staff: Naa-san, Uchida-san, Santo-san
Design: Kurachi-san
Editor: Hiraoka-san

Keigo MAKI

## TRANSLATOR'S NOTES

### *"Quit callin' me that,"* page 16

Inuzuka is a little touchy about people using his full name because "Inu" on its own means "dog."

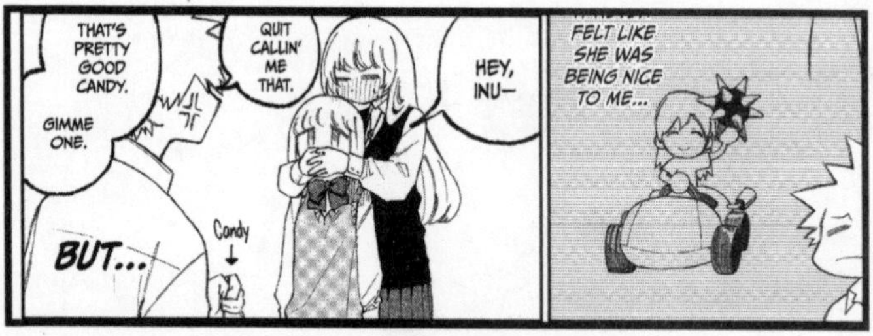
FELT LIKE SHE WAS BEING NICE TO ME...
HEY, INU—
QUIT CALLIN' ME THAT.
THAT'S PRETTY GOOD CANDY.
GIMME ONE.
Candy
BUT...

### *"Everyone knows she's a lone wolf,"* page 28

The first part of Kamiya's name (kami) is written with the character for "wolf" (okami).

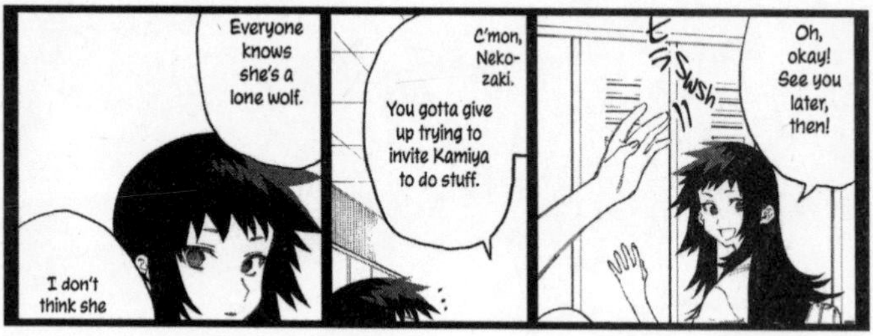
Oh, okay! See you later, then!
Swsh
C'mon, Neko-zaki.
You gotta give up trying to invite Kamiya to do stuff.
Everyone knows she's a lone wolf.
I don't think she

# PERFECT WORLD

### Rie Aruga

A TOUCHING
NEW SERIES
ABOUT LOVE AND
COPING WITH
DISABILITY

An office party reunites Tsugumi with her high school crush Itsuki. He's realized his dream of becoming an architect, but along the way, he experienced a spinal injury that put him in a wheelchair. Now Tsugumi's rekindled feelings will butt up against prejudices she never considered — and Itsuki will have to decide if he's ready to let someone into his heart...

"Depicts with great delicacy and courage the difficulties some with disabilities experience getting involved in romantic relationships... Rie Aruga refuses to romanticize, pushing her heroine to face the reality of disability. She invites her readers to the same tasks of empathy, knowledge and recognition."
—Slate.fr

"An important entry [in manga romance]... The emotional core of both plot and characters indicates thoughtfulness... [Aruga's] research is readily apparent in the text and artwork, making this feel like a real story."
—Anime News Network

KC/
KODANSHA
COMICS

**The adorable new odd-couple cat comedy manga from the creator of the beloved *Chi's Sweet Home*, in full color!**

*Praise for Chi's Sweet Home*

"Nearly impossible to turn away... a true all-ages title that anyone, young or old, cat lover or not, will enjoy. The stories will bring a smile to your face and warm your heart."

—School Library Journal

# Sue & Tai-chan
### Konami Kanata

Sue is an aging housecat who's looking forward to living out her life in peace... but her plans change when the mischievous black tomcat Tai-chan enters the picture! Hey! Sue never signed up to be a catsitter! *Sue & Tai-chan* is the latest from the reigning meow-narch of cute kitty comics, Konami Kanata.

KC KODANSHA COMICS

# A SMART, NEW ROMANTIC COMEDY FOR FANS OF *SHORTCAKE CAKE* AND *TERRACE HOUSE!*

A romance manga starring high school girl Meeko, who learns to live on her own in a boarding house whose living room is home to the odd (but handsome) Matsunaga-san. She begins to adjust to her new life away from her parents, but Meeko soon learns that no matter how far away from home she is, she's still a young girl at heart — especially when she finds herself falling for Matsunaga-san.

# THE SWEET SCENT OF LOVE IS IN THE AIR! FOR FANS OF OFFBEAT ROMANCES LIKE *WOTAKOI*

Sweat and Soap © Kintetsu Yamada / Kodansha Ltd.

In an office romance, there's a fine line between sexy and awkward... and that line is where Asako — a woman who sweats copiously — meets Koutarou — a perfume developer who can't get enough of Asako's, er, scent. Don't miss a romcom manga like no other!

Knight of the Ice ©Yayoi Ogawa/Kodansha Ltd.

# SKATING THRILLS AND ICY CHILLS WITH THIS NEW TINGLY ROMANCE SERIES!

A rom-com on ice, perfect for fans of *Princess Jellyfish* and *Wotakoi*. Kokoro is the talk of the figure-skating world, winning trophies and hearts. But little do they know... he's actually a huge nerd! From the beloved creator of *You're My Pet* (*Tramps Like Us*).

Chitose is a serious young woman, working for the health magazine *SASSO*. Or at least, she would be, if she wasn't constantly getting distracted by her childhood friend, international figure skating star Kokoro Kijinami! In the public eye and on the ice, Kokoro is a gallant, flawless knight, but behind his glittery costumes and breathtaking spins lies a secret: He's actually a hopelessly romantic otaku, who can only land his quad jumps when Chitose is on hand to recite a spell from his favorite magical girl anime!

# Young characters and steampunk setting, like *Howl's Moving Castle* and *Battle Angel Alita*

A boy with a talent for machines and a mysterious girl whose wings he's fixed will take you beyond the clouds! In the tradition of the high-flying, resonant adventure stories of Studio Ghibli comes a gorgeous tale about the longing of young hearts for adventure and friendship!

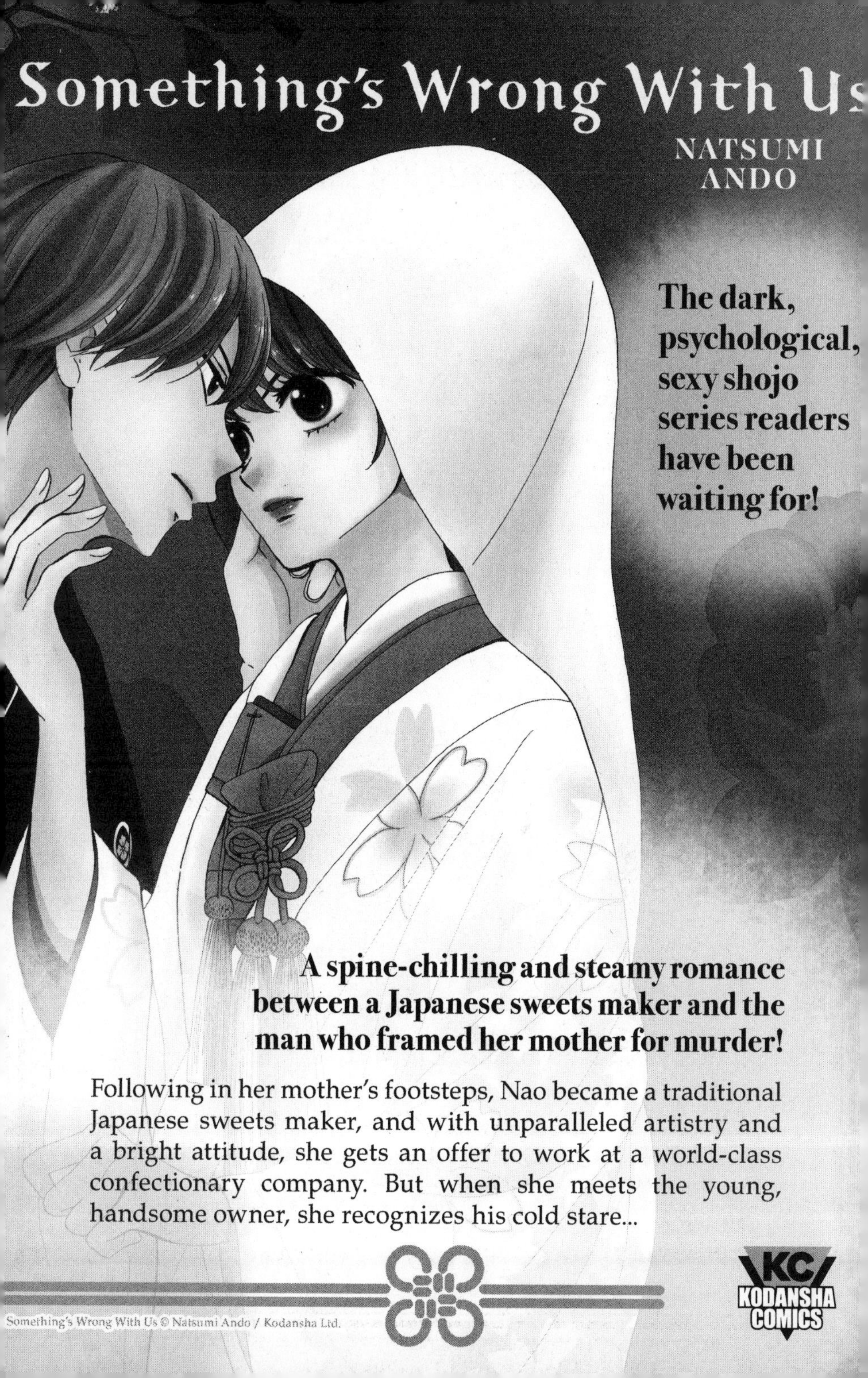
Something's Wrong With Us
NATSUMI ANDO
The dark, psychological, sexy shojo series readers have been waiting for!
A spine-chilling and steamy romance between a Japanese sweets maker and the man who framed her mother for murder!
Following in her mother's footsteps, Nao became a traditional Japanese sweets maker, and with unparalleled artistry and a bright attitude, she gets an offer to work at a world-class confectionary company. But when she meets the young, handsome owner, she recognizes his cold stare...
Something's Wrong With Us © Natsumi Ando / Kodansha Ltd.
KC KODANSHA COMICS

# The boys are back, in 400-page hardcovers that are as pretty and badass as they are!

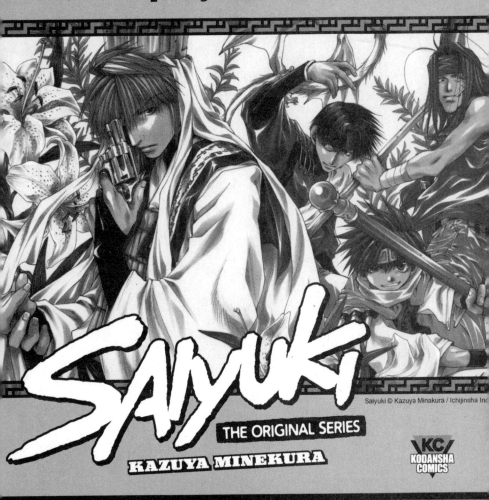

Saiyuki © Kazuya Minakura / Ichijinsha Inc

# SAIYUKI
## THE ORIGINAL SERIES
### KAZUYA MINEKURA

## "AN EDGY COMIC LOOK AT AN ANCIENT CHINESE TALE." —YALSA

Genjo Sanzo is a Buddhist priest in the city of Togenkyo, which is being ravaged by yokai spirits that have fallen out of balance with the natural order. His superiors send him on a journey far to the west to discover why this is happening and how to stop it. His companions are three yokai with human souls. But this is no day trip — the four will encounter many discoveries and horrors on the way.

## FEATURES NEW TRANSLATION, COLOR PAGES, AND BEAUTIFUL WRAPAROUND COVER ART!

A picture-perfect shojo series from Yoko Nogiri, creator of the hit *That Wolf-Boy is Mine!*

Mako's always had a passion for photography. When she loses someone dear to her, she clings onto her art as a relic of the close relationship she once had... Luckily, her childhood best friend Kei encourages her to come to his high school and join their prestigious photo club. With nothing to lose, Mako grabs her camera and moves into the dorm where Kei and his classmates live. Soon, a fresh take on life, along with a mysterious new muse, begin to come into focus!

# LOVE IN FOCUS

Love in Focus © Yoko Nogiri/Kodansha Ltd.

Praise for Yoko Nogiri's *That Wolf-Boy is Mine!*

KODANSHA COMICS

"Emotional squees...will-they-won't-they plot...[and a] pleasantly quick pace."
—Otaku USA Magazine

"A series that is pure shojo sugar—a cute love story about two nice people looking for their places in the world, and finding them with each other." —Anime News Network

# Magus of the Library

### Mitsu Izumi

## MITSU IZUMI'S STUNNING ARTWORK BRINGS A FANTASTICAL LITERARY ADVENTURE TO LUSH, THRILLING LIFE!

Young Theo adores books, but th
prejudice and hatred of his villag
keeps them ever out of his reach
Then one day, he chances to mee
Sedona, a traveling librarian wh
works for the great library of
Aftzaak, City of Books, and
his life changes forever...

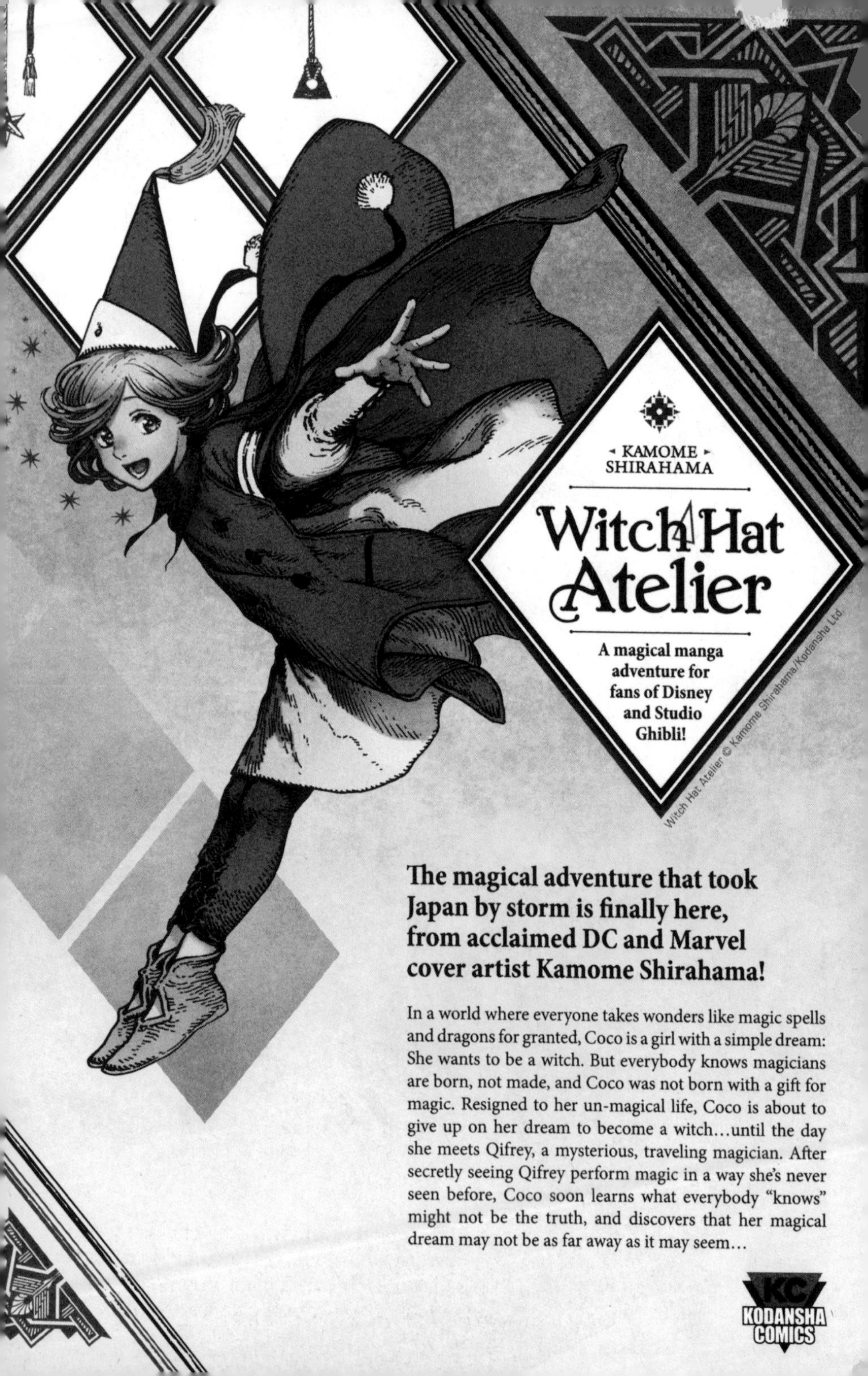
KAMOME SHIRAHAMA
Witch Hat Atelier
A magical manga adventure for fans of Disney and Studio Ghibli!

*Anime now streaming on Amazon Prime!*

The prestigious Dahlia Academy educates the elite of society from two countries; To the East is the Nation of Touwa; across the sea the other way, the Principality of West. The nations, though, are fierce rivals, and their students are constantly feuding—which means Romio Inuzuka, head of Touwa's first-year students, has a problem. He's fallen for his counterpart from West, Juliet Persia, and when he can't take it any more, he confesses his feelings.

Now Romio has two problems: A girlfriend, and a secret…

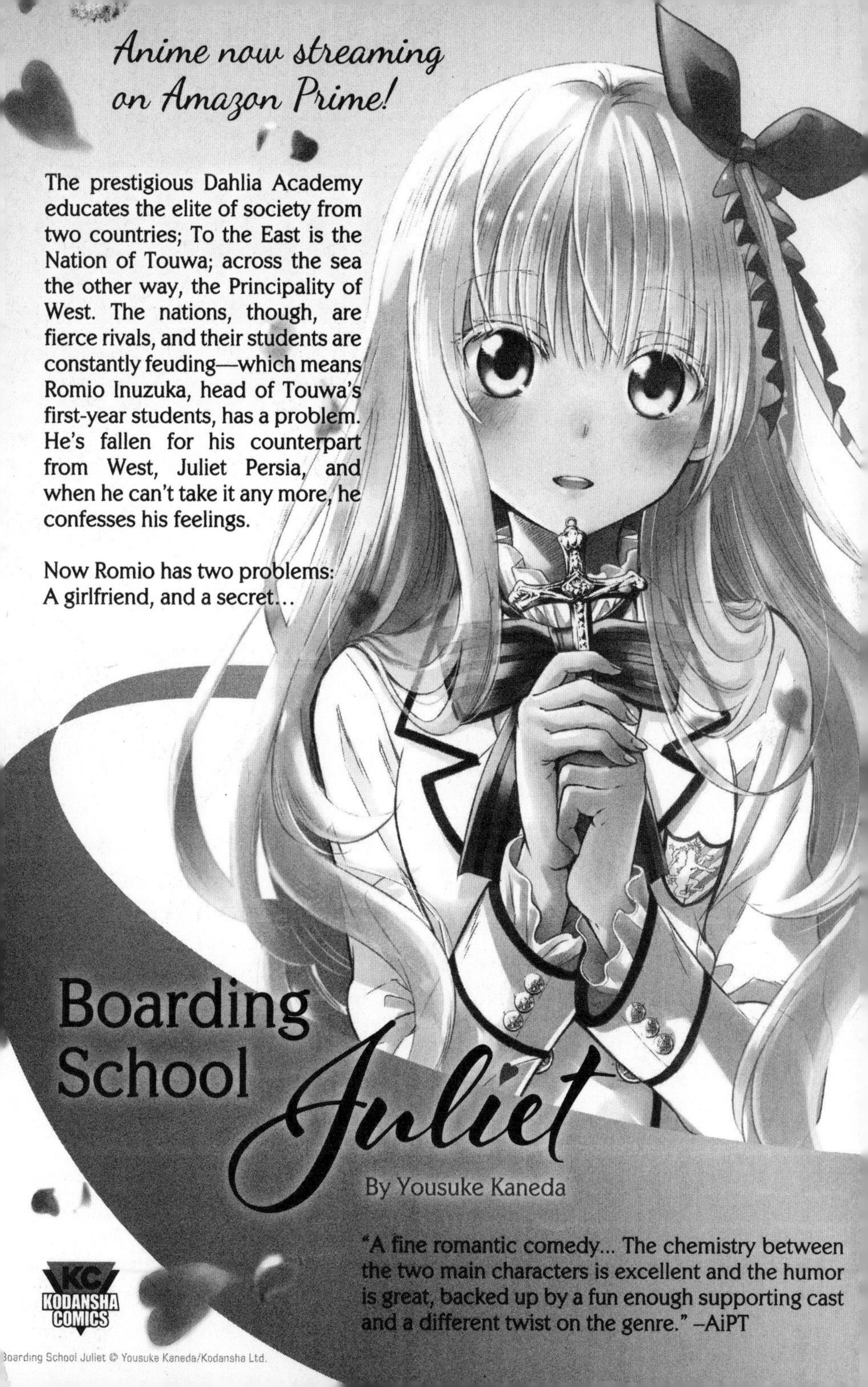

# Boarding School *Juliet*

By Yousuke Kaneda

"A fine romantic comedy… The chemistry between the two main characters is excellent and the humor is great, backed up by a fun enough supporting cast and a different twist on the genre." –AiPT

KC KODANSHA COMICS

A Kodansha Comics Trade Paperback Original
Shikimori's Not Just a Cutie 5 copyright © 2020 Keigo Maki
English translation copyright © 2021 Keigo Maki

Published in the United States by Kodansha Comics, an imprint of Kodansha USA Publishing, LLC, New York.

Publication rights for this English edition arranged through Kodansha Ltd., Tokyo.

First published in Japan in 2020 by Kodansha Ltd., Tokyo.

ISBN 978-1-64651-211-9

Printed in the United States of America.

www.kodansha.us

3rd Printing
Translation: Karen McGillicuddy
Lettering: Mercedes McGarry
Editing: David Yoo
Kodansha Comics edition cover design by My Truong

Publisher: Kiichiro Sugawara

Director of publishing services: Ben Applegate
Associate director of operations: Stephen Pakula
Publishing services associate managing editor: Madison Salters
Assistant production manager: Emi Lotto, Angela Zurlo
Logo and character art ©Kodansha USA Publishing, LLC